Another Round?

ANOTHER ROUND?

STEVEN PARISSIEN

canelo
AUGUST

First published in the United Kingdom in 2025 by August Books

This edition published in the United Kingdom in 2026 by

August Books, an imprint of
Canelo Digital Publishing Limited,
20 Vauxhall Bridge Road,
London SW1V 2SA
United Kingdom

A Penguin Random House Company
The authorised representative in the EEA is Dorling Kindersley Verlag GmbH.
Arnulfstr. 124, 80636 Munich, Germany

A CIP catalogue record for this book is available from the British Library.

Ebook ISBN 978 1 83598 159 7
B Format Hardback ISBN 978 1 83598 163 4
B Format Paperback ISBN 978 1 83598 156 6

Cover design by Emily Courdelle

Cover images © Adobestock

Printed and bound in Great Britain by Clays Ltd, Elcograf S.p.A.

Look for more great books at
www.augustbooks.co | www.dk.com

1

MIX
Paper
FSC® C018179

To Julia

Contents

Acknowledgements

Many thanks go to all who advised on or helped in the planning of this book, in particular Kerry Fretwell, and not forgetting Paul Donnelly, Alison Starr and John Deards. Particular thanks go to Richard Milbank, with whom the concept of this book was devised (fittingly, in a pub) and who has been such a generous supporter of my work over the years. Thanks, too, to Martina O'Sullivan, Hannah Taylor and all of the August Books team, and of course to my genial and supportive agent, Charlie Viney.

Introduction

The history of Britain is, perhaps more than any other nation, defined by its alcoholic choices. Our favourite drinks have presented a revealing mirror to the society and politics of the time, as well as to our own, personal journeys. To paraphrase Ludwig Feuerbach's well-rehearsed aphorism, here in Britain we are what we drink.

Alcoholic intake per capita in Britain remained in the global top ten from 1700 to 1950 – whether that's an occasion for personal celebration or national shame is entirely up to you to decide – and we are still comfortably placed in the top twenty today. The British may not be at the top of the table across the board, though: we are only eighth in terms of worldwide per-capita beer consumption, for example – behind countries such as China, America, Germany and (who would have thought it?) Vietnam – and, remarkably, Britons are only the fourth-biggest consumers of gin, just behind the Dutch and the Belgians and way behind the Spanish. But we are, though, the world's second-biggest consumers per head of champagne (after France itself) by a country mile.

Given our high consumption of booze, it is hardly surprising that Britain's culture and social habits have, over the centuries, been moulded and defined by the enormously broad variety of alcoholic drinks we have consumed. The French may drink more alcohol than us, but they have invariably chosen to focus predominantly on their own native products – creating an indissoluble link between *terroir* and taste, palate and politics that is the envy of food and drink producers elsewhere in the world. In contrast, Britain's relationship with its favourite alcoholic beverages – from beer to sherry, from wine to cocktails, from gin to alcopops – has always been a more complex story. It is a convoluted narrative that has resulted in a fascinating interplay of social interaction, product innovation, marketing ambition and public pretension.

This book interprets some of the key developments in Britain's post-war history through the prism of the nation's ever-changing drinking habits, as these preferences have evolved over eight decades. And it is surprising how much our attitudes and behaviours have changed over the years. Who would be seen drinking, for example, a Babycham and brandy, a cocktail unmistakeably evocative of 'Never Had It So Good' 1950s Britain, in a public place today? Yet someone is drinking Babycham somewhere: the drink's manufacturers claim that they now sell over 15 million of their small, individually-sized bottles a year, while there's a pub in Oxford that has even begun serving Babycham and brandies again.

While Babycham may still be with us, though, many of the drinking habits of past decades are rarely revisited, and our custom of resorting to the prop of alcohol for every conceivable occasion has all but disappeared. Some of our staple drinks have faded from history, along with the hopes and dreams they once incarnated; others have been miraculously revived and re-marketed to appeal to the retro-chic passions of younger generations. The go-to favourite tipples of yesteryear, which made overnight successes and even the odd flagship brand out of what were often uninspiring, mediocre or downright dishonest concoctions, say as much about the expectations of contemporary British society at that time and the way individual Britons saw themselves as did the actual *taste* of the drinks.

-

In *Another Round?* we trace the story of Britain through the medium of alcoholic drinks, exploring how the twelve profiled products encapsulated British political and societal values of their time. The stories of the rise and fall (or occasionally of the unstoppable ascent) of the brands we re-encounter here become metaphors for the history of Britain and its people. Britons may not drink more than many other nations, but our consumption of alcohol types and brands has changed out of all proportion since 1945. British tastes have diversified massively over the past eighty years, as consumers' expectations have amplified and their opportunities have broadened. The limited variety of alcoholic drinks available in the pub of the immediate post-war years – pint of beer for the gentleman, port and lemon for the lady – is now, thankfully, a distant memory.

The drinks selected for this revealing journey represent, I believe, some of the most successful and influential marketing success stories to emanate from post-war Britain. All of these narratives tell peculiarly British tales, allegories of the social and political context that spawned their (often unlikely) success. Their story is the story of post-war Britain – for better or worse.

I have tried, within the parameters of the format, to present a range of chronologies, of drink types and of manufacturers. The resulting lineup ranges from the venerable gin and tonic and that 1950s classic we have already mentioned, Babycham, to four notorious alcoholic brands that span four decades and which have always generated vociferous opinions, both for and against: Watney's Red beer, Blue Nun Liebfraumilch, Buckfast Tonic Wine and the WKD range of alcopops.

-

In 2004 Britons' alcohol intake peaked at a recorded all-time high of 11.6 litres per adult per year, around double that of fifty years earlier. Britons still, though, only drink half as much as they did at the peak of Victorian consumption in the 1870s. (And no, Victorian Britain was not full of drunks. Much of this alcoholic intake was worked off through walking, in a time before public transport or the car, or through strenuous manual labour.) Revealingly, though, wine consumption in Britain soared by almost 800% per cent from 1960 to 1995, from 3.6 pints per head per year to 32.1 pints. This extension of the wine franchise helped to democratise wine drinking – a trend accelerated by Labour chancellor Stafford Cripps' 56 per cent reduction in wine duty of 1949 and the Macmillan government's provision of licences to supermarkets to sell wine and spirits in 1962.

Naturally, our thirst for alcohol has not made us the healthiest nation on earth. Today 17 million working days are said to be lost each year in the UK due to hangovers and 'drink-related illness', while the cost to the National Health Service of dealing with more serious diseases and conditions that alcohol can cause or exacerbate continues to mount. But while British politicians are understandably less keen to be publicly associated with alcohol than they once were, the same is not true of Britain's celebrities. Famous names flock to be associated with a new range or brand of booze. British-based chat show host Graham Norton has for many years been a shareholder in New Zealand-based Invivo Wines; Cara Delevingne and her sisters own their own vegan prosecco brand, Della Vite; Gary Barlow helps create and market his own Spanish wines; David Beckham is the brand ambassador for Haig's blue-bottled new Club brand of light whisky; while British pop star Rita Ora has developed her own brand of Mexican tequila, Próspero. It is not just a simple case of using a familiar face to sell a particular product. The consequent interweaving of image, brand and reputation means that these drinks also help to ensure the star's continuing relevance and visibility in a merciless and unpredictable media landscape.

Such celebrity endorsements do, however, at least help Britons to dismantle traditional class and social barriers to drinking certain types of alcohol. Real ale and lager are, for example, no longer just seen as a male preserve; nor is the gin and tonic viewed as the tipple of the upper-middle classes. Ease of access has also helped to make consumption more egalitarian. The increasing roles that supermarkets play in alcohol retailing – supermarkets now account for well over 70 per cent of all alcohol sales in the UK – has not only promoted domestic drinking; it has also helped to make wine and spirit buying less stressful and more straightforward. No longer do wine buyers have to put up with the intimidating stare and condescending tone of the traditional wine merchant; now they can look, linger and choose whatever they wish in their own time.

A good example of how our alcohol shopping habits have changed over fifty years can be found in that old high street favourite, Marks and Spencer (M&S), the iconic British chain of department stores. M&S was originally founded to sell just clothing and household goods; it only began selling food in 1931, though it did go on to pioneer the sale of ready meals in the 1960s and 1970s. But M&S waited until 1974 to offer wine to its customers – and, even then, only after a hesitant in-store trial embracing just two wine brands. As drinks historian Jennifer Regan-Lefebvre has observed, during this trial Marks and Spencer 'seemed to be targeting nervous consumers ("Do you enjoy wine but find buying it a confusing, hit-or-miss affair?"), who are presumed to be female.' Even after the trial's results seemed to vindicate the enthusiasm of M&S shoppers for wine, the store's subsequent range was deeply conservative, featuring three 'party wines' that were cautiously described as 'a trio of attractive, reliable wines carefully blended to appeal to British palates and bottled in litres for drinking continental style at informal get-togethers with family and friends.' M&S's appeal was clearly targeted more to an aspirational lifestyle than to budding wine enthusiasts. And, as Regan-Lefebvre notes dryly, 'These unknown varietals of imprecise origin were sold by the litre.' Passing over M&S's blithe assumption that Europeans invariably drank their wine by the litre, it is worth noting that, when M&S did decide to extend their range of wines, they chose only bargain-basement stars of the 1970s party scene that are mercifully no longer with us: a German Liebfraumilch and a Yugoslav Riesling.

–

Another Round? does confirm many of the familiar stereotypes we love to recall and to ridicule. But it also charts how class consciousness in our choice of alcohol types, marques and brands has largely evaporated over the decades since 1945. The phenomenal growth of supermarket and off-licence chains in the 1960s and 1970s made alcoholic drinks of all types, from champagne to brown ale, available to everyone. In 1985 that celebrated historian of the industrial age, Professor Asa Briggs, published a commercial history especially commissioned by the Victoria Wine Company, a large, cut-price British network of off-licences founded, as its name suggests, way back in the Victorian era. Briggs's study 'showed that 40 percent of its customers in 1981 were drawn from social classes C2, D and E (which correspond to manual occupations, skilled through unskilled)', thus proving that 'Whether or not the class structure of Britain had changed in the post-war period, there is evidence that wine had its own place in working class culture… [and that Victoria Wine was] building on consumption trends that had been already established.' Today wine consumption is not based on class or background, but on price and image.

-

This book employs the iconic drinks of the period to take us on a rollercoaster ride through many of the key episodes in our island's post-war story. The decline of gin drinking in the 1950s and 1960s, for example, is presented as an allegory of Britain's withdrawal from empire, which started with the partition of India of 1947. Each successive imperial retreat brought scores of British military personnel and civil servants, most of them habitual gin and tonic drinkers, back from Asia and Africa to their home shores, where they found that their values were often at odds with the locals'. The rise and fall of Britons' taste for sherry is simultaneously linked to

Britain's political and economic decline in the Macmillan, Douglas-Home and Wilson years, as old-fashioned brown drinks signally failed to meet the social expectations and 'white heat' aspirations of the Swinging Sixties. We explore the globalisation of the British beer industry and the grassroots response to the corresponding diminishing of choice and character by what has since been hailed as the most successful pressure group in the post-war world: the Campaign for Real Ale. We also examine how the huge growth in package holidays that, allied to the UK's joining of the EEC in 1973, opened the door to new continental tastes – and how these tastes were cleverly exploited by products that in truth were often grotesque parodies of their supposed European models. We revisit the cocktail culture of the 1980s, popularised at least in part by the newly revitalised 'Special Relationship' between the UK and the US, as Ronald Reagan and Margaret Thatcher brought the two nations closer together than they had been at any time since 1945. And we rediscover that same decade's phenomenon of the widely publicised race to import the first Beaujolais Nouveau into the country: a manifestation of the ultra-competitive, over-hyped and over-active 'me' culture of the 1980s.

Nearer to our own time, we follow the disheartening trajectory of Blair's Britain between 1997 and 2007 – a time that promised so much but delivered so little – as reflected in the rise of the alcopop, through the story of a morally compromised product whose youth-focused styling and marketing effortlessly triumphed over content and value. And we see how, in the wake of the Brexit vote of 2016, the adult drink of choice of the 2020s became, somewhat bizarrely, an Italian aperitif suggestive of the

European cultures that a majority of Britons had just rejected.

-

This book abounds with ironies and paradoxes, incongruities and absurdities. Everyone will have their own, personal choice of drinks that they can cite as a mirror to Britain's post-war journey. I hope you find this very personal interpretation of our recent history both entertaining and enlightening.

Chapter 1

THE END OF EMPIRE

THE G&T

Gin has come a long way since its pernicious Georgian reputation as 'mother's ruin'. The terrible consequences of the Gin Craze of the eighteenth century led to destitution, prostitution, disfigurement, imprisonment and death. During the second half of the Victorian era, however, gin suddenly became respectable. Having been universally regarded as the scourge of working-class society, it was, owing to a remarkable stroke of fortune, unexpectedly recast as one half of that felicitous and engaging duo: gin and tonic. The G&T became the drink of Indian Army officers serving out in the British Raj – and subsequently the customary tipple of British Colonial Service officers and administrators serving across all of the pink bits[1] on the globe. These scions of empire habitually consumed their G&Ts when they retired to their shaded verandahs at the end (or even the middle) of the day.

The gin and tonic consequently evolved into a metaphor for empire. Resonantly symbolic of The Empire Where The Sun Never Sets (a ringing phrase first coined in Britain by the diplomat Lord Macartney in 1773),[2] and a fusion of that most English of spirits with a carbonated tonic ingeniously devised to ward off disease, the G&T was one of the essential foundations of British imperial rule. Wherever you found Britons overseas on imperial missions, you encountered the gin and tonic, too. And as the empire's representatives returned to Blighty[3] at the end of their service, they brought their G&Ts with them. It's just that their gin verandahs were now located in Leatherhead or Leamington rather than Lucknow or Lagos.

After 1945, however, this imperial image haunted the gin trade. By the 1960s the classic gin and tonic was frequently perceived by younger drinkers as old-fashioned, elderly and tainted with the stigma of outmoded imperialism – much, indeed, as was Britain herself.

The declining fashionability of gin in 1950s and 1960s Britain can be seen as an allegory of Britain's withdrawal from empire. As the British disengaged from their imperial possessions – starting with the precipitous withdrawal from the Indian sub-continent in 1947 and the surrendering of their Palestinian mandate in 1948, leaving a legacy of devastating turbulence, mass murder and civil war in the wake of their hasty retreats – the reputation of the G&T correspondingly slumped. Each successive withdrawal brought scores of British officers from the colonial civil service and armed forces, most of them confirmed gin-and-tonic drinkers, back to their home shores. None of which, though, served to make gin – and particularly not gin and tonic – a chic feature of the supposedly hip Britain of the Swinging Sixties. By the early 1970s, as the British government closed all of the nation's military bases sited 'east of Suez',[4] gin's image among the under-40s was irredeemably antiquated. The G&T was seen as a drink for old fuddy-duddies. And at the same time, the image of solid gin brands such as Booth's and Plymouth was, like the British economy of the time, at rock bottom.

Ironically, though, it was just those same imperial associations that helped the G&T to revive so spectacularly at the end of the twentieth century. Old colonial stereotypes helped gin distillers to trade on the drink's colourful and resonant heritage, while the spirit's innate Britishness proved an invaluable marketing tool. At the time of writing, gin is the fastest-growing sector of the spirits market, both in Britain and worldwide. You can barely find a pub or a bar these days without shelves groaning with craft gins and 'authentic' tonic waters.

-

Gin originated simply as a flavoured grain spirit – a close cousin to schnapps and vodka. While spirit distilling was pioneered (like so much else) by medieval monasteries, spirits such as gin were more widely drunk by Northern Europeans, who lived in countries whose chilly climates were not conducive for growing grapes, from the sixteenth century onwards.

The drink's name comes from the French for juniper, *genièvre*, the principal flavouring or 'botanical' of the spirit – a term that in Georgian Britain was often anglicised as 'geneva' or even the anthropomorphic 'Madam Geneva'. (More prosaically, British gin was often called 'Old Tom', presumably because the scent of juniper was reminiscent to some of cat pee. Each to their own.) Juniper was not the only organic ingredient to be added to gin, though. Today's 'botanicals', as they are called, can include angelica, cardamom, coriander, ginger, citrus peel, liquorice, nutmeg and, to fix these flavours in the spirit, orris (iris) root. In the eighteenth century, though, many of the ingredients added to 'bathtub' gin to mask its dubious origins were less benign, and included turpentine and sulphuric acid. All gins, though, were at this time sweetened with sugar. Dry gin, like dry champagne, was very much a late-Victorian innovation, as British palates turned away from sweet drinks to less cloying and supposedly more sophisticated styles.

Gin was, thanks to the influence and proximity of its native Netherlands, distilled in England in large quantities from the middle of the seventeenth century. And by 1700 gin had become the principal British spirit, for good or (more frequently) ill.

-

Gin's breakthrough moment came in 1688, with the accession to the English and Scottish thrones of the Dutch king William III, who was both impeccably Protestant and conveniently married to the daughter of the ousted Catholic monarch, James II. The drinking of gin – a habit that the British had, after all, picked up from the Dutch – now became a patriotic gesture. Not only was gin drinking supportive of both the new sovereign's country of birth and Britain's new ally; it also supported a native industry and, crucially, was also appropriately anti-French.

Britain was at war with France for most of the reigns of William III and Queen Anne, William's successor and sister-in-law; in fact, Britain seemed to be fighting France during much of the Georgian era. War with France inevitably brought with it a ban on the importation of French brandy, a move that caused native gin consumption to soar correspondingly. William III's government went even further: the 1690 Distilling Act raised taxes on beer but actually lowered them on home-made spirits – which effectively meant just gin. Beer taxes were hiked yet again, in 1694, to pay for the escalating and ruinously expensive French war. As a result, by 1700 a glass of beer was, astonishingly, more expensive than an equivalent glass of gin. This strange and potentially dangerous state of affairs was made worse by a series of poor harvests during the 1690s: beer, like whisky, needed high-quality barley to be successfully brewed, yet gin could be distilled from any old manky grain. Gin was on the rise.

By the 1720s the Gin Craze was in full spate in London and in Britain's port cities. Gin consumption rose from 500,000 gallons in England in 1689 to 11 million gallons in London *alone* by 1733. The late, great social historian Roy Porter calculated that by 1740 the average weekly consumption of gin in London was two pints *each* for every man, woman and child in the capital, and that every eighth house in London sold gin – as opposed to a mere 1 in 10 houses across the rest of the UK. In 1751 the novelist and anti-gin campaigner Henry Fielding estimated that gin was 'the principal sustenance' of 100,000 in London. In this context it was hardly surprising that, for twenty-eight years after 1723, the death rate in London actually outstripped the birth rate, and that, of those unfortunate children who were born to London's gin-sodden mothers, many were increasingly being born with deformities – while at the same time the capital's consumption of milk and other staple foods was declining alarmingly.

Gin of doubtful quality could be bought in every city back street or alleyway. It was even available anonymously by an ingenious, through-the-wall drawer service – the ancestor of the modern-day cash machine. This was often advertised by an image of a cat (to signify that 'Old Tom' could be found here) and operated by what was, intriguingly, called the 'puss and mew' system. The punter's spoken 'mew', accompanied by the requisite cash payment, would lead the vendor to open the through-the-wall drawer; the retailer would take the proffered coins and send a flask of the gin back down the chute.

William Hogarth's celebrated print *Gin Lane* of 1751. Hogarth graphically illustrates the damage that 'Mother's Ruin' can do – the only business that is flourishing in this

apocalyptic vision is the pawnbroker – in an attempt to persuade his audience to adopt healthier drinks such as beer, the subject of his companion print *Beer Street*.

Madam Geneva's merciless rampage through urban Britain seemed to be halted in its tracks by the 1751 Gin Act. This important legislation was the result of years of pressure brought by the reforming brothers Sir John and Henry Fielding and the runaway success of William Hogarth's damning paired prints *Gin Lane* and *Beer Street*. But with the outbreak of war with the French in 1778, and again in 1793, and the resulting prohibition of imports of French brandy, gin consumption rose yet again. It is revealing that some of today's best-known gin producers originate from the time of the French Revolutionary War – notably Coates' Plymouth distillery, founded in 1793, and that classic London Dry brand, Gordon's, founded in 1796.

Nor did gin drinking decline after the Battle of Waterloo finally brought the French wars to an end in 1815. The development of thick, strong plate glass enabled the creation of ever-larger windows, made without any internal glazing support, for the first time. Simultaneously, the introduction of gaslight into domestic and commercial interiors revolutionised after-dark activity indoors, while the Spirits Act of 1825 slashed the duty on gin by 40 per cent in order to stimulate trade. The combination of these three factors resulted in the notorious 'gin palace' of the early nineteenth century: an alluringly lit proto-pub whose attractive etched-glass windows were enticingly illuminated by gaslight. Inside the gin palace, as you might expect, were available copious quantities of gin, served by handpumps on the bar counter in order to speed up service. (This latter innovation was later mimicked by the beer-serving public houses set up by the Duke of Wellington's 1830 Beer Act to specifically combat the popularity of the gin palace.)

George Cruikshank's print *The Gin-Juggernath* of 1834 is a compelling allegory of the power of the brightly-lit and gaudily-decorated gin palaces of that era to ruin lives.

Charles Dickens describes a typical London gin palace in terms of admiration and disgust in his *Sketches by Boz* of 1836:

> *The extensive scale on which these places are established, and the ostentatious manner in which the business of even the smallest among them is divided into branches, is amusing. A handsome*

plate of ground glass in one door directs you 'To the Counting-house;' another to the 'Bottle Department;' a third to the 'Wholesale Department;' a fourth to 'The Wine Promenade;' and so forth… Then, ingenuity is exhausted in devising attractive titles for the different descriptions of gin; and the dram-drinking portion of the community as they gaze upon the gigantic black and white announcements, which are only to be equalled in size by the figures beneath them, are left in a state of pleasing hesitation between 'The Cream of the Valley,' 'The Out and Out,' 'The No Mistake,' 'The Good for Mixing,' 'The real Knock-me-down,' 'The celebrated Butter Gin,' 'The regular Flare-up,' and a dozen other, equally inviting and wholesome liqueurs.

–

Forty years after Dickens' account, however, the reputation of gin had been transformed. Gone was the evil, adulterated back-street killer of the previous century. As if by magic, in its place was conjured a thoroughly British spirit that now stood for empire, industry and, would you believe it, health. Beer-centric public houses had now largely replaced the gin palaces of the 1820s and 1830s, largely thanks to the financial incentives established for beer retailers by Wellington's 1830 Act – a far-reaching piece of legislation that explains why so many pubs are named after public figures of the 1830s such as George IV, William IV, Queen Adelaide, Queen Victoria and, of course, the Duke of Wellington himself.

However, far more important to gin's apotheosis as a reputable drink for modern times were, firstly, a more upmarket approach to the way in which it was packaged and sold and, secondly, its unlikely association with health-giving properties.

As glass technology raced ahead in the early nineteenth century, green and later clear glass bottles became increasingly used for spirits designed for home consumption – which was now a rapidly growing market. An understandable desire to see what you were buying, allied to the emergence of recognisable national gin brands, helped to accelerate the abandonment of ceramic vessels and the adoption of clearly branded glass containers. The latter were also crucial in creating an export trade. For much of the 1840s, the extrovert gin distiller and pioneering Arctic explorer Sir Felix Booth spent much of his considerable fortune pushing a private members' bill through parliament designed to remove duties on export gin. His efforts finally paid dividends (both literally and metaphorically) in the Gin Act of 1850; tragically, though, Booth only had a few weeks to enjoy his legislative success before he died of a heart attack in a Brighton boarding house. But Booth's Gin was, together with its rivals from Gordon's and Tanqueray, now able to be exported abroad in clear glass bottles.

Even more unexpected than the early Victorian technological advances in retail packaging, which in turn helped to launder British gin's reputation, were gin's unlikely associations with health and wellbeing – a strange quirk of fortune for the formerly insidious spirit. In 1824 one Dr Johann Siegert, a German-born military doctor who was then serving as Surgeon-General in the Military Hospital at Angostura in Venezuela, invented a herb-based cure for seasickness that he first called 'Amargo Aromatico' but later renamed the easier-to-pronounce 'Angostura bitters'. Visiting ships of the Royal Navy soon came upon Siegert's remedy and by the late 1820s were promoting it widely across the service. While rum had traditionally been the tipple of British sailors, Royal Naval officers preferred gin. Thus was the pink gin born: gin mixed with a few drops of Siegert's Angostura bitters to ward off on-board stomach disorders much as the gimlet, gin and lime juice, was frequently taken to keep scurvy at bay.

Then in 1858 came an even bigger break for the much-maligned spirit: the momentous invention by London mineral water manufacturer Erasmus Bond of 'aerated quinine tonic water'. The magic ingredient of Bond's new tonic, cinchona bark, had long been known as a prophylactic for malaria, the deadly, mosquito-borne disease that killed thousands every year across the British Empire. As early as the seventeenth century, Spanish Jesuits in Peru observed the native Quechua Indians using the bark of a shrub of the Rubiaceae family to combat fevers. But it was not until 1820 that two French scientists, Pierre Pelletier and Jean Caventou (the same pair who had, three years earlier, discovered the existence of chlorophyll in plants), found a way of extracting the crucial medicinal element, quinine, from the cinchona bark. Soon the British, too, had got in on the act, as was their way, and had begun to produce quinine on a large scale at the Royal Botanic Gardens in Kew.

By the end of the 1840s the British East India Company was importing about 700 tonnes of cinchona bark a year as a malarial preventative for their soldiers and civil servants across the sub-continent. However, quinine was horribly bitter, and hardly the most palatable of medicines. Bond's clever idea of softening its blow by combining the drug with soda water and sugar made it instantly acceptable to the British in India. And what better way to promote the intake of quinine than to add the officers' favourite snifter, gin, to Bond's health-giving tonic water. Better still, his invention could now be backed by the British government, which had just wrested the administration of India from the failed East India Company in the year Bond's commercial tonic water had first appeared – and a year after the Indian rebellion had sent a shudder through the British population of the Raj. Fittingly, Bond himself, after the untimely death of his wife, went to live with the family of a Southwark gin distiller, neatly reflecting the genesis of what was to become a world-famous drink.

Bond himself failed meet the demand for his tonic from the British Army in India; but a far bigger rival could: the Bristol-based firm founded by German-born chemist Johann Jacob Schweppe,[5] whose Indian Tonic Water of 1870, containing thirty milligrams of quinine per pint, became the market leader overnight. Never mind that you would need to drink around seventy litres of tonic water to ensure lasting protection against the malarial mosquito; it was the concept that mattered. The spectacle of Britons in India drinking tonic water with their daily ration of gin after dinner soon became a familiar ritual, one first mentioned in print in an account of the Sealkote (Sialkot) races near Lahore in *The Oriental Sporting Magazine* of 16 November 1868.

During the Fifties tonic water manufacturer Schweppes (founded in Geneva in 1783 but based in London from 1792) was still associating the consumption of the traditional gin-and-tonic with the armed services. The impressively-hirsute and rather contemporary-looking 'Commander' was actually based on a real person: Commander Edward Whitehead (1908-78) was a Royal Navy officer who had served in the Second World War

and who from 1950 worked for Schweppes as the public face of Ogilvy and Mather's advertising campaigns. Whitehead rose to become President of Schweppes USA and was awarded a CBE in 1961.

The gin and tonic was born at exactly the right moment. In the same year as Erasmus Bond's tonic hit the shelves, the dreaded phylloxera louse arrived in French vineyards, having (unbeknownst to anyone) hitched a ride on some imported American vine cuttings. Its disastrous effect on the French wine trade was not observed until 1865; and by then it was too late. Wine production in France was wrecked for years, while by 1880 the distilling of French cognac had virtually ceased. The brandy and soda, so long the staple of gentleman's clubs and the go-to drink for the middle classes before and after dinner, was now almost unobtainable. Eager to take its place in both the bar and the living room was the gin and tonic, a combination that has never looked back. The G&T even stole the clothes of its predecessor, being served in the cut-glass tumbler previously reserved for brandy and soda. The age of the gin and tonic had arrived.

During the ensuing decades the gin distillers went from strength to strength. Many small producers of weaker gin brands were wiped out in an instant in 1879, when Benjamin Disraeli's government decreed that, to be sold as 'gin', a spirit had to be of at least 37.5 per cent alcohol by volume (ABV). Nine years later, as the drinking public was turning definitively to dry, 'London' styles, as opposed to the old sweetened gins (even though 'London Dry Gin', then as now, has no legal definition nor protection), the Bloomsbury distiller Charles Tanqueray merged with its London rival Gordon's to produce the world's largest gin combine.[6]

In Delhi as in Devon, the gin and tonic was the default drink of both the British gentry and of its aspirational middle classes. Nothing, it seemed, could halt the onward march of Britain's burgeoning gin industry – not even America's Prohibition of 1920–33, which actually saw the consumption of gin *rise* in the US, thanks to imports from Britain and, particularly, the British Dominion of Canada. Gin remained the staple drink of London bars, Surrey drawing rooms and Indian gymkhana clubs right up to the Second World War.

–

As we have seen, however, gin's imperial baggage soon proved to be a disadvantage in the brave new world of post-war Britain, a country where America's trendy gin-based Martini culture had never really caught on and where the G&T was beginning to be seen as yesterday's drink.

The immediate aftermath of the war and the early years of imperial retreat, though, actually saw gin sales recover from their wartime nadir. Indeed, the G&T still seemed to be essential to the fabric of British middle-class life. After all, Winston Churchill himself – back in office as Britain's prime minister in 1951 – is supposed to have affirmed that 'The gin and tonic drink has saved more Englishmen's lives, and minds, than all the doctors in the empire' (though no one can find any documented evidence of this helpful remark). And after India, Pakistan, Ceylon and Burma had become independent in 1947–8, followed by Sudan in 1956, Ghana in 1957 and then over twenty imperial territories in the ensuing decade, hundreds of gin-and-tonic-drinking colonial administrators returned to the green hills and grey skies of Britain. The British Colonial Service actually expanded in the years after the Second World War, reaching a peak of about 18,000 posts in 1954; but nearly all of these administrators returned to Britain, along with nearly all of the 468 British staff who still remained in the Indian Civil Service (ICS) in 1947 following years of deliberate Indianisation.

British Army officers turned for home, too. Prior to the partition of what had been British India in 1947, 13,500 out of 22,000 officers in the old Indian Army – which in 1945 stood at an amazing 2.5 million men and constituted the largest volunteer army in the world – were British. Now, as Professor Yasmin Khan observes, while 'a few hundred, at the request of the undermanned Pakistani army, stayed on to train Pakistani soldiers… the majority swapped their uniforms for civilian positions in Britain.' (The same did not, incidentally, apply to the Royal Indian Navy, which, following the nationalist naval mutinies of 1946, retained very few British senior officers at independence.)

Some British officers and civil servants actually stayed in post after the army left; men such as Justice Donald Falshaw, who only retired as chief justice of the Punjab High Court in 1966, and Paul Scott's fictional 'Tusker' Smalley, the irascible former Indian Army colonel who subsisted on Carew's gin[7] in Scott's evocative novel *Staying On* of 1977. But they were few in number. Increasingly isolated and out of touch, like Scott's Colonel Smalley, they eked out a twilight existence in an ever-changing world-turned-upside-down that they increasingly failed to recognise.

Gin's reliance on associations with the services and the empire to market itself increasingly limited its market for younger audiences, who saw the gin-and-tonic as the drink of crusty old colonels who had lately returned from India or Kenya.

So post-war Britain – or at least the leafy Home Counties – was suddenly inundated with returning colonial and army officers, most of whom were habitual G&T drinkers. This, surely, would have been good for British gin sales. But, crucially, none of these returnees were young. British Colonial Service and ICS staff were invariably of advanced years – by 1943 the ICS had given up recruiting new staff from the UK, as no one under fifty wanted to join. Confirmed devotees of the G&T they may have been; but their custom only served to underline that the gin and tonic was fast becoming an imperial relic of an age that was fast disappearing.

This is not to say that the G&T suddenly disappeared from British life. Rather, the drink began to fade away gradually, as it was eclipsed by trendier drinks-of-the-moment such as vodka and white rum.

James Burrough's Beefeater gin was, with shrewd prescience, heavily promoted in both Britain and America at the time of the televised 1953 coronation of Queen Elizabeth II. But for Burrough it was really the American sales that counted. The US was a promising market in which to expand gin sales, as it was already well acquainted with the gin Martini and lacked any historical baggage – images of fusty, red-faced British colonels sozzled by tiffin-time – that might curtail G&T consumption.

The G&T even featured in post-war literature. It featured in Ian Fleming's James Bond spy thriller, *Dr No*, of 1958, in which Bond added the juice of a whole lime (an unheard-of luxury in contemporary Britain) to gin and tonic and also invented a new gin-based Martini, the Vesper, which combined vodka and Lillet Blanc vermouth with a gin base. Significantly, though, Bond's usual Martini was made with vodka, not gin.

Sixteen years later, the renowned poet Philip Larkin's poem 'Sympathy in White Major', from his 1974 collection *High Windows*, hymned the gin and tonic with unambiguous enthusiasm.

However, neither Fleming nor Larkin were exactly the sort of cool role models who might encourage the younger generation to take to the G&T. Both men fitted Professor Lisa Jardine's description of Larkin as 'a casual habitual racist, and an easy misogynist', and neither were exactly Labour voters. And both were increasingly out of step with the times.

-

From the mid-1950s, sales of vodka began to catch and then overtake those of traditional spirits such as gin. In 1954 the vodka market outstripped that of gin in the US for the first time. The same happened in the UK in the early 1970s – perhaps, not uncoincidentally, at almost the same time as Britain was withdrawing her forces from the former East of Suez imperial territories (Singapore, Malaya and the Trucial States on the Persian Gulf) at the end of 1971.

By 1971 white spirits such as vodka and white rum were all the rage. Perceived as dry, sophisticated, international and classless, they echoed the egalitarian emphasis of 1960s culture and the forward-looking philosophy embodied in Harold Wilson's celebrated 'White Heat of Technology' speech of 1963. Though it was technically a 'white drink' too, gin was rarely considered in the same breath. As gin expert Geraldine Coates has remarked, by this time gin 'was perceived as old hat and middle-aged, the drink of the Home Counties bridge-playing set.'

As Britain entered Margaret Thatcher's 1980s, gin sales in the UK continued to fall. The dispiriting response of the big distillers, though, was to retrench rather than to innovate.

Diageo dropped the strength of some of their leading brands, including the market leader Gordon's, from 40 per cent ABV to the legal minimum strength of 37.5 per cent. This short-term palliative may have shored up Diageo's profits, but it did nothing to enhance brand image or the viability of the sector in the longer term.

In hindsight, the reductions in the strength of gin to which some leading producers resorted in the 1980s and early 1990s were actually going the wrong way. For by the end of the 1990s the gin market had recovered spectacularly, through new or spin-off brands promoted not on their mixability, nor outmoded notions of an inherent social cachet, but on alcoholic strength, heritage and, most importantly, taste. The marketing emphasis of these new brands highlighted the captivating story of gin's botanicals, rather than underlining the spirit's suitability to blend anonymously, vodka-like, with whatever mixer was to hand. At the same time, these new gins were not afraid to cite gin's rich imperial legacy in order to conjure a strong brand narrative.

The Gin Revival of the late twentieth century was effectively launched by the appearance in 1986 of Bombay Sapphire. Created by Grand Metropolitan's International Distillers and Vintners (IDV) subsidiary, and originally distilled by Greenall's of Warrington,[8] the new brand concept adapted from IDV's old Bombay Dry marque in a novel format that provided British gin with an exciting new direction. Bombay Sapphire's distinctive, pale blue bottle, easily recognisable on any bar back, together with the innovative stressing of the product's botanicals, virtually created a new premium gin sector on the spot.

Following Bombay Sapphire's instant success, other distillers followed IDV's in upgrading some of their well-known existing brands. The biggest turnaround was for Plymouth Gin. Plymouth boasted the oldest surviving gin distillery in the UK (their Blackfriars site in Plymouth's historic Barbican district was well established as early as 1697, although the current firm was founded a century later) and by 1900 was the largest gin manufacturer in the country. From the 1860s it was beloved of cocktail aficionados as well as naval officers, and until 2015 it even enjoyed a Protected Geographical Designation (PDO), like champagne and Stilton. However, with the decline of gin in the 1950s, Plymouth was gradually forgotten. Its Coates family owners sold up in 1953 and the distillery was subsequently bought up by Whitbread in 1975 and by Allied Domecq in 1991. Allied already had a flagship gin in the shape of Beefeater, though, so they relegated the venerable Plymouth brand to the lower divisions as a basic running gin, which was now made from cheap cane spirit rather than traditional grain. However, with the renewed interest in gin's heritage, salvation was at hand. In 1996 Plymouth was rescued from Allied's uncertain grasp by the founder of the small St Peter's Brewery in Suffolk, brand authority John Murphy, who restored it to its original recipe and strength (41.2 per cent). The gin's runaway success attracted first Vin and Sprit (the makers of Absolut vodka) and subsequently Pernod Ricard, who restored Plymouth to its rightful place on the bar backs and supermarket shelves of Britain.

–

Since the millennium there has been a veritable explosion in the number of gins available across the UK, as well as a surge in interest in the absorbing history of the G&T. In 2018 the Office for National Statistics announced that UK sales of gin had rocketed an astounding 267 per cent, from £130 million to £461 million, over the preceding decade, and predicted that the UK 'gin boom' showed no signs of stopping. And they were right. UK gin sales have passed half a billion pounds in value since 2009, with Britain now producing almost three-quarters of all gin made in Europe.[9] One hundred new gin distilleries were founded in the UK alone in 2022 (the Covid pandemic having, unsurprisingly, helped to grow home consumption of G&Ts), with a further fifty being added in 2023. Traditional (i.e. British-style) gin is estimated to grow by around 5 per cent over the next five years, says the International Wines and Spirits Record.

Not all of this growth is down to heritage styles, of course. The range of flavoured gins has grown exponentially, from mint to ginger and from cherry to rhubarb. (Though there is nothing new about flavoured gins: historically these gins were often seasoned with saffron.)[10] Often these brightly coloured additions to the bar and supermarket shelf have been devised and promoted as spin-offs of familiar brands. Thus Diageo's well-established Tanqueray gin has, over the last thirty years, been transformed into 1997's Malacca version, a sweeter drink made with grapefruit (discontinued in 2001 but reintroduced in 2012); 2002's No.TEN, a stronger version of the original brand, at 47.3 per cent, and distilled four times to produce an acclaimed, award-winning super-premium gin that has adapted Tanqueray's green cocktail-shaker bottle of the 1930s in a more contemporary idiom; 2011's Rangpur, a variant that unashamedly trades on the brand's Raj heritage and which features lime juice, ginger and bay leaves; 2013's Old Tom, a sweetened nod to an even more distant gin history; 2019's Blackcurrant Royale, clearly aimed at the younger, female market; and, in a sign of the times, 2021's alcohol-free version, 0.0. At the same time, Bombay Sapphire has spawned Bombay Sapphire East, with lemongrass and black pepper; Star of Bombay, with bergamot and ambrette (hibiscus) seeds (and a strength of 47.5 per cent); Bombay Bramble, which includes blackberries and raspberries; and Bombay Sapphire English Estate, featuring mint, rosehip and hazelnut. All of these adaptations hark back to a British gin heritage that, for decades after 1945, were seen as an embarrassment rather than an asset.

These days, it is now gin that is eclipsing vodka, rather than the other way round. In 2014 drinks expert Paul Gallagher cited 24-year-old gin convert Rebecca Palmer, who 'describes herself as coming through university "at the tail-end of the vodka drinking generation"':

> *'When I was at university we all drank vodka,' she said. 'I think that's because that is what everyone had been doing for years and my parents and grandparents were gin drinkers so I didn't want to drink what they were drinking. Now we are a little older I think most of my friends are choosing gin over vodka. I think it's the 20- and 30-somethings that are really getting into gin now, and obviously the classic gin drinkers of the older generations are still drinking it too, so it is spanning a range of ages, which is great.'*

Gallagher's subsequent in-depth research on London's premier bars (well, someone has to do it...) revealed that, even as early as 2014, premium gin was regarded as the most important spirit in a venue's portfolio. With gin on a seemingly unstoppable rise, the prevalence of gin in the on-trade is even more widespread today.

The growth of gin drinking has, of course, generated a G&T revival too. There are now pubs and bars across Britain that only serve gin and tonics: here customers are greeted by a formidable and even forbidding wall of gins when they enter, and both the tonic and the resulting G&T's organic embellishment are carefully chosen to match the distinctive characteristics and featured botanicals of the chosen gin. As recollections of Britain's troubled retreat from empire fade from the national memory, the G&T is once more the height of fashion.

Chapter 2

THE RISE AND FALL OF CHAMPAGNE PERRY

BABYCHAM

Britain in the early 1950s was still struggling to emerge from the shadow of war, bankruptcy and austerity. Wartime rationing was still in force: the supply of sugar and sweets was still regulated until 1953 and the availability of meat was controlled until 1954, while coal rationing did not end until 1958. As historian Dominic Sandbrook has remarked: 'At the beginning of the 1950s… Britain had been threadbare, bombed-out, financially and morally exhausted. Its major cities were still bombsites, it was almost impossible for many families to borrow money, rationing was harsher than ever, and there was an acute shortage of decent housing.' The nation was in dire need of cheering up – and what better way than through a cheap and cheerful alcoholic drink that didn't take itself too seriously.

In the immediate post-war years, most British-made top-end luxury goods were earmarked for export rather than domestic consumption. Thus the much-heralded 1946 design exhibition at the Victoria and Albert Museum in London, optimistically entitled 'Britain Can Make It', was unofficially dubbed 'But You Can't Have It!'

by those who had been lucky enough to see it. Christian Dior's radical, fabric-heavy 'New Look' fashions might have swept the world of haute couture after 1947, William Haynes's Jaguar XK120 of 1948 might have been one of the best-looking and finest-engineered sports cars ever created (no less a global celebrity than Clark Gable bought the first production model), while Scottish smoked salmon might have fetched eye-watering prices in global markets after 1945. However, very few Britons could afford such unattainable indulgencies.

Alcohol had not been rationed during the Second World War but was only intermittently available. On the outbreak of war distilleries were closed by government order so as to save grain for food, and compelled to distil just for industrial use. While some producers reopened after restrictions were lifted in 1944, seventy whisky distilleries did not survive the hostilities. Even as late as 1948 some pre-war gin and whisky distilleries had not yet managed to reopen. Those that did concentrated on exporting their wares to the dollar-rich United States, where the former arsenal of democracy had seamlessly metamorphosed into the acme of conscious consumption. The UK's brewing industry, too, was in a sorry state. During the war, beer had often been watered down from its pre-war strengths; now there was no longer a war on, though, this widespread dilution was continued. Many pre-war beers, indeed many breweries, also failed to reappear after 1945.

By the time of Queen Elizabeth II's coronation in 1953, however, British manufacturing was getting back on its feet. New ranges of packaged foods, new British-made car models and chic but affordable clothes were now within purse-range of the domestic consumer. In this coronation year the number of televisions sold to private homes soared as Britons sought to watch the ceremony – the first-ever televised coronation – in the comfort of their own homes.

That same year, one little-known Somerset brewery hit upon a novel idea: offer those average Britons just emerging from austerity a festive, sparkling tipple that was cheap but fun. Thus was born Babycham: the celebratory drink that looked like champagne, but wasn't. But not only did Babycham's bubbles come at a fraction of the price of genuine French bubbly – a luxury that very few New Elizabethans could afford – it also pioneered daring, new, American advertising and marketing methods. Perhaps most importantly, it was the first British alcoholic drink to be aimed squarely at women.

The styling of the bottle and the glass both helped to enhance Babycham's appeal to post-war women desperate for something chic, stylish and out of the ordinary. Many British women were, in the early 1950s, increasingly going out in the evenings (in groups, though; never alone) and wanted something affordable that they could drink that was, at the same time, stylish and classy. Babycham's creator, Francis Showering, noted that, in the pubs of 1950s Britain, 'Every man knew what he wanted, a pint of beer, but the ladies had little choice and they often ended up with a port and lemon. The new drink was perfect for them.' More recently, historian Penny Dade summarised Babycham's appeal to women in a similar vein: it was, she remarked, 'a short, not-too-alcoholic drink for women who did not drink beer but could not afford whisky and other spirits.' Social historian David Kynaston similarly observed that

> *...for women who were not teetotallers, there was by the early 1950s a new, sparkling drink available in the form of the affordable (1s 3d), brilliantly marketed 'champagne' perry with the appealing Bambi deer symbol. Babycham's creator Francis Showering... at last freed women from the dismal and expensive alternatives of, in an obituarist's words, 'milk stout, sweet cider or the sickly VP wines.'*[11]

As biographer Philip Norman later asserted, somewhat more bluntly, in his autobiography *Babycham Night*: 'Babycham was the first drink a woman could order in a bar without feeling a tart or a crone.'

Babycham came to epitomise the Brave New World of mid-1950s Britain, a time when wartime rationing was a thing of the past, British was still best, British ingenuity still seemed to lead the world, and anything seemed possible. Babycham's innovative brand design, marketing methods and advertising techniques brought flashy and flamboyant American techniques to the staid world of British beverages as its makers exploited not just the expanding potential of magazines and radio but, crucially, the revolutionary medium of television advertising.

-

The Showering family of Shepton Mallet had run a modest brewery in Kilvert Street since the seventeenth century. By 1945 the firm was concentrating on producing (unrationed) cider rather than beer, and was effectively run by the four Showering brothers: Arthur, Herbert, Ralph and Francis, all of whom had been educated at the town's grammar school. Arthur, the eldest, was the brewer; Herbert was destined to become the firm's chairman; Ralph soon displayed a talent for marketing; while Francis specialised in product development.

The four brothers worked together surprisingly well, each contributing their own particular expertise. In the years after the war's end, Herbert was keen to expand the business, while Francis, who had trained as a chemist, was eager to deploy a new, sterile filtration process he had helped to develop in order to improve the shelf quality and appearance of the brewery's perry products. This breakthrough had been the brainchild of the University of Bristol's Long Ashton Research Station, a research centre that was already famous for having invented the vitamin C-rich, blackcurrant-based wartime children's drink Ribena. Perry had always been difficult to make consistently in large quantities, as the fruit rots if not processed within days of ripening. Francis Showering overcame this by juicing the pears and using Long Ashton's clever new filtration process to enable Showerings to make perry all year round.

Francis also encouraged the propagation of the Williams pear, a species long grown and eaten as a dessert pear in southern England but which for centuries had been distilled in Europe, particularly France, to make pear eaux-de-vie. The brothers grafted Williams stock onto traditional, high-tannin perry cultivars such as Barnet and Blakeney Red and planted thousands of acres of the resulting hybrid at local farms they had bought expressly for this purpose in and around Shepton Mallet. The juice from these pears, when fermented, produced its own carbon dioxide; this, in turn, gave the product its gentle, natural sparkle.

The result was a wholly new alcoholic fizzy drink with a modest strength of 6 per cent alcohol by volume (ABV). Packaged in full-sized[12] bottles as well as fashionable, handbag-sized eight- and four-ounce versions and even tiny two-ounce ones, it was originally named 'Champagne de la Poire' by its proud parents. In that guise it was tested at the Three Counties Agricultural Show and other regional agricultural fairs, where its popularity quickly established that the Showerings had a hit on their hands. The tests also demonstrated, though, that the family needed to change a couple of things. Firstly, the packaging. The small eight- and four-ounce (10cl) bottles, which neatly filled a whole wine glass, could be used up in one go; however, the 'champagne' in the full-size bottles rapidly went flat after the bottle had been opened. As a result, the firm began to concentrate on the smaller sizes.

In addition, at the agricultural shows most of the locals had found pronouncing the French vowels of the 'sophisticated' brand name distinctly challenging. Accordingly, the Showerings sensibly resolved to abandon their rather pretentious-sounding francophone monicker. But to what?

The history of alcoholic drinks rather appropriately abounds with myths and legends, from Dom Pérignon inventing champagne (why on earth would you put a blind monk in charge of the cellars?!) to the cautionary tale that the wormwood in absinthe could make you mad (it couldn't: predictably, it was the alcoholic volume that did that). Even the relatively modest sparkling perry that is Babycham is not immune to such folklore. There are, for example, various competing traditions concerning how the drink was eventually named. One story has it that the prizes it had won at the south-western agricultural shows earned it the nickname of 'Baby Champ'. (But then, would there really have been prizes for a Best Perry?) Another version has the factory's transport manager asking his colleagues, 'Where would you like the baby cham [champagne] sent to?' Meanwhile, old advertising hands attest that it was the ad agency that dreamed up both the brand name and the deer logo (even though Showerings' ad agency wasn't formed until 1951). In the absence of any documentary evidence, the jury is out. What we do know is that the Babycham name was adopted and registered as a trademark in 1950, just in time to allow the Showerings to test the drink on pubs and off-licences in the Bristol area.

Babycham was an innovatory product in so many ways. It was, thanks to Herbert Showering, a standard-bearer of modern marketing as the first alcoholic brand to be specifically promoted to women. Babycham was inexpensive and not terribly strong; yet it also promised the post-war woman a glamour and exuberance that was all too often sadly lacking in a grey, impoverished post-austerity Britain starved of both. Moreover, the drink's small bottle was not only attractively coloured but was also easy to grasp and pour. And at the epicentre of Showerings' marketing message was a brand assurance that promised the prospect of a champagne lifestyle at a beer price. Babycham was, Showerings advised their female customers, best served in an attractive, undeniably feminine French champagne coupe – the historic glass shape associated with fashionable female society and which had allegedly been based on the shape of Queen Marie Antoinette's breasts. (We have no idea how or when this rumour started: it only became current long after the doomed French queen's execution in 1793.) Coupes were soon being customised by Showerings, plastered with the brand's deer logo; thus was a kitsch collectible born.

Babycham offered the aspirational female Briton of the 1950s a fleeting illusion of glamour and sophistication at the price of an average pub tipple. While most women of 1953 may not have been able to afford a Dior New Look dress or a pair of Salvatore Ferragamo stilettos, they could certainly afford a Babycham. It was at least a start.

–

The instant success of the Showerings' creation encouraged the family to phase out their production of beer (in 1952) and cider (in 1953) in order to concentrate on their sparkling perry. The Showering brothers were, nevertheless, wary of putting all their commercial eggs into one bottle (to mangle a metaphor). Accordingly, they adapted Babycham's four-ounce bottles to serve an alternative miniature drink that was also aimed at women: a sparkling rosé of vaguely Mediterranean origin that the Showerings called, for some reason, 'Rosayne... The exhilarating pink wine with the exciting champagne sparkle!' Unlike Babycham, though, Rosayne signally failed to capture the public's imagination following its 1954 launch. Its appeal was probably limited by the unintentionally suggestive print ads produced for the drink's unveiling, which featured the weak tagline 'Tonight's the night for Rosayne' beneath an illustration of a socially ambitious yet scantily clad good-time girl. British women of the 1950s didn't want to go *that* far.

Undeterred by Rosayne's failure, the Showerings were determined that the promotion of Babycham should be as bold and innovative as possible. Accordingly, the brothers resolved to secure the best advertising talent around. And so they went to London, to visit the leading advertising agency of the time, the celebrated Anglo-American firm of J. Walter Thompson (JWT) at their impressive offices at the prestigious address of 40 Berkeley Square, in the heart of London's prestigious, aristocratic Mayfair quarter.

There are many versions of what happened next. The most credible story is that Herbert and Francis Showering (Francis had been managing director of the family firm since 1949) simply turned up at JWT's imposing reception desk without having made a prior appointment. In their country clothes and with their Somerset accents, the Showerings apparently failed to impress the receptionist of London's biggest and most distinguished agency. She was just about to dismiss them out of hand when she remembered that JWT had recently agreed to loan the unoccupied top floor of their well-appointed office block to a fledgling new agency, Masius Wynne-Williams.[13] Accordingly, she directed the brothers upstairs, to the far smaller, newly established agency – which, she curtly suggested, might suit their aspirations better. Which, indeed, Masius duly did.

–

Jack Wynne-Williams was one of the most colourful and successful of the legendary London ad men of the 1950s and 1960s. Handsome and impeccably dressed, suave and persuasive, inspirational and intuitive, he was the sort of cocksure creative famously celebrated by the fictional TV series *Mad Men*: London's very own combination of Bert Cooper, Don Draper and Roger Sterling. Former Masius creative director Paul Donnelly, who worked on the Babycham account for years, recalls Wynne-Williams padding silently around the offices in his impeccable suits and monogrammed slippers. And in an interview with the *Guardian* of 2008, long-serving Masius executive and legendary motor racing commentator Murray Walker noted reverently of Wynne-Williams that

> *He was an inspirational leader, a charismatic personality who had the common sense and brains to pick the right people to work for him, outline what he required of them and then leave them alone to get on with it. He was very quick to praise people if they did a good job but equally quick to kick them up the backside if they didn't. He was urbane and suave and had this curious mix of being laid back but at the same time demanding; I suppose he was an iron fist in a velvet glove who inspired great loyalty through his approach.*

In order to secure the account and impressed by the Showerings' ambition, which seemed to match his own, Wynne-Williams agreed to take on the Babycham business without commission as a sign of goodwill, at least for the first year. It was a gamble that paid off handsomely. Babycham stayed with Masius for thirty years, while the agency helped to make the brand into a national phenomenon. A grateful Herbert Showering apparently joked to Jack Wynne-Williams at their first meeting that Showerings would buy him a Rolls-Royce once Babycham had reached 1 million pounds in annual sales. Twelve months later, during a meeting at the Shepton Mallet offices, Showering silently passed Jack Wynne-Williams a set of Rolls-Royce car keys over the conference table.[14]

Together, Showerings and Wynne-Williams' Masius advertising agency revolutionised the staid, predictable, male-oriented world of 1950s Britain. Babycham became Britain's first food or drink brand created by advertising alone; a product whose ebullient marketing ushered in a new era of American-style consumerism. As the British economy and Britain's global presence both receded during the later 1950s and 1960s, Britons increasingly turned to the solace afforded by the explosion in consumer choice. For those looking for something new to drink at an affordable price, Babycham was at the head of the queue.

Image was key to Babycham's success. And first on the agenda was the drink's brand identity. Ralph Showering, the family's marketing expert, worked with Masius's creatives to develop an instantly recognisable logo in the American mould: a leaping golden-yellow fawn wearing a big blue bow round its neck – colours that matched those of the bottles. The endearing animal worked up by Masius's art department[15] as the Babycham logo was a cross between a Chinese water deer and the title character that illustrator Marc Davis had devised for Disney's much-loved animated film *Bambi* of 1942. Chinese water deer could, oddly enough, actually be found grazing in the fields near Shepton Mallet: the Showerings had bought three of these beasts from the 11th Duke of Bedford[16] and eventually amassed a whole herd of them. Masius's artists eliminated the devilish tusks of the Shepton Mallet water deer, though; and, borrowing from Davis, they added cute vestigial antlers to create an endearing, Disneyesque composition.

An early Masius Wynne-Williams print ad for Babycham of the mid-1950s. The female drinker, the company deer and the coupe glass are all there, even if the overall composition is a bit chaotic. (Is the deer about the jump into her glass?)

Frustratingly, while the little deer mascot looked nothing like a baby chamois – a chamois is actually a rather ungainly goat-antelope – Showerings' own staff, thinking of the drink's brand name, persisted in calling the deer a 'chamois', much to the chagrin of its creators.

The eyecatching new deer logo featured in Masius's new press ad campaign of autumn 1953[17] and, apart from an unfortunate hiatus during the 1990s, has been with us ever since. It was soon being applied not just to champagne coupes and bottles but also to ashtrays, coasters, serving dishes, cutlery holders and personal jewellery – all of which are now highly collectable. A wide range of promotional point-of-sale items were also commissioned, including oversize plastic mascots with detachable big blue bows for bar counter display.

Even more groundbreaking was Masius and Showerings' audacity in harnessing a wholly new advertising vehicle – one from which many British manufacturers initially shrank. The Independent Television Network (ITN) first launched in Britain at 7:15 p.m. on 22 September 1955. To start with, no alcoholic product dared embrace the airwaves. But the instantaneous impact of this exciting new advertising medium soon inspired both agency and client. Masius's first television ad for Babycham aired later that autumn, constituting the first-ever commercial for an alcoholic drink ever shown on British television. And while this first ad was a relatively simple and swiftly assembled animated piece, Masius's subsequent television commercials were increasingly slick and costly. The sixty-second film the agency produced for 1956, which boasted impressive, Disney-style animation that dissolved into a real-life couple at its conclusion, was directed by legendary French film producer and advertising director André Sarrut.

From its very inception, the Babycham brand was built on Masius's advertising. Together, the Showering brothers and Jack Wynne-Williams demonstrated just what could be achieved with what was, after all, an affordable but inessential luxury in post-rationing Britain. Manufacturing equipment at the Shepton Mallet plant had to be upgraded regularly to keep up with the plant's burgeoning order book, despite the fact that the site already featured the fastest bottling line in the world. To meet the soaring demand, Showerings also bought a number of new farms across Somerset on which to plant new pear orchards to supply the Shepton Mallet factory. By 1966 Babycham output in Shepton Mallet had reached 108,000 bottles an hour, while new bottling plants were being opened in Ireland and Belgium; and at its peak the Somerset factory was churning out 144,000 bottles each hour. As early as 1959 Showerings was accounting for all of the UK's perry pear crop, compelling the firm to augment their product with juice from European pears.[18]

Babycham epitomised the unstuffy, American-influenced and increasingly gender-aware current that was seeping into 1950s Britain. Babycham's marketing also managed to project an aura of affordable exclusivity. As early as 1953 the sparkling drink was being advertised as 'the genuine champagne perry' best served 'sparkling in its own glamorous [champagne] glass' in order to head off any potential Babycham clones. When, in 1965, the now-legendary *Good Food Guide* founder Raymond Postgate derided Babycham in an article for *Holiday* magazine as a drink that 'looks like champagne and is served in champagne glasses [but] is made of pears' he uncharacteristically missed the point. Only the very dimmest punters actually believed that Babycham really *was* champagne.[19] Despite Postgate's inappropriate censure, the tagline 'The genuine champagne perry', along with the familiar request 'I'd love a Babycham', both lasted well into the 1980s.

In the hands of the Showerings and Jack Wynne-Williams' rapidly expanding Masius agency, the marketing of Babycham became even more inventive, and even a little bizarre, during the Swinging Sixties. During that decade campaigns promoted 'Babycham Babe' beauty contests across Britain's seaside resorts. They also introduced an unlikely point-of-sale *Girl's Survival Guide* – '24 tips for sparkling success from Babycham' – printed on coasters and bar-counter leaflets. The *Guide*'s gushing prose told young women to bear in mind that there were four (just four) key priorities for dealing with both life and men: *Your Lair, Your Prey, Your Ammunition* and *In the Jungle.* Follow-ups to the *Guide* included a 'Babe Starter Beauty Kit', free with four Babycham bottle foil tops; the *Babycham Guide to Palmistry*; a *Babycham A Passion for Fashion* guide; and *The Babycham Girl Zodiac* series. For older drinkers, the firm cheekily promoted a *Babycham Cocktail Guide*, which featured such unlikely 'sparkling' concoctions as the 'Babycham Florida' (Babycham and orange juice, of course), the 'Babycham Stinger' (Babycham, brandy and Angostura bitters)[20] and, for those braver souls, 'Babycham Black Mist' – Babycham mixed with Guinness, a cheap and cheerful riff on Black Velvet. In 1968 Masius Wynne-Williams went even further and announced a cross-media campaign across press, cinema, TV and radio to announce the fantasy drama world of 'Babychamland' – the Barbie-like home of the Babycham. Sadly, though, the little deer's new kingdom was short-lived.

The brief existence of Babychamland notwithstanding, the continuing success of Babycham persuaded the Showerings to revisit the spin-off market fourteen years after Rosayne had sunk like a lead balloon. In 1968 they repurposed the four-ounce bottle once again – this time for a product they called 'Pony', 'the little drink with a big kick'. Pony was far from being a Babycham derivative, though. It was instead a dark, murky and incredibly sweet British 'sherry', presumably borrowed from their corporate cousins at Vine Products, makers of those downmarket Christmas perennials VP and QC sherries. In the event, though, there proved to be a limit to the appeal of a miniature bottle of cream sherry from Somerset, made from wine concentrate from God knows where. Pony's sales barely reached a trot and the brand was finally led to the knacker's yard around 1975.

–

The 1970s was the Age of Colour in Britain, as the irresistible spread of colour television ownership – and indeed the introduction of numerous American-made colour television programmes, since British companies had precious few colour series ready when the time came – was instrumental in encouraging Britons to become more curious and marketing-aware consumers. Colour television had been first introduced into the UK by BBC Two in 1967 – a mere sixteen years after the US had first introduced colour television broadcasts. By the mid-1970s it had become widespread in Britain: 1976 was the year in which colour TV sets first outnumbered black-and-white ones in the UK. In 1957 only 44 per cent of UK households had owned a television at all; by 1970 that had soared to 92 per cent, and by the end of the 1970s it was nearing 100 per cent – with the vast majority of them being colour. And with the advent of colour television came new advertising opportunities.

Given that Babycham's attractive gold and blue packaging, not forgetting the sparkling, pale-golden perry itself, filmed very well, both Showerings and Masius Wynne-Williams were keen to expand their advertising reach on television as this new Age of Colour dawned. Masius also sought to capitalise on the new wave of nostalgia for 1950s music and products sparked by Warren Casey's 1972 hit musical *Grease* and George Lucas's celebrated 1973 acclaimed cult film *American Graffiti*. However, the era of Disneyesque animated whimsy was now seemingly over. The appeal of the engaging little deer, in particular, had begun to fade and the fawn was relegated to a supporting role in Masius's new TV spots, which tended to be live-action advertisements with a harder edge and a more visible brand strategy. Masius's fizzy new mantra was 'Babycham's got sparkle, Babycham's got life', with the deer logo added only as a closing afterthought – although the eternally imploring 'I'd love a Babycham' was always somewhere in the background.

And paralleling the Western world's cultural drift from 1960s innocence to 1970s cynicism, and reflecting the somewhat predatory sexism of this troubled decade, Masius's ads were now fronted not by the charmingly petite deer nor a doting dating couple, but by the suave, handsome 'ladies' man' Patrick Mower, an actor then best known for playing a series of compelling but calculating and hard-bitten TV cops. In 1966 Mower had even been auditioned for the role of James Bond – but was judged to be too young.[21] He may not have won the highly coveted role of the world's most famous spy, but Pinewood's loss was Shepton Mallet's gain. In Masius's new TV and cinema commercials Mower found himself parachuted into Bond-like scenarios: frequenting parties, surrounded by beautiful women, and pressing an ice-cold Babycham coupe against the bare leg of a woman as she sunbathed. As you did then. Not quite 007, perhaps, but at least it paid Mr Mower's bills.

All of this Americanised marketing paid handsome dividends. Babycham's sales tripled between 1962 and 1971, enabling the Showerings to punch considerably above their weight on the national corporate stage. In 1968 they ensured that Babycham became a key element in a far larger drinks conglomerate: the leviathan Allied Breweries, one of Britain's soon-to-be-notorious 'Big Six' brewing combines that now dominated the beer and pub industries. However, this was not meant to signal that retirement was on the cards for the effervescent Showerings. In fact, quite the opposite. After taking the family firm public in 1959, Francis Showering had augmented its portfolio through the acquisition of Gaymer's Cider, Vine Products (VP, of downmarket sherry fame), Whiteways of Whimple and Britvic fruit juices. In 1966 Showerings even acquired the venerable sherry and wine importers Harveys of Bristol, whose august directors had for years looked down their noses at the Babycham *arrivistes* nearby. And in 1968 the unstoppable Showerings effectively took control of Allied Breweries itself. Francis Showering became a key director of the new company, while in 1975, at the height of Babycham's success, his nephew Keith became Allied's chairman and chief executive, which he remained until his sudden death in 1982. (By that time

Keith Showering had in turn merged Allied with the food and catering giant J. Lyons to create the food and drink behemoth of Allied Lyons.)

In the meantime, the Showerings batted away a legal attempt of 1978 by the French champagne industry to prevent Babycham's lighthearted use of the term 'champagne' in their marketing. As it turned out, the EU's Protected Designation of Origin rules of 1992 stopped any further reference by Babycham's makers to 'champagne', anyway. By that time, though, Babycham's new owners had long since ceased making any such comparison. And the drink was well past its peak.

-

It was in the early 1980s that Babycham's sales began first to fall, and then to plummet. During this decade the drinks market was becoming more sophisticated and diverse, with women turning more to wine and cocktails than to retro tipples of sparkling pear juice poured from dinky little bottles. The Babycham brand and its winsome fawn logo now seemed rather old-fashioned. If it was remembered at all, it was now associated with celebrations such as birthdays or Christmas. No longer was it seen as a regular treat.

To address Babycham's shrinking market share, Allied Lyons resorted to the time-honoured panacea of firing its advertising agency, Masius (later known as D'Arcy-MacManus and Masius). Old personal loyalties now counted for little: Jack Wynne-Williams was dead and Francis Showering, now in his seventies, was semi-retired, although he still featured on the Allied board as vice-chairman. However, Masius's successor agency, the celebrated Charlotte Street firm of Saatchi & Saatchi (famous for its recent work on British Airways, Silk Cut and particularly Margaret Thatcher's Conservative Party, which included the notorious 'Labour Isn't Working' slogan) fared little better. Saatchi's new 1986 campaign boldly addressed popular concerns about Babycham's increasing social irrelevance head on. Their 30-second TV commercial features a traditionally dressed couple with upper-class, received pronunciation accents entering a packed, trendy bar; having requested a Babycham, they are met with a stunned silence – only broken when a cool, Black patron steps forward to declare that 'Hey, *I'd* love a Babycham.' The ad's finale shows the bar's fashionable customers all energetically demanding their own glasses of Babycham. And while the concluding pack shot does feature the old deer mascot, the animal is wearing sunglasses, black tie and a distinct attitude.

Reality, however, failed to match Saatchi's fiction. As sales of Babycham continued to nosedive – from 144 million bottles in 1977 to a mere million bottles in 1993 – Allied Lyons predictably lost confidence in the brand. Francis Showering emerged from retirement, aged seventy-nine, to try to buy his family firm back from the conglomerate; yet the Allied board refused, preferring to accept a more generous offer from Australian winemakers Accolade Wines. Francis Showering recovered from this setback to form a new drinks company, Brothers Drinks, with his four sons Matthew, Francis, Jonathan and Daniel. Brothers' flagship brand was a blast from the past: a traditional, flat perry with a punchy 8 per cent ABV called Straight 8.

On the face of it, Accolade – best known for its Hardy's branded wines – made an odd home for the forty-year-old sparkling perry. As subsequent events were indeed to prove. Having brutally axed the classic deer logo (in 1993) and repackaged the drink in an oddly shaped blue bottle (which was itself quietly dropped two years later), Accolade then took a further seven years to decide what to do with their stumbling Babycham brand. Their first, somewhat left-field idea was to launch a range of Babycham-branded clothing in 2000 in partnership with trendy streetwear label Shopgirl. A press release even enthusiastically trumpeted the purchase by Dannii Minogue of a pair of Babycham trainers. Few, though, cared to follow Dannii's lead. Then in 2002, Accolade's British subsidiary Matthew Clark, better known as a drinks supplier than a strategic powerhouse, finally woke up to the retro-chic potential of the drink itself, as opposed to the limited appeal of Dannii Minogue's trainers. Their subsequent campaign, however, took nine years to appear, and once again ignored the product's heritage and potential to concentrate, bizarrely, on clothing and footwear. In 2011 Accolade, now owned by a private equity firm called CHAMP (the link with Babycham's brand origins never seemed to occur to them), proudly announced that a Lancashire-based footwear supplier called the Jacobson Group had been granted a licence to design, develop and distribute Babycham-branded footwear, accessories and apparel across the UK, Europe and North America. Even more curiously, these products were to be aimed at women in their twenties – most of whom had never even heard of Babycham.

In the following years Accolade lurched from strategy to strategy for Babycham, all of which saw minimal success. In 2013 the Babycham bottle was redesigned yet again, reverting to something like the original gold foil top. This, Accolade's press release claimed, 'comes after research showed consumers considered the previous bottle "old-fashioned"' – forgetting that Babycham had actually been launched nationally in 1953 with a similar gold foil neck wrapper. This 'new look' would, Accolade suggested, 'establish a clear position for Babycham, notably extending the franchise to the 25–45-year-old female target audience.' When that redesign seemed to have little effect on sales, Accolade reverted to the tired old model of stretching the brand as far as it would go. In 2014 they launched two new 'flavour extensions' for Babycham: cream soda and cherry soda. The firm tried desperately to justify their new brand direction, explaining that 'The new flavours celebrate Babycham's 1950s heritage with flavours that were popular as soft drinks back then but with a special Babycham twist for today' – confusing the soft drink markets of the 1950s with adults' alcoholic choices of sixty years later. Unsurprisingly, the cream soda and cherry soda variations soon went the way of Coca-Cola's notorious 'New Coke' of 1985, which had also meddled disastrously with a classic recipe. Like New Coke, cherry and cream soda Babycham were both consigned to the dustbin of history.

Meanwhile, the Showering family was quietly biding its time. In January 2016 the brothers bought back the original Showerings cider mill in Shepton Mallet. ('It's great to have been able to buy back our grandfather's factory,' declared Matthew Showering at the time.) And in 2021, in the aftermath of Covid, they finally showed their hand: after ditching Matthew Clark and selling Hardy's Wines to an even bigger American financial services multinational, Accolade sold Babycham to Brothers Drinks 'for an undisclosed fee'.

Babycham had finally returned home. The Babycham legacy clearly meant a lot to the Showering family. As Matthew Showering noted in a company press release 2021, 'It's very special, as it almost defines our family. It changed everything.' He confirmed that the years of brand extensions and tie-in accessories were over:

> *We will get closer to the original production method and recipe, as some things got chiselled away for speed with mass production. And we are going towards the original look too, so we'll have quite a retro feel, which, oddly, will make it more modern.*

Symptomatic of the Showerings' journey back to the future was their installation of the original statue of the Babycham fawn, now immaculately restored, in a prominent location immediately outside the main entrance to the firm's Shepton Mallet headquarters. This fifteen-foot sculpture had sat on top of the Showerings factory roof for decades, and after enduring years of wind, rain and snow it was inevitably in a poor condition. The rescue and renovation of its cute antlers, its broad, winning smile and its oversize blue bow suggested that the Showerings fully understood the appeal of the past. While nostalgia cannot resurrect the wide-ranging manufacturing base of 1950s Britain, it can at least conjure up a sparkling drink that has lasted for seventy years – and has outlasted much of British industry.

Chapter 3

DRINKING SHERRY AND DREAMING OF ENGLAND

HARVEYS BRISTOL CREAM

Although it actually comes from Spain, there's always been something peculiarly British – indeed English – about cream sherry.[22] Like the English themselves, it is overflowing with paradoxes. It's a style of wine that few Spaniards would touch: most Spanish drinkers rightly view cream sherry as a British invention, and prefer instead paler and drier amontillados, finos and manzanillas. Yet today cream sherry still accounts for 75 per cent of sherry sales in the UK. And most of that is accounted for by the legendary brand that was and is Harveys Bristol Cream.

A strong, fortified wine ('fortified' means that the drink has been stiffened with the addition of spirits)[23] that boasts a generous alcoholic strength of between 17 and 20 per cent ABV, cream sherry has been regarded for decades by its some of its, how shall we say, older and more traditional UK consumers as a genteel tipple that barely counts as alcohol at all. And while its fortification levels and high sugar content do mean that, once opened, it is likely to last longer than most table wines, cream sherry continues to be regarded by its more aged British demographic as a seasonal treat that is only to be uncorked at Christmas, and which is consigned to lurk at the back of the drinks cabinet for the rest of the year. Yet after a couple of Christmases even the most powerful cream sherry will start to wilt and decay.

Cream sherry as a trope is inexorably intertwined with historic definitions of the English and Englishness. Popularly associated with doting grandmothers, over-sociable vicars and, in particular, that much-loved (though frequently abused) dessert cherished by Britons in the years before and after the Second World War: sherry trifle, in which the madeira cake pieces or sponge fingers ('lady-fingers' or 'boudoir biscuits' if you were posh: they were much the same thing but just more expensive) were placed at the bottom of the bowl, then liberally doused with sweet sherry before being covered with fruit and custard. Ironically, though, while Harveys Bristol Cream[24] may remain the ultimate choice for a British trifle, it is nevertheless a Spanish wine invented and drunk by Britons that is today owned by a Filipino multinational conglomerate. More cream sherry, vicar?

To many older readers, sherry drinking in Britain – particularly of Bristol Cream, still by far the nation's favourite sherry – is invariably redolent of a vanished Britain of good manners, discreet civility and instinctive hospitality, a nation familiar today only through the novels of writers such as Charles Dickens, Somerset Maugham and Agatha Christie. (Dickens was a particular fan of sherry: he left over a hundred bottles of brown sherry to his heirs when he died, and purportedly fed his pet canary a thimbleful of the stuff every morning.) But is it a part of our future, too?

During the 1950s and 60s, Harvey's targeted both their American and UK markets by exploiting their brands' histories to the hilt – though perhaps citing Aintree's Grand National was not the best way to interest American consumers. The handsome and distinctive bottle label design, common to all of Harvey's sherries, lasted until the 1980s.

The word 'sherry' comes from the Andalusian town from where it originated: Jerez de la Frontera in south-west Spain, sited only a few miles inland from the Mediterranean. The earliest English word for sherry, though, was 'sack' – which, counter-intuitively, comes not from the Latin (*sicco*) nor Spanish (*seca*) words for 'dry', as you may think, but from the Jerez term *sacas*, meaning to draw out wine from a *solera*. The solera is the foundation, both literally and figuratively, of traditional sherry production: *criaderas* (tiers) of butts (that's barrels to you) designed to facilitate the labour-intensive blending of the older wines, extracted from the barrels below, are over time added to the younger wines above, while at the same time receiving some of the newer wine from further up the scale. The aim of this fractional blending policy was to create a consistent style of sherry every year.

Sherry was being exported from Jerez to England as early as the fifteenth century. By the seventeenth century, 'sherris-sack' was a familiar sight in British taverns, denoting sherry from Jerez, rather than from the other Andalusian centres that made fortified wine by the solera system, such as Sanlúcar de Barrameda (on the coast north of Cadiz) and Montilla (south of Cordoba). The word 'sack' appears frequently in the diaries of Samuel Pepys; indeed in 1663, having finished his naval business in Tangier, Pepys visited Sanlúcar on the way home and found a thriving colony of British sherry (sack) merchants there. A century later, though, the term 'sherry' had replaced 'sack' across the nation.

Until recent times, most Spanish sherry arrived in Britain through the ancient south-western port of Bristol.

There the pre-eminent sherry shipper was, by the mid-nineteenth century, Harveys: founded in Bristol's Denmark Street in 1796 and from 1871 known as John Harvey & Sons. As we'll see, though, sadly little remains of Harveys' legacy in the city today. The company's former offices are now a bar... sorry, 'an upmarket wine, sherry and cocktail lounge'.

One of Harveys' bestsellers for decades was a sweetened dessert sherry of the type known since the early seventeenth century as 'Bristol Milk'. When, at the height of the English Civil War in 1643, Parliamentarian commander Colonel Nathaniel Fiennes was cashiered from the army for failing to hold Bristol against the Royalist army of Prince Rupert, his prosecutors declared that 'the Bristol garrison might have held out, especially being furnished with a good store of Bristol Milk.' Sherry guru Julian Jeffs also cites historian Thomas Fuller's posthumously published *History of the Worthies of England* of 1662, which observes that 'Some will have it called Milk because... such Wine is the first moisture, given infants in this City.'

Bristol Milk was such a lucrative product for Harveys that in 1882 the shipper launched an upmarket, richer and more expensive version, which contained older olorosos (rich, dark, aged sherries) than its milky forebear as well as a larger dose of the intensely sweet and inky-dark Pedro Ximénez wine from Montilla. The resulting blend was called, inevitably, Bristol Cream. As we've already seen, almost every innovation in the drinks trade seems to be shrouded in a fog of apocryphal marketing myths, and this is no exception. The tale of Bristol Cream features a female visitor to Harveys' premises who, having tasted both Bristol Milk and its premium derivative, exclaims that 'If the first was Bristol Milk, then this must surely be Bristol Cream!' Of course.

By the 1920s, Harveys Bristol Cream was easily the best-selling sherry in Britain. Its reassuringly sweet, rounded richness made it a firm favourite with older drinkers, while the application of the word 'cream' spawned a whole new market sector, as the term 'cream sherry' was adopted by a range of imitators – from the Jerez bodegas (sherry warehouses) of Domecq ('Celebration Cream', now renamed 'Solera Cream') and Williams & Humbert ('Canasta Cream') to the Cypriot 'Emva Cream' and the low-budget, British-made QC and VP brands. In 1996, however, the European Union definitively ruled that only products made in Jerez could be called 'sherry'. This spelled the beginning of the end for Cyprus and British sherry, whose sales were already waning. VP and QC still just about survive, described merely as 'Creams', while Emva Cream, which after 1996 became just a 'fortified wine', lingered on in the UK market until 2023.

The sherry sales boom of the last decades of the nineteenth century may well have been at least partly inspired by Harveys' new premium cream sherry. However, the sherry boom was about to bust. In 1894 the phylloxera louse, which as we have seen had already wrought havoc in French vineyards, arrived in Jerez, devastating the vines there and bankrupting many smaller growers. It was not really until the 1930s that Spanish sherry production began to recover, while only in the 1950s did sherry exports to Britain begin to climb towards the levels of pre-1894.

The second sherry boom came almost exactly a century after the first. John Harvey and Sons, and particularly their flagship 'cream sherry', prospered during the third quarter of the twentieth century, enjoying sales far in excess of anything they had seen before. The reassurance and comfort of what was perceived as a quintessentially English drink appealed to a nation that had virtually bankrupted itself during the Second World War and, following years of austerity and imperial retreat, looked to familiar consolations and touchstones in order to conjure the illusion of a simpler and less challenging age. Although, to cite US Secretary of State Dean Acheson's cruel but justified claim of 1962 that post-war Great Britain had 'lost an Empire but not yet found a role', there was comfort and cheer in a glass of Harveys Bristol Cream, which could at a stroke (or should I say a sip) invoke the simpler world of centuries gone by.

Unlike its Spanish rivals, Harveys did not initially own its own Jerez bodega but bought its wine from other sherry houses in the city. As a result, the firm could conceivably end up being a victim of its own success, if insufficient supplies of other companies' sherry meant it could not meet current demand. Accordingly, in 1958 Harveys entered into an agreement with the elderly sherry broker Zoilo Ruiz-Mateos to guarantee a regular supply of sherry for their flourishing Bristol Cream brand. It turned out, though, to be a deal with the devil, from which Harveys were lucky to emerge unscathed.

After Zoilo died in 1962, his two sons, Zoilo junior and José María, encouraged Harveys to go even further and agree that their new holding company, Rumasa, would provide Harveys with all the sherry it needed for the next hundred years – an astonishingly ambitious and, as it turned out, rash assurance. Barely was the ink dry on the new and highly lucrative Harveys contract than Rumasa was using it as collateral to acquire a slew of Jerez bodegas, including famous names such as Garvey and Williams & Humbert, along with Rioja wines, banks, hotels, shipping companies, supermarkets, construction companies, department stores and manufacturing concerns of all shapes and sizes. Rumasa, run from Antonio Lamela's strikingly ugly paired Madrid towers then known as the 'Torres de Jerez' (The Towers of Jerez, or more risibly the Towers of Sherry), was the commercial wonder of the age. At its peak it employed over 60,000 people, controlled about a third of Jerez's bodegas, and had made José María Ruiz-Mateos the richest man in Spain. Protected by a web of friends and allies – including well-placed Francoists and the secretive and powerful religious cult Opus Dei – Rumasa seemed untouchable. Who cared if much of the Rumasa empire had been built on credit rather than capital? Or that three-quarters of its supposed 800 companies were mere cosmetic shells? By 1982 Rumasa accounted for 2 per cent of the Spanish nation's entire Gross Domestic Product. It was simply too big and too well connected to fail.

Except that it wasn't. Spain's transition to democracy after the death of General Franco in 1975 culminated in the election in 1982 of a socialist government led by Felipe González. And one of González's first targets was Rumasa's corrupt empire, which was forcibly confiscated and dismantled in 1983. José María Ruiz-Mateos initially escaped arrest; but eventually he was captured, tried and imprisoned.

After serving his time, the irrepressible Ruiz-Mateos even built yet another sherry-to-property combine, provocatively called Nueva Rumasa. (He also founded his own political party, won election to the European Parliament and bought a football team.) Predictably, though,

Nueva Rumasa met the same fate as its predecessor: in 2011 it succumbed to a mountain of accumulated debts and to ubiquitous fraud. Not only was Ruiz-Mateos still facing several outstanding criminal charges when he died in September 2015; two years later his first wife was convicted of fraud, while other members of his family also remained under investigation.

Many celebrated and renowned names in sherry disappeared in the wreck of Rumasa. Thankfully, though, Harveys of Bristol had already disembarked from that particular ship. In 1966, as we've seen, Harveys had been bought by neighbouring Somerset drinks giant Showerings. Allied Breweries' buyout of Showerings itself two years later provided Harveys with all the capital it needed to establish its own presence in Jerez. The firm thus politely withdrew from the Rumasa contract, citing quality control issues. And, having already vacated their historic offices in Bristol's Denmark Street for a vast if soulless complex at Whitchurch on the outskirts of the city, they bought their very own bodega in Jerez: the former premises of Mackenzie and Co, the old Scottish shippers who had for years supplied Harveys with the sherry for Bristol Cream, at least until the 1958 Rumasa accord. Nine years later they added the next-door bodega of Marqués de Misa, too, while following the collapse of (old) Rumasa, Harveys also bought two of the combine's most buoyant sherry producers: Palomino (named after the grape from which sherry is made) and Terry. The future for sherry in Britain, and for Harveys in particular, looked bright.

–

This early Sixties print as is unusual in stressing Bristol Cream's Spanish heritage. While Harvey's Bristol Cream went from strength to strength, the mass-bottling of its subtler parent, Bristol Milk, was discontinued in the mid-1970s.

In the event, however, sherry consumption in Britain was never to reach the giddy heights of the 1970s ever again. UK sherry sales peaked at 750 hectolitres in 1979; thereafter it was just a sorry tale of uninterrupted decline. Today annual sherry sales in the UK stand at a seventh of what they were in 1979, at just over 100 hectolitres – back to the levels of 1920. Harveys Bristol Cream still commands an enviably large portion of the British sherry market; but that market has, for the past forty years, been inexorably shrinking.

Margaret Thatcher's successive governments of the 1980s generally preferred to look forward rather than backward, in business as in politics. In Thatcher's Britain there was no place for sentimentality or nostalgia: the Iron Lady preferred to cite Ronald Reagan's ultra-capitalist, neo-liberal America as a more suitable corporate model for the future than what she saw as the out-of-date paternalism not just of Victorian Britain but also of the post-1945 cross-party consensus.

Thatcherite philosophy even permeated the alcoholic drinks sector. During the 1980s sales of bright, white, American-inspired drinks such as vodka and tequila soared, together with those of Americanised cocktails such as the Margarita and the Harvey Wallbanger. Meanwhile, traditional sticky brown drinks of the past such as Bristol Cream were pushed even further to the back of the drinks cabinet or the supermarket shelf. Sherry – and especially the cloyingly sweet, dark-brown cream sherry that your grandmother drank – began to be seen not as the reassuring and uplifting drink of yore but simply as a tired and increasingly irrelevant old vestige of time-worn traditions.

Britain's sherry importers tried desperately to respond to the drink's decline by jettisoning as much of the baggage of the past as they could. Spanish Sherry Shippers, an industry alliance that included Harveys, even launched a national campaign to persuade British drinkers to drink their sherry chilled or with ice, as in Spain. But it didn't work.

Not before time, Harveys also took aim at the ludicrously small 'Elgin' schooner glass traditionally associated with sherry drinking in Britain. With its small capacity, narrow waist and outward-curling lip, the tiny 'schooner' (invariably filled to the brim at wedding receptions or wakes) was absurdly ill-suited to drink, or even to sniff, sherry – and any other kind of drink, too. The glass could not be swilled to release the aromas of its contents; the schooner glass just spilled its meagre contents with every hand movement.

The Elgin schooner (no relation to its Australian, beer-toting 'schooner', a far more capacious glass) was one in a long line of unnecessary, 'must-have' new products that the British glass, ceramics and cutlery industries had dreamed up in the late nineteenth and early twentieth centuries: accessories such as fish knives or game casserole dishes that were devised by their manufacturers merely to extend their product lines and enhance their profits. Even the Elgin schooner's name was spurious. 'Schooner' was allegedly derived from the seagoing vessels used to ship sherry to Spain; indeed, online descriptions of the glass still recycle this myth. Yet in truth sailing schooners were actually far too small to ever be used for this type of trade. The small schooner glass was thus yet another instance of the creation of a fake product heritage, one designed to generate a new orthodoxy to mislead credulous consumers. And the prefix 'Elgin'? Well, that was yet another aristocratic-sounding brand name designed to lend this impractical affiliate of the glasses cabinet a spurious antiquity.

The Spanish had long preferred the well-proportioned 'copita' glass for drinking sherry, the copita's ample bowl and concave rim helping to concentrate the wine's aromas. Harveys now sought to persuade their customers to do the same. An American TV commercial of 1984 for Harveys Bristol Cream even employed British comedy legend Peter Cook to exhort party guests to 'throw away those silly little glasses' in order to be able to serve Bristol Cream over ice. Though that didn't work, either.

Early in the 1980s, Harveys went one step beyond in order to modernise the image of sweet sherry. In a brave if ultimately doomed strategic ploy, they sought to introduce Bristol Cream into the rapidly expanding, American-influenced cocktail market. Their vehicle for this was a new 'mixer sherry', Harveys Eleven, introduced in 19081. Eleven came in a tall, green wine bottle adorned with vaguely art deco graphics – a package that was deliberately distinct from the firm's traditional squat, brown bottles and staid, polygonal paper labels. Eleven appeared to be far more American than British. The contents, too, were nothing like Bristol Cream: although still as shatteringly sweet as the firm's flagship brand, Eleven's new sherry blend was pale cream rather than dark brown – enabling it to be positioned as a 'light' alternative, thereby exploiting the fashionability of supposedly drier and more sophisticated white drinks. Or so the brand strategy hoped. Eleven was positioned as a chic cocktail ingredient that would mix well with tonic or (piling sugar upon sugar) lemonade. Sadly, though, it didn't really work well with either. Although it was tested for a year in the Reading area, Eleven never reached beyond the Thames Valley. Following disappointing market research results, it was quietly euthanised.

Having survived the rollercoaster monetarist economics of 1980s Britain and the ebbing tide of the sherry market, in 1994 Harveys Bristol Cream reiterated its proud Bristol heritage by adopting a bottle made of traditional Bristol Blue glass. That same year, however, Harveys suddenly found themselves competing with an old rival from Jerez from the same stable. Allied Lyons (as Allied Breweries had become) succeeded in deftly absorbing the Pedro Domecq sherry empire on the death of the ill-starred Franco loyalist Álvaro Domecq y Díez.[25] Now the two famous sherry brands jostled for attention not just on the supermarket shelves but in the boardroom, too.

Barely a decade later, Allied Domecq was itself bought up by the Paris-based global drinks giant Pernod Ricard. As was becoming common with millennial corporations, Pernod Ricard swiftly divested themselves of those brands they did not want, in this instance to Fortune Brands. This, regrettably, included Harveys. Fortune Brands was an American conglomerate from Illinois whose drinks division was named after its best-known marque, Jim Beam bourbon. Beam Global Spirits & Wine, though, was clearly at a loss in deciding what to do with Harveys sherry. As wine critic Jancis Robinson astutely observed:

> *In 2005 the American company found itself the owner of the two most famous names in sherry, Harveys and Domecq, and, according to most observers of the sherry scene, proceeded to run them into the ground. Poor little sherry with its shrinking market was a sort of corporate football, of relative insignificance compared with the lucrative, globally famous spirits brands that were seen as*

the real prizes in the sharing of the spoils in the boardrooms of the world's biggest drinks companies.

Beam's only attempt to revitalise their sherry portfolio came in 2006, when they launched two bizarre new sherry 'variants' of what they called 'Aperitivo' sherry, blended with orange juice and red berry juice. Harveys Orange and Harveys Pink were professedly 'aimed at women over the age of 35', presumably in a bid to exploit the female market at which Eleven had been bravely levelled twenty-five years earlier. At 15 per cent ABV, the colourful pair were weaker than their Jerezano ancestors and thus, in theory, could prove palatable to a female audience more concerned with limiting their alcohol intake. Beam's promotional blurb enthused that

> *Exclusive to the UK and developed by the renowned Harveys Bodega in the scorching heat of Jerez in southern Spain, Harveys Aperitivo comes in two flavours – Pink and Orange. Both flavours are best poured over ice, topped up with soda water (or lemonade) and finished with a couple of red berries (Pink) or a slice of orange (Orange). Harveys Orange is a delicious blend of two grape varieties – Palomino and Muscatel – with an aroma of bitter orange, tangerine and aromatic herbs. The delicious result is a low ABV (15%) and low calorie (62 kcal) light, zesty and refreshing serve, made with 100 per cent natural flavours.*

Beam also informed the trade press, rather unconvincingly, that 'the decision to introduce the ready-mixed orange variant was inspired by the popularity among consumers of its original Harveys Bristol Cream when served with ice and orange.' Few, however, were either convinced or converted: the fruity pair were dropped after just a year's trial. Their launch did, nevertheless, at least remind drinkers about Bristol Cream, which, in the context of a declining sherry market, actually witnessed a heartening 20 per cent growth in sales during 2006.

The sole lasting legacy bequeathed by Beam's brief stewardship of Harveys sherry was the barely heralded development of a premium range of aged sherries under the VORS (Very Old Rare Sherries) designation: Very Old Oloroso, Very Old Palo Cortado, Pedro Ximénez and the award-winning Very Old Amontillado. This was the achievement not of Beam's executives but of the scion of yet another rival sherry dynasty: Beltrán Domecq y Williams. Beltrán also oversaw the expansion of Harveys-owned soleras and completed the corporate move from Bristol to Jerez.

In the familiar, voracious corporate cycle that saw gluttonous big fish being eaten by even bigger and more ravenous predators, the corporate shark that was Beam Global was in turn gobbled up by a Japanese orca: the spirits-based conglomerate Suntory, the third biggest distillers in the world after Diageo and Pernod Ricard. Yet again, though, Harveys found itself on the discard pile. In 2014, only a year after its acquisition of Beam Global, Suntory sold Harveys (along with Domecq sherry and Fundador brandy) to Andrew Lim Tan's Filipino multinational, the Alliance Global Group. And once more Harveys found itself housed in a spirits subsidiary. This time it was assigned to Alliance's Emperador division, named after the world's best-selling brandy. Here Harveys was, just as before, to be managed by spirits executives who, like Beam's, had little experience of the sherry market – in this instance the venerable Glasgow whisky firm of Whyte & Mackay. Almost the only thing the two marques had in common was that Whyte & Mackay had been founded in the same year, 1882, that Harveys Bristol Cream had been launched.

Whyte & Mackay had, since 1971, passed through even more hands than Harveys, being passed from pillar to post by some of the most notorious corporate marauders of post-war Britain. In 1971 they were bought by House of Fraser tycoon Sir Hugh Fraser and were subsequently acquired by 'Tiny' Rowland's infamous Lonrho group (in 1981), by former boxer Billy Walker's rickety Brent Walker empire (in 1988), and by Fortune Brands (in 1990), where Whyte & Mackay actually, if briefly, served as a stablemate to Harveys sherry. Whyte & Mackay was then sold to the Tchenguiz brothers and their associate Vivian Imerman, who sold it to the Indian drinks company United Spirits in 2007. United Spirits then almost sold Whyte & Mackay to Diageo in 2013 but, frustrated by the opposition of the whisky blender's senior managers, who must have been fed up to the back teeth with this ownership merry-go-round, offloaded it instead to Alliance Global in 2014. Confused? Well, so was the drinks industry – to say nothing of Whyte & Mackay's own staff.

The fate of both Harveys sherry and Whyte & Mackay whisky – two traditional British brands that encapsulated longstanding cultural traditions of, respectively, England and Scotland – parallelled the plight of so many British companies and British institutions by 2000. The result of the dash for privatisation at any price during the Thatcher and Major years was that foreign firms were able to snap up venerable British companies at bargain-basement prices.

While the French or German administrations of varying political hues consistently sought to protect their most cherished corporate brands and to safeguard their proud industrial heritage, successive British governments cheerfully allowed overseas buyers to acquire quintessentially British brands, products and services whose identities and appeal had for decades relied on their identification with Britishness, however you might define this. In the automotive world, for example, BMW now owned those ultimate British icons the Mini and Rolls-Royce, their German rivals at Volkswagen owned Bentley,[26] Jaguar and Land Rover – premium marques whose credibility rested on the image of traditional British craftsmanship – were sold to the Indian industrial giant Tata, while the rights to the historic 'MG' name, for decades associated with the inimitably British sports cars built at the Oxfordshire town of Abingdon, were bought by the Chinese.

–

The drinks and car industries were by no means the only sectors in which British ownership was, by at the turn of the twenty-first century, fast becoming a thing of the past. In 1998 Malayan United Industries bought a majority shareholding in the legendary firm that had clothed so many British women in the 1980s, Laura Ashley, while the following year the famous old British shipping line Cunard passed into the hands of the Miami-based Carnival cruise operator and James Bond's shoemaker, Thomas Church of Northampton, was bought by the Milanese Prada Group. This list goes on and on. Britain's Brexit vote of 2016 was partly fought on the Leave camp's celebrated slogan 'Take Back Control'. Yet many of the things Britons consume, use or wear were, both before and after 2016, already far beyond British 'control'.

That's all very well, you may say, but surely we now live in a globalised society; and, after all, what does it matter where things are now made? Well, it matters if you are working to produce them. And it matters if brand identity is promoted through a notional yet fraudulent Britishness (or Englishness, if we are talking about Harveys Bristol Cream) that actually has little to do with who owns it or where it is made. Interestingly, though, almost no other European nations have, to paraphrase former Prime Minister Harold Macmillan, sold the family silver.[27] It appears to be a peculiarly British trait, rather at odds with a nation that allegedly prizes its heritage more than any other Western nation.

Perhaps Britons are, after all, less proud of or interested in their island history than everyone thinks. As an example, the former contents of Harveys' famous Bristol Wine Museum, originally curated in 1960 for the firm's historic Denmark Street premises, are now redisplayed in the nicely restored brick Old Distillery at the old Domecq bodega in Jerez, recently renamed after Emperador brandy.

Today, Emperador's Whyte & Mackay subsidiary, the one that manages Harveys sherries, is at least based in Glasgow. And, far from Bristol though it may be, it is certainly making an attempt to make Harveys Bristol Cream relevant to the twenty-first-century consumer. Currently Whyte & Mackay are reviving the old 1980s campaign to encourage drinkers to try Bristol Cream chilled or over ice – though this time round the suggestion is 'with a slice of orange'. To achieve that, they have introduced a rather improbable gimmick: the newly redesigned

Bristol Cream bottle features a 'thermochromic' ink logo that turns blue as the sherry hits the appropriate (cold) serving temperature. Whyte & Mackay claims that 'by refreshing the Harveys "The Bristol Cream" bottle and label with a new thermochromic ink feature, it not only modernises the design, but provides a clear call to action for the consumer to re-think Harveys Sherry.' Careful not to alienate older customers with this frankly odd promotional stunt, though, Whyte & Mackay hastily adds that, while 'we want to encourage our consumers to drink Harveys as it is enjoyed in Spain and make space for the new, cooler serve in their fridge', the brand 'still has its place in the classic trifle recipe.' At the same time, though, the drink's redesigned bottle (which, with its bulging shoulders, looks rather muscular and aggressive) reveals that Harveys' new owners have, disappointingly, decided to downplay their Bristolian heritage. The emphasis on the sherry's revised label graphics is on the Harveys name, which carries the subtitle of 'Solera Sherry'. Only lower down the bottle, in a smaller typeface, does the blue label feature the phrase 'The Bristol Cream'.

This abandonment of Bristol has been in train for a while. In 2006 Beam Global shifted Harveys' registered office from Bedminster in Bristol to Great Marlborough Street in London. By then Harveys' Whitchurch offices and bottling complex were long gone. (Today the former bottling warehouse accommodates a film studio.) Today all of Harveys' sherries are both made and bottled in Spain, in one large, late-nineteenth-century Jerez bodega called El Brigadier. This holds around 6,000 butts of solera sherry, ranging from two to twenty years of age and mostly destined for Bristol Cream. El Brigadier is supplemented by an additional twenty-five smaller bodegas in and around Jerez; indeed, at the time of writing Harveys (or rather Emperador) owns about 10 per cent of the vineyards around the town.

Emperador and Whyte & Mackay continue to focus largely on the popular Bristol Cream brand. There is now only one dry sherry available from the firm (Harveys Fino, the descendant of the old brand Luncheon Dry), whereas in 1980 there were several. If it were not for Beltrán Domecq's impressive VORS quartet of aged sherries, the Harveys range would now look rather depleted. The commercial emphasis on Bristol Cream, though, has undoubtedly paid its new owners dividends. Harvey's Bristol Cream, as we have seen, now accounts for around 75 per cent of all sherry sales in the UK.

The sector as a whole, nevertheless, continues to shrink. In 1979, the year of Peak Sherry, over 150 million litres of the drink were exported from Spain. Yet in 2022 the equivalent figure was just over 30 million – a decline of 80 per cent.

Much has been written in the national press and in trade magazines about the supposed 'sherry renaissance' of the 2020s. But so far this hasn't really translated into sales. For example, *en rama* sherries – unfiltered, cloudy finos with a sharper, even raw taste – may be fashionable in a few bars in the larger British cities, but you can't find them in any of the big supermarkets. Spain, where the drink is of course made, is now sherry's biggest market – whereas, until the end of the twentieth century, Spanish consumption was always eclipsed by Britain's. Surprisingly, at the time of writing in 2024, even the Dutch drink more sherry than we do.

These days many Andalusian sherry producers are making as much money out of selling their old, seasoned sherry casks to the whisky, bourbon and rum industries, in order to lend these spirits that highly sought-after sherry character, as they do retailing sherry itself. Sometimes they make even more profit from their casks. In 2021 (admittedly at the height of the Covid pandemic), Jerez bodegas sold around 84,000 seasoned sherry casks to spirits producers, while only the equivalent of 64,000 casks were sold for actually drinking.

But where does all of this leave Harveys Bristol Cream? The brand certainly enjoys robust sales in Britain; but how can its sweet, cloying taste and conventional image be reconciled with the young British drinkers of the future? Bristol Cream is, as we have seen, a brand popularly associated with older drinkers. But as this demographic typically doesn't drink very much – possibly just sampling Bristol Cream at Christmas, or as a miniature nightcap served in one of those infuriating schooner glasses – the inevitable disappearance of this market segment (to put it euphemistically) may not, in the event, make much difference to Bristol Cream's prospects.

Younger drinkers do seem to prefer drier wines – although, as we will see, over the last eighty years Britons have always been partial to astoundingly sweet drinks, often in defiance of pronounced international trends. Sales of sweet sherries are, globally, in steep decline, while those of the drier and fashionably paler styles – fino, manzanilla, palo cortado, amontillado and dry oloroso – are proving more buoyant.

Salvation for Bristol Cream might, though, lie in the rising popularity of the intensely sweet wine from Montilla that has bucked the supposed trend to ever-drier drinks. Pedro Ximénez (known in the trade simply as 'PX') is the name of both the grape and the dark, sticky, almost black wine it produces, which has customarily been used to sweeten sherry – and is a key ingredient in Bristol Cream. The grape may have originated in France or in Germany, and might have been, it is said, introduced to Spain by Emperor Charles V's zealous regent Cardinal Ximénez (except that the cardinal's first name was Francisco, not Pedro) or by one of Charles V's German soldiers, called Peter Siemens, which translates into Spanish as Pedro Ximénez (except that Herr Siemens had lived many decades before Charles V was born). Wherever it came from, it was definitely being grown in Spain by the seventeenth century. PX's unmistakeable, concentrated-raisin taste and pleasingly viscous texture have, in recent years, enabled it to come out of the shadows. No longer is it regarded as merely a sherry additive, nor just a supplier of richly aromatic casks for finishing whisky or bourbon. PX now stands on its own as a celebrated dessert wine and as a key component in fashionable new desserts such as the 'PX Affogato', a combination of espresso coffee, ice cream and PX that is taking Western restaurants by storm.

PX's apotheosis could chart a path for Bristol Cream's future: as a dessert wine – a drinks sector that is currently doing remarkably well – or as a crucial ingredient in dessert cuisine. It could even serve as a pivotal constituent of new British cocktails. As Britons have had to adapt to a world in which the traditional Christmas schooner of cream sherry, the sherry decanter on the sideboard and Grandma's sherry trifle are increasingly seen as faintly ludicrous relics of a thankfully bygone age – and as British-owned heritage marques are becoming an increasing rarity – so, doubtless, will Harveys Bristol Cream learn to acclimatise to a world that knows little, and cares less, about the brand's proud British and Bristolian heritage.

Chapter 4

RESISTING THE RED REVOLUTION

WATNEY'S RED

The takeover fever to which Britain succumbed following the nation's economic Indian summer of the 1950s was perhaps best epitomised by the corporate greed and acquisition fever demonstrated by the country's big brewers. For the latter, as indeed for much of British industry during the Swinging Sixties, their commercial axiom was invariably that 'bigger is better'. Modest local breweries that had survived the Great Depression and two world wars now fell victim to the playground bullies who coveted not their beers, which soon disappeared from view, but their invaluable tied pub estate, which offered new outlets from which to sell their standardised and thus more profitable national brands.

By 1970 the majority of Britain's breweries and pubs were in the hands of the so-called 'Big Six': Allied Breweries, Bass Charrington, Courage, Scottish and Newcastle, Whitbread and Watney Mann. The last of these, perhaps unfairly, has come to symbolise the worst excesses of the drinks industry during this period. For it was during the 1960s and early 1970s that first Watney's, and then its new owner, the multinational property developer Grand Metropolitan, attempted to foist their ubiquitous national keg mega-brand, Watney's Red, down the throats of the nation's pubgoers. As Britain's first keg beer (in hindsight not a very welcome accolade), Watney's Red[28] was backed by a massive media campaign that, astonishingly, even associated the beer with China's Chairman Mao – just at the time when Mao's horrific Cultural Revolution was killing or imprisoning millions of his own countrymen.

Leo Burnett's poster ad, designed to advertise Red Barrel's relaunch simply as 'Watneys Red', bizarrely hitched the brand to authoritarian and repressive communist dictatorships in what must be one of the most ill-judged campaigns of the late twentieth century. Mao's China was then in the midst of his terrifying and chaotic 'Cultural Revolution.' Russian premier Leonid Brezhnev, though, was evidently felt to be too anodyne for Burnett's photocall, so a lookalike of Nikita Kruschchev (whom Brezhnev had toppled from power in 1964) was substituted.

However, by the mid-1970s the seemingly unstoppable tide of Watney's Red and its keg cousins had, to everyone's surprise, been reversed by the most unlikely of opponents: a grassroots consumer revolution that had been created from the ground up. The Campaign for Real Ale (CAMRA), founded in a pub in 1971 yet soon being supported by strategically placed allies in the national media, led the charge against the nation's outsize brewers, demanding that traditional cask beers be reintroduced. And, astonishingly, CAMRA won. Grand Metropolitan closed Watney's brewery and discontinued the toxic Red brand in 1979.

-

Watney's actually started as a reasonably respectable small brewery in Victorian London. Based in Westminster (near the site on which Victoria Station was to emerge), in 1889 they also acquired the Mortlake Brewery, two miles upstream on the River Thames and, then, still in Surrey. Nine years after that they merged with Combe Delafield and Reid breweries to form the mega-brewer Watney Combe and Reid. The Combe family was represented on the Watney's board well into the twentieth century. Indeed, war hero Simon Harvey Combe (who had won a Military Cross at Anzio in 1943) was the combined firm's chairman between 1950 and 1965. However, Combe was, in the spirit of the age, never one to be sentimental about the past. In an augury of things to come, his own Combe brewery in Long Acre and the Reid brewery in Clerkenwell were both immediately shut down following the merger, and all production was concentrated at Watney's Stag Brewery in Victoria.

Once Simon Combe was installed in the driving seat, Watney's – along with, it must be said, the rest of what became the Big Six of the beer world – embarked upon a determined campaign of ruthless takeovers and chillingly hardboiled rationalisations. His first target was Hammerton's of Stockwell in south London, which was bought in 1951. Then followed a far larger prize: Tamplin's of Brighton. In 1955 came Henty and Constable of Chichester and the biggest fish landed so far: Mann, Crossman & Paulin of Whitechapel in east London. That same year Combe even attempted to effect a merger with his equally ambitious and empire-building rivals at Bass in Burton-on-Trent. If his scheme had worked, it would have created a massive combine, way ahead of its time, which would have been one of the largest brewers in the world.

Simon Combe was not one to rest on his laurels. He was clearly a believer in the hoary old adage that 'you can't stop progress', a monotonously popular phrase during a period that witnessed the thoughtless destruction of countless heritage assets that could have been easily adapted to modern specifications. In 1959 Combe demolished Watney's own, historic Stag brewery in Victoria as part of a highly lucrative deal with developers by which the old brewery buildings would make way for a series of depressingly mundane and cheerless offices. Combe then shifted the company headquarters to Mortlake. Over the next few years, Combe's Watney's targeted a second series of sizeable regional breweries for acquisition, familiar names that included Wilsons of Manchester, Phipps of Northampton, Steward & Patteson of Norwich, Drybrough of Edinburgh and Ushers of Trowbridge. Watney's even bought three breweries in Belgium. Just three of Combe's acquisitions of 1960 – Phipps, Wilsons and Ushers – added a staggering 3,200 public houses to Watney's retail estate, while the Norwich breweries that Watney's absorbed in 1963 added another 2,000. In 1973 journalist Christopher Hutt observed that, while in 1959 Norfolk had boasted six independent breweries, by 1970 these had all fallen to national predators: five had been bought by Watney's (it was perhaps not a coincidence that Norfolk was Simon Combe's home county) and just one by Whitbread. Crucially, only one of them was still brewing beer.

The results of the Big Six's mammoth spending spree were catastrophic for beer drinkers in many parts of the country. But Britain's brewing grandees were not interested. *Guardian* journalist Richard Boston later observed that 'The cannibalistic way in which the Big Six developed reminds one of W. S. Gilbert's "The Yarn of the 'Nancy Bell'", in which the starving crew are reduced to eating one of their number, and then another, and then another, until the entire crew is incorporated in a single survivor.'

The creation of ever-larger economic units and the suppression of competition did not, however, necessarily guarantee commercial success. While mega combines were seen as the panacea for failing industries in the late 1960s, many of them subsequently came to grief. In 1967, for example, Britain's steel producers were forcibly amalgamated into the giant British Steel Corporation, yet twenty years later the ailing giant was forcibly privatised by the Thatcher government. Similarly, in 1968 Thoresen and Townsend combined to form a ferry conglomerate that was soon investing in ambitious property schemes across the world, while the five main shipbuilding firms on the River Clyde joined forces as Upper

Clyde Shipbuilders. However, the Townsend Thoresen brand was hastily buried after the ferry disaster nineteen years later, while Upper Clyde Shipbuilders lasted only three years before liquidation.

Most notorious of these late-1960s mergers was the creation of British Leyland in 1968. In 1950 Britain had been the largest car exporter in the world; but eighteen years later the UK's auto exports had been surpassed by France, Italy and Japan. Yet the decision to meet these foreign challenges by consolidating most of Britain's mass-carmakers was not a success. The new British Leyland (BL) auto combine seemed unable to offer anything new. The Austin and Morris divisions still retained their separate dealerships, which needed to be supplied with a range of appropriately badged cars, while BL's portfolio featured far too many car factories: forty-eight in 1968, many of which were ponderously old-fashioned and operated by antiquated piecework agreements. BL's new models were dismal, too: the 'new' Morris Marina of 1971, the last car to use the Morris name, was created mostly by cannibalising existing models and was likened by critics at the time to 'a skip on wheels'. By 1974 BL was broke, and had to be bailed out by the new Labour government in Harold Wilson's Second Coming.

Bigger was thus not always better – and certainly not for the consumer. For the brewers, big brewing combines and pub estates seemed to facilitate economies of scale. But for the drinker, choice was minimised and prices went up. And overheads meant that even the big brewers often made less profit on their much-vaunted national brands than their country cousins. In 1977 the Labour government's Pricing Commission report on the brewing industry stated that 'The large national breweries charge higher prices for their beer than regional and small companies' but concluded that 'despite the fact that their prices are higher, the large national brewery conglomerates make a significantly smaller net profit margin on their beer' than their regional rivals. Of the Big Six's vast promotional spending of the late 1960s and early 1970s, the heyday of Watney's Red, the Commission pointedly asked, 'to what degree has the customer benefited from the massive expenditure by the large brewers, most of which, after all, he [sic] has paid for in higher prices for his beer.'

Not only did Watney's and their fellow giants close breweries. They also replaced familiar and much-loved local brews with their bland national brands. Newly acquired tied houses – pubs that were anchored to the brewery that owned them, which could thus dictate what drinks the pub would serve – gave Watney's a far broader platform from which to sell their wares. And top of the list for the rampaging and confident Big Six brewers were their nationally promoted flagship beers. These ranged from Whitbread's Tankard (their keg offering) and Trophy (a name initially used to re-badge beers from the breweries Whitbread had smothered under its notorious commercial 'umbrella') to Allied's famous Double Diamond – or 'DD' as the marketeers preferred to call it. The most notorious of these bland, over-packaged and over-promoted beers, though, was Watney's own Red Barrel – which in 1971 metamorphosed into just 'Watney's Red'.

–

By 1971 Watney's Red *was* Watney's. Everything was riding on its success. The brewery's former range of eighty beers had been brutally culled in 1969–70 to just feature thirty-five products. Without question, the beer that Watney's preferred to promote on its bar counters and in its export trade was invariably Red – and its heavy advertising spend clearly reflected that.

Significantly – and, as it turned out, disastrously – Watney's Red had never been a traditional, cask-conditioned ale. Red Barrel had originally been devised in 1931 as a filtered and pasteurised beer, one in which the working yeast had been killed off, depriving it of a complex taste and character, but which was easier to transport and to keep. This filtering process made the beer particularly suitable for overseas export and for sale in sports clubs where turnover was low and experienced cellar staff were thin on the ground. The first UK client for Watney's first titled 'container beer', a term later changed to the less industrial-sounding 'keg beer', was East Sheen Lawn Tennis Club, in 1935. Then in 1950 Red Barrel also began to appear in bottled form, as the take-home trade soared.

Fully fledged 'keg' Red Barrel came a few years later. Chilled, filtered, pasteurised, carbonated 'keg' beer – fizzy, cold, reliable but unutterably dull and insipid – was first introduced into pubs by the Flowers Brewery of Stratford-upon-Avon in 1955. Watney's quickly followed Flowers' lead, introducing a keg adaptation of Red Barrel into their pubs the following year to make it the first national keg brand. By 1961 Red Barrel was the highest-selling beer in the country. Easier to transport by lorry and to maintain in the cellar, it made the brewers more money than those troublesome old cask-conditioned ales. Accordingly, Watney's cask beer was phased out in all of the firm's tied houses during the 1960s.

In the place of the traditional, cask-conditioned ales crafted by well-loved brewers such as Tamplin's and Webster's, Watney's now offered mass-produced keg beers such as Red Barrel and the large, dustbin-like cans of Special Bitter (branded as 'Party 4' and 'Party 7', according to size) for home drinking. First introduced 1968 as Britain's first bulk container for beer drinkers at home, Party 7's success seems incomprehensible today. Basically just a huge cannister of pressurised beer – not a mini-keg with a special tap, such as you can find now – its thick metal sheath was notoriously difficult to prise open. Partygoers frequently resorted to a screwdriver to access the can's contents; the consequent uncontrolled explosion inevitably soaked most of the kitchen (or wherever you were) in sticky beer. As one commentator has recently observed, Party 7 'was among the least welcome sights at a Seventies party, along with Hirondelle wine and your friend's collection of Boney M records.'

The journalist Richard Boston was clearly thinking of Red Barrel when he paraphrased economist J. K. Galbraith's authoritative *The New Industrial State* of 1967 while charting the dictatorial behaviour of Britain's ever-growing brewing combines during the 1960s:

> *Galbraith argues that, instead of responding to the demands of the market, these large corporations on the contrary accommodate the consumer to their needs. Instead of producing what people are asking for they come up with something that is convenient for them to produce and then, with the help of massive and sophisticated sales techniques, create a demand for it.*

Watney's Red Barrel seemed to fit Galbraith's template exactly. It was easy to make and to store, as it didn't need experienced landlords or cellarmen who had learned how to keep live and temperamental 'real ale'. And, as outlined by Galbraith, it was ultimately promoted on a vast national scale.

Initially, however, the early Watney's ads failed to match with the brand's ambitions. During the 1960s, Watney's beers had been marketed in an energetic if uninspired fashion around the catchy if hardly compelling slogans 'What we want is Watney's' and 'Roll Out Red Barrel'. Meanwhile, however, their rivals had been stealing a marketing march on them. Courage's national keg brand, Tavern, did very well when promoted with the memorable tagline 'It's what your right arm's for' (though a Tavern campaign of 1969 that featured the actress Andria Lawrence coyly admitting that 'It's too strong for me, but I like the men who drink it' did not, unsurprisingly, last as long). Tankard, the keg brand that Whitbread had launched just a year after Red Barrel, deployed the illogical but effective slogan 'The pint that thinks it's a quart' to imply the beer's suitability for session drinking. Mystifyingly, this seemed to work well with the brand's male audience, and the ads (which featured actor Tim Stern, soon to star as the doomed Laurence in Mike Leigh's play *Abigail's Party* of 1977) ran for years.

Most successful of all of this era's beer adverts were the campaigns devised by London ad agency Young & Rubicam (Y&R) for Allied's Double Diamond keg brand. Ros Levenstein's pithy catchphrase 'I'm only here for the beer!' was soon accompanied by the 'works wonders' jingle, which, while a maddening earworm, is still remembered today, with much affection (or perhaps anguish).

When Watney's resolved to reformulate, rebrand and relaunch their flagship brand in 1971, they sought to bridge this advertising gap. Partly thanks to Y&R's memorable ads, Allied Breweries' sweeter and stronger, Burton-brewed rival Double Diamond, 'DD', was soon racing ahead of Red in terms of sales. In response, Watney's hired a new advertising agency, the American firm Leo Burnett, to devise a whole new strategic direction for Red and a £0.5 million relaunch campaign.

Predictably, Burnett's new marketing strategy had little to do with the characteristics of the beer itself. Watney's themselves had already been quick to emphasise that Red was blander and sweeter than its predecessor:

> *What we've done is to give the beer a new smooth pleasant taste. We've also given it a much better head and altogether a more attractive appearance. Gone is any suggestion of bitter after-palate; instead, there is a pleasant malty mealiness.*

For beer writer Roger Protz, though, the new recipe was reminiscent of little more than 'liquid Mars Bars... sweet, gassy and lacking any noticeable hop character.' Either way, there was not much for the new agency to build on there. Instead, Burnett turned, curiously, to the longstanding political associations of the colour red. To that end they launched a nationwide campaign extolling the virtues of Watney's 'Red Revolution'. Posters and print ads proclaiming 'Long Live the Red Revolution!' featured lookalikes of some of the most notorious totalitarian dictators of recent times: Fidel Castro, Mao Zedong and Nikita Khrushchev.[29] The inclusion of a 'Mao', brandishing the *Little Red Book* that had been designed as the revolutionary bible for his vicious and brutal Red Guards, was spectacularly ill-judged and inappropriate. Today it is estimated that Mao's Cultural Revolution, which lasted from 1966 until his death a decade later, accounted for the deaths of between 1 and 2 million Chinese people. Portraying this callous mass murderer as a jolly figure of fun was bad enough; having him supposedly endorse a lacklustre British keg beer was even more offensive. Burnett had created what must surely rank as one of the most tasteless ads in the history of British marketing.

The 'Red Revolution' did not end with advertising. Watney's pubs across the land were drastically remodelled to carry large, identical, bright-red fascias with bold white graphics, irrespective of the age, design or architectural merit of the building or the architectural context of the location. This new brand image was the work of a London design consultancy, the Design Research Unit, which included celebrated architect and designer Misha Black among its luminaries and which had recently been responsible for the 1965 rebrand of British Rail, including the invention of its famous double-arrow logo. Their Watney's work, however, seriously misfired. The British pub had for two centuries been at the hub of the British way of life. And much of the pub's importance derived from its individual character and unique architectural form. Pubs depended not just on their beer, their food or their landlord for their success, but also on how they looked, both inside and out. They defined communities, providing a sense of place, identity, belonging and continuity in an ever-changing landscape. Making them all look alike did no favours to historic pubs, nor to their customers. Yet in 1971 Watney's future seemed to be painted only Red. Watney's Peter Crossman even predicted confidently that cask beer would be totally extinct by 1978. In the event, though, it was Watney's, not real ale, that became extinct.

-

The consumer group primarily responsible for the demise of both Watney's Red and its 'Red Revolution' pubs – and indeed, for the Watney's brand in its entirety – had only just been born when Watney's Red sprang onto our pub bar counters. The Campaign for Real Ale (originally called the Campaign for the Revitalisation of Ale, which turned out to be too difficult to pronounce after a pint or three) was founded on 16 March 1971 over a drink in an Irish bar by four British journalists: Michael Hardman, Graham Lees, Jim Makin and Bill Mellor. CAMRA wasn't the first consumer group to protest against the disappearance of traditional, cask-conditioned ales; the Society for the Preservation of Beers from the Wood had been launched in that traditional cradle of protest, Epsom in Surrey, eight years earlier.[30] However, CAMRA's wider brief proved appealing for a generation of Britons who were fed up of being told what they could choose by vast industrial combines motivated solely by profit.

CAMRA was about as far as you could get from the corporate world epitomised by Watney's owners Grand Metropolitan and Courage's bosses at Imperial Tobacco. The first CAMRA members were really just the founders' friends, and their first office was based in a spare room at Graham Lees's mother's house in Salford. When the organisation held its first conference in 1972 – at another crucible of radicalism: Nuneaton in Warwickshire – the founders were pleased that a hundred delegates had actually turned up.

However, CAMRA was soon eagerly embraced by key figures in the traditional beer world – notably Christopher Hutt, author of *Death of the English Pub*, who succeeded Hardman as CAMRA's second chairman; John Hanscomb, the first editor of the *Good Beer Guide*; and Frank Baillie, author of *The Beer Drinker's Companion*. When *Guardian* journalist Richard Boston espoused their cause publicly in his weekly national beer column, membership soared – to 10,000 by the end of 1974 and 30,000 by 1991. Today CAMRA boasts almost 150,000 members, and has been described as the most successful consumer campaign organisation in Europe.

CAMRA's ire was not specifically directed at Watney's Red in particular. As a subsequent CAMRA chair, James Lynch, later admitted: 'In truth [Red] was neither any worse nor any better than any of the other national keg brands. Bland, brown, devoid of any character and ridiculously fizzy.' CAMRA members were indeed happy to target any beer or brewery they felt merited their condemnation. One early CAMRA conference, for example, saw members wearing badges announcing that 'DD IS K9 P'.

However, the fact that Watney's was the pioneer of keg beer, and was treating both their tenants and their pubs in a decidedly cavalier fashion, made the company a prime target for the campaigners. Christopher Hutt engaged in a very public battle with Watney's head of PR, Ted Handel, on the letters page of the *Financial Times*, while the first edition of the *Good Beer Guide*, published in 1973, explicitly advised drinkers to avoid Watney's 'like the plague'. Meanwhile, the eponymous hero of cartoonist Bill Tidy's *What's Brewing* comic strip 'Kegbuster', which first appeared in 1972, frequently took aim at 'Grotneys' and their goon-like marketeers, the 'Grotney Hardmen'.

The big brewers initially laughed off CAMRA's attacks as mere pinpricks and derided CAMRA members as 'cranks'. The public, they confidently declared, preferred keg beer. And as the attacks grew, they simply tried to ignore them. In Richard Boston's words, though, 'Their behaviour uniquely combined that of an ostrich with King Canute's.' CAMRA wouldn't go away; in fact it was just getting stronger. This particular David would not let Goliath alone.

CAMRA was not the only challenge Watney's was facing in the early years of the 1970s. Back in 1959 property tycoon Charles Clore had tried to take over Watney's with a bid of £21 million. He was successfully rebuffed; but Watney's were worried that another corporate raider from outside the hallowed ranks of the 'Beerage' – the late-Victorian term coined to reflect the overweening influence of the captains of the brewing industry – might one day succeed. The pace of mergers and takeovers across British industry at the end of the 1960s merely heightened their fears. Accordingly, in 1972 they seized International Distillers and Vintners – as its name suggests, a wine and spirits firm – and added yet another traditional brewer, Webster's of Halifax. These two acquisitions, they hoped, would safeguard them from further unwelcome takeover bids. But they didn't. Later that same year Maxwell Joseph's massive leisure empire Grand Metropolitan made a hostile takeover bid for Watney's, offering a whopping £413 million in the biggest commercial takeover bid that Britain had yet seen. Grand Met had already bought up the London brewers Truman from under Watney's nose. Equally disturbing was the purchase of the Courage brewing empire early in 1972 by another giant, non-brewing predator from outside the Beerage, Imperial Tobacco. Could Watney's be next?

Watney's also faced a revolt from within. Since 1970 the brewer's most loyal tenants had been systematically evicted by Watney's from the brewery's most successful pubs to make way for more easily manipulated salaried managers. The reactions to these astonishingly callous acts ranged from the outraged and appalled to the utterly resigned. Christopher Hutt interviewed some of the dispossessed tenants such as James Crossland, from the Hope at Brixton, a Watney tenant for nineteen years. He had asked the Watney's representative who broke the shocking news to him why on earth he was being sacked. 'It's the march of time and part of the company's new policy,' he was told.

Watney's tenants fought back by forming a Watney Mann Tenants Association. One of their most powerful leaflets read, 'If Watney's expect Watney tenants to keep Watney's Watney's, then they should keep Watney tenants tenants. Loyalty cuts both ways.' Prime minister Edward Heath's ringing phrase of 1973, accusing corporate raider Roland 'Tiny' Rowland of exposing 'the unacceptable face of capitalism',[31] could equally have applied to Watney's policy of evicting its most enterprising and successful pub landlords for short-term gain. But Heath's *laissez-faire* Tory government did not wish to intervene in the dispute. It was only the perceived need to keep bad publicity to a minimum, in order to fend off Grand Met's likely takeover bid, that compelled Watney's to finally reduce the scale of evictions and improve the proffered compensation for the discarded tenants.

In the event, by the time concessions had been wrung out of Watney's by the Tenants Association it was way too late for the brewery. Watney stakeholders ultimately succumbed to Maxwell Joseph's enticing share offer and early in 1973 Watney's brewing kingdom became part of Grand Met's vast empire.

However, the war was not yet over. Prior to their hostile takeover proposal, Watney's had bought the long-established London brewer Truman, Hanbury and Buxton. In their bid document, Grand Met now explicitly reassured Watney's staff that 'It will be our policy to allow the brewing businesses of Watney and Truman to continue as separate and autonomous units' and that 'no rationalisation of the activities of Watney and Truman will take place.' But guess what? It wasn't true. Barely one year later, the two brewing businesses were fused into 'a single profit centre'. Jobs were lost and competing pubs closed, with the loss of all hands.

In the event, though, all of Watney's desperate corporate twists and turns ultimately counted for nothing. Just as Watney's Red seemed to have a bright new future as the flagship keg brand for Grand Met's huge pub estate, the wheels started to fall off both the brand and the brewery.

By 1973, despite – or perhaps because of – the generously financed relaunch of two years earlier, Red's sales were actually falling. The beer not only failed to overhaul the new market leader, Allied's Double Diamond; now it fell even further behind. In response, having surreptitiously weakened the strength of their beers during the 1960s, Watney's took a leaf out of both Allied and Whitebread's books and actually reversed their policy by increasing the strength of Red and other key beers. But this didn't do anything to improve Red's unexceptional taste. As John Keeling, a technician at Watney Mann, later admitted: 'What drove [Watney's] was how to use science to make beer cheaper, not better.' Excessive pasteurisation had made the beer highly oxidised, Keeling volunteered. But even though the result was a beer that tasted stale and cardboard-like, Watney's 'didn't seem to care about that, because they weren't as interested in flavour' as they were in profits.

In the mid-1970s, Britain – along with the rest of the world – was transforming itself in response to the recent oil crisis. The Arab coalition's failures during the brief Arab–Israeli War of 1973 had prompted the Middle Eastern oil producers to penalise those Western countries which had supported Israel. As a result, Western pump prices quickly rose by 40 per cent and kept rising, causing vast queues at petrol stations as drivers filled up their tanks in panic. A blanket national speed limit of 55 mph and tougher standards for fuel consumption for new cars were established in Britain and the US. Global governments, along with industries worldwide, had to acknowledge that the age of cheap fuel was over, and tighten their belts accordingly. The fundamental tenet of Western consumerism, that resources were endless and abundant, was no longer relevant in a world in which environmental and consumer concerns began to play a far bigger part in daily life. Bigger was now not always going to be better. The age of the dinosaur was over: the world now belonged to the small mammals.

–

In 1975, as North Vietnamese troops entered the Presidential Palace in Saigon, as President Gerald Ford's new

US administration attempted to grapple with the fall-out from Richard Nixon's disgrace and resignation, as Margaret Thatcher replaced Edward Heath as leader of the Conservative Party, as Britain entered a double-dip recession, and as the government was forced to bail out a bankrupt British Leyland, it was clear that the socio-economic assumptions of the past were no longer valid.

Watney's new owners could see this coming, too. After Michael Webster, the last Watney family member to lead the brewer, stepped down in 1974 from his post-takeover role as chairman of Grand Met's newly forged Watney, Mann and Truman division, wiser heads prevailed. By 1975, sales of Watney's Red had fallen behind not just those of Double Diamond but also those of its other Big Six rivals: Worthington E, Courage Tavern and Younger's Tartan Special. CAMRA's jibes were beginning to take real effect: the national media poured scorn both on the tarnished Watney's brand and on Watney's excruciatingly standardised red pubs. Then, in a brave and unprecedented move, Grand Met publicly admitted that the brewery rationalisation of the past twenty years, along with the recent focus on the Watney's Red brand alone, may have been a mistake. Hallelujah.

The man behind this astonishing *volte-face* was certainly no board-room radical. Marketing expert Anthony Tennant was a patrician Old Etonian who had pursued the customary route of Cambridge and the Scots Guards. However, rather than continuing to follow the familiar path to the City of London, Tennant began his working life with the London advertising agency Mather and Crowther (later Ogilvy & Mather), where he worked with the legendary advertising guru David Ogilvy. In 1970 Tennant was appointed marketing director of Truman's brewery; given his experience there, after 1972 his in-depth knowledge of both the marketing world and of the brewing sector served him well in the new Grand Met universe. Although Tennant eventually lost out in his 1986 bid for the Grand Metropolitan chairmanship, he embarked on what appeared to be a charmed, stellar career, ultimately advancing to become chair of the prestigious auction house Christie's in 1993. Unfortunately, all of his marvellous achievements were undone by his dramatic fall from grace in 2001, following a US indictment resulting from the Sotheby's/Christie's price-fixing scandal. At least, unlike his opposite number at Sotheby's, he escaped jail.

It was Tennant's wisdom and foresight that prompted Grand Met to withdraw their marketing support for the failing Red brand in 1975. Nor did Tennant stop there. In 1976 he persuaded Grand Met to magically revive axed brewery names such as Ushers of Trowbridge and disinterred much-loved old beer brands. Now the evil empire of Grand Metropolitan was actually helping CAMRA to make cask ale fashionable again. Watney's even introduced their *own* cask beer, the unremarkable London Bitter, in 1978. Simultaneously, the insensitive red corporate imagery bedecking Watney's pubs was removed. As Richard Boston later wrote: 'Early in 1975 many of their pubs in London were repainted in any colour other than red. The company appeared to be trying to camouflage its pubs, to conceal the fact that they were Watney's houses.'

Watney's Red itself was finally put out of its misery in May 1979. The 'beer of the future', the keg that was going to see off cask-conditioned ales for good, was now no more. As the final nail in Red's coffin, Grand Met later bought a highly successful and award-winning regional brewer, Ruddles of Rutland, and actually promoted its real ales on counters that once boasted bright Red taps. CAMRA went from strength to strength, while Watney's name was erased, at least in the UK. (There's a moral in there somewhere.) Exhausted by it all, Grand Met eventually sold all of its brewing interests to Courage, in 1991.

Watney's, though, has not completely disappeared. Sales of Red continued in the US and Europe for some years after 1979; even today, the Belgian brewer Alken-Maes still produces a Watney's Red Barrel beer of 6 per cent, while Canadian firm Sleeman's issues a lager of the same name at 3.9 per cent. Surprisingly, in 2016 a British firm that specialised in acquiring expired brewery names, Brands Reunited, revived the Watney's name in the UK. They did not, though, resuscitate either Red or Red Barrel; instead, they merely devised a range of modern pale ales to be brewed at Sambrook's Wandsworth plant. In an interview of 12 June 2019 with the online industry publication *The Drinks Business*, Brands Reunited's Nick Whitehurst asserted that that his new beer sold under the old Watney's name today was a far cry from the notoriously bland and below-par product of the 1970s:

> *The nostalgia and history of Watneys give us provenance, but what we've done is taken this heritage and reinvented the brand to appeal to a whole new generation of drinkers... Now we're modern, relevant and have a business model to make Watneys a key brand in the craft beer market.*

Even the ever-optimistic Whitehurst admitted, however, that there was no place for Red in his lineup, aside from the manufacture of some retro Red Barrel memorabilia. While seeking to capitalise on nostalgia, he understandably recoiled from the negative connotations of the old Watney's name. Perhaps some things are, after all, better left forgotten.

Chapter 5

DON'T MENTION THE WAR

BLUE NUN

Blue Nun was *the* wine of the 1970s: the British and American market leader that offered a veneer of European sophistication and protection from wine snobbery. It was the *safe* wine: a wine that was 'correct with any dish', one that could rescue you from any potential dinner-party faux pas or career-wrecking social gaffe. It was the wine that aspirational middle-class couples took to dinner parties, that Reggie Perrin of *The Rise and Fall…* and Margo Leadbetter of *The Good Life* would probably have served to their guests. When, in Mike Leigh's classic play *Abigail's Party* of 1977 (since voted one of television's all-time greats by the British Film Institute), the unforgettable Beverly ('shoulders like a lifeguard, and a walk to match', as Alan Bennett admiringly wrote of the Demis Roussos-loving host) served white wine throughout the doomed evening, most probably it was Blue Nun.[32]

But where exactly did the Blue Nun hail from? Which country's grapes had actually created the wine? Only unobtrusively did its producers acknowledge that Blue Nun was actually *German*.

The reasons for the winemaker's reticence were not hard to fathom. Thirty years after the cataclysmic events of 1939–45, Britons were still fighting the Second World War – at least in popular culture. Boys' comics were still chock-full of strip-cartoon sagas featuring gung-ho British Tommies ('give it to 'em, good and hot!') battling valiantly against fanatical but invariably doomed Nazis ('Clever Schwein, I'll get you for— arrggghh!'). A year after Britain joined the European Economic Community (EEC) in 1973, Dundee-based publishers D. C. Thomson (who already published a war-heavy boys' title in the shape of *The Victor*) unveiled yet another new comic set almost entirely in the Second World War: *Warlord*, a weekly replete with impeccably British, stiff-upper-lip heroes such as Lord Peter Flint ('a minor aristocrat and sporting daredevil'). In response, in 1975 D. C. Thomson's great rival, IPC Magazines, launched yet another contender into the crowded market for graphic military tales in which the British continued to trounce the Germans. *Battle Picture Weekly* (the title says it all, really) introduced readers to Second World War heroes such as D-Day Dawson, Major Eazy and Johnny Red. Meanwhile, during 1975–6 IPC's venerable *Valiant* comic introduced yet more adventures set in the Second World War, including 'The Boy Who Went To War' ('Underage poacher Danny Dougan forges his age to join the British Army in World War II. His outdoorsman skills soon make him invaluable in fighting Germans in Crete.'), 'Death Wish', starring embittered sergeant Joe Bannon, and 'The Black Crow' ('a British secret agent carries out perilous missions in German-held Europe while Gestapo officer Major Klaus von Steutsel attempts to stop him'). Young readers of these titles could be forgiven for thinking that the Second World War had never ended.

The 1970s was the heyday of the Airfix plastic model kit, too, and the Airfix range was always dominated by Second World War models and always topped by the legendary Supermarine Spitfire, the scourge of the German Luftwaffe. It was also the era of Palitoy's Action Man, first introduced in 1966 yet still clad in a Second World War uniform.

The war never seemed to go away on the television, either. British TV drama of the 1970s seemed to be obsessed by it. Over on ITV, the instant classic *A Family at War* of 1970–2, particularly memorable for the evocative sandcastle title sequence set to Vaughan Williams' music, touchingly depicted the trials of an average Liverpool family between 1938 and 1945, while a less successful follow-up, *Pathfinders* of 1972–3, focused on British wartime bomber crews. On the BBC, *Colditz*, the hugely popular series of 1972–4 about a prisoner-of-war camp, was succeeded by the wartime escape network of *Secret Army* of 1977–9 (created by the same producer as *Colditz*, former wartime pilot Gerard Glaister, but these days perhaps best known for being affectionately parodied by the long-running series *'Allo 'Allo!* of 1982–92).

It was the same for television comedy of the 1970s, too. Britons' enduring nostalgia for their wartime experiences and their relentless suspicion of the Germans was perhaps best reflected in two classic moments of television genius during this decade: Captain Mainwaring's legendary exclamation, 'Don't tell him, Pike!' from *Dad's Army*[33] and Basil Fawlty's outrageous treatment of his German hotel guests ('Listen, don't mention the war. I mentioned it once but I think I got away with it') in an episode of John Cleese and Connie Booth's classic comedy *Fawlty Towers*.[34] The show concluded with the insulted

German visitors shaking their heads in disbelief as they left Fawlty's appalling hotel, wondering out loud, 'How ever did *they* win?'[35]

Sichel went to great pains to stress Blue Nun's quality and, in particular, its consistency. In this 1973 print ad they contrast their 'classic German white wine' with

cheap, generic 'plonk.' The overt mention of Germany is unusual, but they still don't mention in the copy that this is a 'Liebfraumilch' – a difficult word to pronounce for many Britons.

To cap it all, at the 1970 World Cup in Mexico, the over-confident English football team – winners of the trophy four years earlier, when they defeated the Germans 4–2 – were now knocked out of the tournament by a resurgent West German team. Yet many Britons simply ignored this result. For years Britain's football terraces resounded to the echoes of 'Two world wars and one world cup, doo da, doo da…' – a chant that was, historian Ruth Wittlinger has suggested, 'an indication of how deeply embedded the Second World War is in the psyche of this country, [even] in generations far too young to have experienced it.'

Yet while Germany continued to be viewed by much of the British public at this time through the archaic prism of the last war, throughout the 1970s the nation's favourite wine was actually German. Albeit a wine cunningly rebranded to look as generically continental and as un-German as possible. Even its name, Blue Nun, failed to identify its country of origin. But the wine's soaring sales suggested that this was just the right strategy for 1970s Britain.

–

Blue Nun arrived in Britain just at the right time. During the 1970s Britons grew wealthier: despite the predictable media stereotypes of this unsettled decade, by 1979 the average family was actually far better off than they had been ten years earlier. In the wake of the country joining the EEC, they sought to use their enhanced spending power to become more sophisticated and European, drinking more wine-based drinks and holidaying at continental, wine-drinking destinations. As Britons moved from Beer Street or Gin Lane to the *Rue des Vins* or the *Weinstraße*, though, they were still happy to poke fun at their Europhile affectations – social aspirations that were so neatly skewered in Collett Dickenson Pearce's wickedly funny TV ads for the Italian vermouth Cinzano of 1978–9,[36] at the end of which the glamorous international jet-setter Joan Collins was always left covered in drink spilled by the hapless average Britisher played by Leonard Rossiter.

Britons were now drinking far more wine than they had in the past. During the 1960s, annual adult consumption of wine per head in Britain had doubled, from 3.6 pints per head per year to seven pints. By the end of the 1970s, though, it had soared to 17.9 pints.[37] Per capita consumption of wine then doubled in the decade after 1975, from five to ten litres per year. All of this triggered what many critics have since called Britain's 'wine revolution'. As historian John Burnett remarked, it was during this time that 'Wine… passed from a drink of privilege to one of mass consumption,' with the result that the nation 'at least partially converted to a Europeanization of taste'.

Much of this may be laid at the door of Britain's invasion of the European continent – not, as had been the case thirty years before, by tank and truck, but this time by car and caravan. Historian Stella Moss has noted:

> *The transformation of mass tourism in the 1970s via cheaper travel and package holidays afforded new opportunities to experience first-hand European habits and cultures, which in turn*

had a marked effect on attitudes towards wine consumption. Moreover, the popularity of continental cuisine, especially from Italy and France, also helped propel interest in wine, as was witnessed in both domestic cookery and restaurant cultures.

As European travel became more common, continental cuisine – and, most importantly, the wines that you could try while you were on holiday – became far more fashionable. Wine drinking was heavily promoted on TV by popular chefs such as Graham Kerr, who was constantly glugging wine with guests plucked from his audience on his syndicated series *The Galloping Gourmet* of 1968–72. Many Britons, inspired both by the 'oui' affirmation in the 1975 referendum on EEC membership and by the weakening pound, eagerly seized the opportunity to try European wine, at home or abroad, for the first time.

At the same time, supermarkets and off-licences increasingly encouraged Britons to drink wine at home rather than in the pub, where bar staff often still viewed European wine with suspicion and bottles were left open for days on end. British supermarkets had been licensed to sell wine since 1962 (although, as we have seen, Marks and Spencer remained obdurately dry until 1974), while the Wilson government's axing of the retail price agreement in 1965 gave a massive boost to wine sales in the high street. Unlike beer, which was still seen very much as a man's drink, to be quaffed in the pub, wine was perceived as being gender-free. Accordingly, women now became more confident in exploring the alcohol aisle.[38]

As ever-larger supermarkets began to colonise Britain's High Streets (Britain's first out-of-town shopping centre, Brent Cross in north-west London, did not open until

1976, but supermarkets did not really begin to desert town centres until the 1980s), so too did off-licences begin to proliferate. In the twenty years after 1965, the number of off-licences in the UK rose from 26,352 to 42,646. It was now far easier to pick up a bottle or two of wine on your way home than it had been a decade earlier.

The 1970 Equal Pay Act had made many women better off – although there was still a long way to go in achieving genuine pay parity – while the spread of wine bars, in which beer was rarely served, gave women who wished to drink away from the home a viable alternative to the male-dominated culture of the pub. As historian David Gutzke has observed, 'wine bars exorcized women's fear of insecurity, embarrassment, humiliation, and absence of what I would call "inviolable public space"':

> *Here, they were not 'fair game' for male attention, salacious comments and mockery. Into wine bars went no leering beer-swilling men who, as 'regulars' imposing and asserting their unwelcome masculinity, would freely hassle women... In redefining gender boundaries, the wine bar gave them sanctuary of an unprecedented kind. They had no compunction – either alone or with company – about patronizing wine bars where owners were mindful of their customers' desires, notably privacy and anonymity in a feminine environment.*

Unlike traditional pubs, wine bars consciously targeted a professional, upwardly mobile, female clientele. Early wine bar entrepreneurs such as John Davy – who opened his first London wine bar, the Boot and Flogger near London Bridge, in 1964, and who by the end of the 1970s had established a successful chain of similar venues across the capital – clearly recognised the way the wind was blowing, and made sure women felt both welcome and safe at their venues. In 1972 London even acquired its first female wine bar owner: Julia Carpenter, who opened a wine bar called Wolsey's in London's Fulham Road that ostentatiously rejected the chauvinistic working environment of the conventional pub and prioritised the hiring of women as bar and office staff.

At the same time, the admission of women into the male sanctuary of wine journalism helped to convince many female consumers that wine drinking need not be the domain of pompous male 'connoisseurs' loudly exchanging the names of obscure French vineyards or incomprehensible viticultural terms. This welcome development in turn helped to underline the gender-neutral appeal of wine drinking in the 1970s. One of the most high-profile of these pioneering critics was Jancis Robinson, whose no-nonsense approach to the enjoyment of wine was exemplified in her highly successful *Wine Book* of 1979, unambiguously subtitled *A Straightforward Guide to Better Buying and Drinking for Less Money*.

-

While wine drinking was increasing across most sectors of British society during the 1970s, though, wine from Germany was still burdened with a challenging image problem in Britain. Not only, as we have seen, were many Britons innately suspicious of anything German – though, as the decade wore on, that did not stop them from buying Volkswagen cars, Siemens ovens or Bosch fridges – there was also an additional obstacle to overcome if German wine was to reach a mass market in the

UK. Traditional German wine labels were notorious for their indecipherable Gothic script, over-complex wine classification system and long and, to untutored British tongues, unpronounceable German names.

To appeal to a British audience ripe for harvesting, the Mainz winemaking firm of Sichel astutely decided to jettison all of that cumbrous Teutonic baggage. Instead of slapping an impenetrable Gothic typeface and long, unintelligible wine designations on the label, Sichel shrewdly deployed an existing English brand name with vaguely continental and socially respectable connotations. The 'Blue Nun' marque dated from 1923 and had originally been used for a diverse range of wines. Helpfully, though, it said nothing about Germany or the Germans. The bottle label spelled out the wine's name in a clear, modern font that implied a historic pedigree in a deliberately ambiguous manner. Sichel also refrained from adding the customary vineyard coat-of-arms or picture of a local castle on the bottle, as was usual for most German wines of the time. Instead, their label design featured six contented nuns, dressed in simple brown habits, cheerfully toiling away in a vineyard on an estate that could have been located anywhere in the world. In later years, five of the nuns were quietly retired and the label was simplified to focus on just one, blue-clad sister: the eponymous 'Blue Nun'.

The wine inside the bottle was also given a lot of thought. Peter Sichel had decided to target his product squarely at the incorrigibly sweet tooth of British and American consumers. Accordingly, his Rhenish wine was additionally sweetened for the UK market – resulting in a product that few Germans would recognise.

Blue Nun was not the first continental wine specifically engineered to appeal to the British palate by adapting a traditional, native wine style to create a sweet, easy-drinking 'everyday wine'. In 1942 Portuguese winemaker Fernando van Zeller Guedes had launched a new viticultural company, the Sociedade Comercial dos Vinhos de Mesa de Portugal (later simplified to 'Sogrape'), with a branded rosé named after the nearby Palace of Mateus – a picturesque rendering of which was inevitably included in the label design. An unashamedly sugary, salmon-pink and slightly *pétillant* mass-market wine, Mateus Rosé first saw success in Brazil and then in the Britain of the Swinging Sixties, where it appealed to Europhile men and women who wanted to seem sophisticated but who also found the wine's pronounced sweetness and attractive colour pleasantly reassuring.

Mateus Rosé's distinctive bottle shape swiftly became a British domestic icon. Guedes had chosen an unusual form that was allegedly based on the flasks used by Portuguese soldiers when they were serving alongside the British armies on the Western Front during the First World War. (A nice pro-Allied touch, that.) The bottle's profile also, Guedes later admitted, helped it to muscle its way to the front of the shelf, as its distinctive squat shape often led to Mateus Rosé bottles being placed in front of taller rivals. And in Britain and America the idiosyncratic bottle was soon being converted into a table lamp or candle holder when empty – a practice clearly designed to remind dinner guests that their hosts had been on a recent continental holiday, even if, in truth, the bottle of Mateus in question may have only been bought at the off-licence round the corner.

Thanks as much to the bottle as to the wine inside, by 1970 Mateus Rosé had become a cultural phenomenon in Britain. Its bottles adorned the dining tables of the middle classes and it was ostentatiously drunk at parties by the likes of rock stars Jimi Hendrix and Elton John – and by none other than Queen Elizabeth II herself. Ever the entrepreneur, Guedes even ensured that Mateus was also at the forefront of the new trend for British couples to book onto vineyard tours as part of their continental package holidays. Stella Moss notes that, in April 1972, *Good Housekeeping* editor Charlotte Lessing specifically recommended a visit to the Vila Real home of Mateus Rosé, where the firm's winning combination of 'old-world manners' and up-to-date 'marketing methods' would, she promised, delight everyone.

The enormous success of Mateus Rosé showed that the British were happy to drink wine if it was sweet and fruity enough, and provided that it possessed an appropriately European pedigree. By 1978 the brand accounted for over 40 per cent of Portugal's entire wine exports, with 3.5 million cases being sold worldwide in that year.

Mateus' example in turn encouraged Britain's ambitious and acquisitive 'Big Six' breweries to make their own forays into the mass-market wine business. In 1968 Bass Charrington brewery's Hedges and Butler subsidiary brought out its own soft, fruity and sweet wines: a range of whites, rosés and reds all branded 'Hirondelle'. The name sounded French, but of course wasn't. As former Hedges and Butler executive Christopher Burr admitted many years later: 'Because the bar we used to drink in after work was in Swallow Street, our bright marketing director came up with the "double entendre"... of Hirondelle, which is the French word for the bird swallow and English for quaffing!' Buoyed by an astute ad campaign beautifully illustrated by the artist Alan Cracknell and based on the matey slogan 'It's about as likely as a duff bottle of Hirondelle', the range was soon selling impressively. Yet Hirondelle had nothing to do with France or the French. Initially the wine originated from Austria, and was imported via Italy's German-speaking South Tyrol region. On the way it had been judiciously sweetened for the British market through the addition of sugary grape juice. After a while, though, Hedges and Butler switched Hirondelle's wine suppliers to winemakers in Bulgaria and Yugoslavia, whose products were substantially cheaper – although following the UK's admission to the EEC in 1973 European strictures forced them to switch back to Austrian wine for a brand that was now entirely bottled in England.

In response to Hedges and Butler's success, another of the Britain's brewing giants, Grand Metropolitan, used their wine and spirits business IDV to develop a branded wine for the British market that was, this time, *genuinely* French. In 1975 IDV launched a wine called 'Le Piat D'Or' with the pay-off line 'Les Français adorent le Piat D'Or.' In truth, no self-respecting *Français* had ever heard of the wine – and, if they had been offered it, would doubtless have been horrified at its insipid sugariness.

Despite challenges from the likes of Piat d'Or, though, it was Sichel's Blue Nun that dominated the market for wine in Britain throughout the 1970s. Like Guedes with Mateus Rosé and Hedges and Butler with Hirondelle, Sichel artificially sweetened the already sugary and fruity Liebfraumilch from the German Rhineland to produce a wine that was both bland and sweet enough to appeal to British palates. Although today the marque survives (quite astonishingly) as a generic name for a wide range of wine varietals, in the 1970s it was classified just as a Liebfraumilch – a designation that denoted a naturally sweet and soft wine from the Rheingau, Mosel and Pfalz regions. As Jancis Robinson notes, in its heyday Liebfraumilch 'accounted for an extraordinary, some would say horrifying, 60 per cent of all German wine exported.'

–

The Blue Nun was no British novice: Sichel had been selling this brand to the British since 1927, the year in which the firm had set up its London office. But it was only during the 1960s that the brand's promotion in the British market became more forceful. Not only did the wine's pan-European branding now seek to downplay the wine's Teutonic origins. Much was also made of the wine's consistency and, crucially, its alleged ability to be served with any type of dish – thus enabling hosts to sidestep the gaffe-ridden minefield of which food should be paired with what wine. Sichel's bold assertion that they had produced 'A wine for every meal' was a brand claim that won many nervous customers on both sides of the Atlantic.

The man behind this ingenious positioning, Peter Sichel, was a colourful and multicultural hybrid of both Germanic and Anglo-Saxon cultures. A scion of the Mainz winemaking dynasty that had originated in Bordeaux (and was, rather appropriately, of British origin), he was educated at an English boarding school, Stowe, after his parents fled Nazi Germany in the 1930s. Interned in Bordeaux after the outbreak of war in 1939, he escaped through Spain and Portugal to the US, where he joined the American Army a week after Pearl Harbor.

Recruited by the Americans' rapidly expanding intelligence agency, the Office of Strategic Services (OSS), Sichel was soon running American agents in Hitler's Reich, using German prisoners of war to infiltrate the Nazi war effort. (Sichel's exploits, which won him the Distinguished Intelligence Medal from the OSS, could easily have inspired a strip cartoon in the likes of *Wizard*, *Victor* or *Battle Picture Weekly*.) After the war, Sichel worked for the OSS's successor, the CIA, in Berlin, Washington and Hong Kong until he belatedly decided to rejoin the family wine firm in 1960.

From New York, Peter Sichel masterminded the marketing campaigns designed to persuade the British and, later, the Americans of the virtues of Blue Nun. He ensured consistency and quality, and limited the brand to a single wine – unlike the numerous varietals that the company had produced under the same name during the 1920s and 1930s.

Thanks to his energetic promotion of the brand to younger American audiences, annual sales of the wine in the US had reached 1.25 million cases and 3 million cases worldwide by the mid-1980s. Sichel hired the US advertising agency Della Femina, Travisano & Partners (DFTP) to introduce the brand not in print, the traditional medium for advertising fine wines, but on television and radio. DFTP hired well-known husband-and-wife comedy duo Jerry Stiller (later famous for his stints on the hit TV shows *Seinfeld* and *The King of Queens*) and Anne Meara, who wrote as well as performed their distinctive and entertaining radio spots:

> *Meara: 'Couldn't you just have left an extra dollar in the collection plate?'*

Stiller: 'May I suggest you have a little Blue Nun at your smorgasbord?'

Meara: 'Oh, I don't think she'd have a very good time. Besides, it's going to be all couples.'

The fact that both Stiller and Meara were both Jewish showed how far Sichel had successfully obscured the wine's German origins. At the same time, DFTP produced a television ad for Blue Nun in which a shifty Lothario with impossibly wide lapels produced a bottle of the aforementioned wine at a series of domestic dinners-for-two, each hosted by a different woman every night. This particular scenario, it must be said, has dated rather less well than Stiller and Meara's timeless schtick.

Behind the humour, Sichel's brand strategy during the 1970s remained consistent: firstly, to downplay any mention of Germany and, secondly, to reassure consumers that the wine's universality would safeguard them from embarrassing social indiscretions. As Jancis Robinson observed in an early edition of her *Oxford Companion to Wine*, Blue Nun 'preyed on the fears of an unsophisticated wine drinking public'. But Sichel's strategy continued to reap big rewards. Blue Nun's advertising taglines may have changed a little from year to year, but their message was always the same. Blue Nun was endorsed as 'A fine wine you can drink right throughout the meal', as a wine that 'Entertains – right through the meal' and as a choice that was always 'Correct with any dish.' Most significantly, it was marketed as a wine that would safeguard you from malicious or judgemental gossip and which would guarantee social acceptance. 'There's always someone who sees and knows and passes on the good news,' proclaimed one UK print ad of the late 1970s.

In Britain, Blue Nun was promoted as an aspirational wine – but at the same time one that was safe and reassuring. That was its genius. Blue Nun was designed to calm first-time wine buyers who were worried about being seen as unsophisticated and gauche in front of friends or colleagues, and to appeal to the sort of person who was still terrified of breaching alleged rules of etiquette and being socially exposed by inadvertently asking for a 'serviette' rather than a 'napkin', calling multi-seat furniture a 'settee' instead of a 'sofa' or describing the dessert course as a 'sweet' instead of a 'pudding'.[39]

The same marketing strategy was still being applied in the early 1980s, when the Blue Nun brand was under pressure from more 'authentic' continental wines such as Piat d'Or. A British TV ad of 1983 showed that Sichel continued to target consumers' fears of appearing foolish or stupid in public: an (unseen) customer enters an old-fashioned wine shop, where there's no reassurance of being able to choose your own wines from the shelves, and is addressed by a pretentious and conceited wine merchant trying to shift a bottle of traditional French wine. It looks like a Burgundy bottle – and, most damningly, there is no colourful picture on the label to help you. Faced with the prospect of Blue Nun, however, the merchant's supercilious sales patter ('a remarkable little vintage with a crisp, delicate flavour') soon breaks down ('well, actually a rather roughish sort of flavour...'), and he is ultimately forced to acknowledge the qualities of Blue Nun ('An exquisite wine. Honestly.'). The ad ends with the converted merchant's enthusiastic admission that, of all his wines, Blue Nun is the 'one you could drink with any kind of food'.

To middle-class British consumers of the 1970s, the sweet, fruity, uncomplicated flavours of Blue Nun (along with Blue Nun imitators such as Reh Kendermann's Black Tower of 1967, with its distinctive tall, black bottle) were just what they wanted. A nation beset by strikes, rising inflation and appalling industrial relations sought solace in a sweet and reliable dinner-party wine that reminded them of their recent European holidays and reassured them of their innate refinement.

Inevitably, though, as Britons grew more confident in their wine purchases, and as their holiday destinations became more ambitious, Blue Nun sales faded. In the later 1980s former Blue Nun customers were moving on to more 'modern', complex and supposedly sophisticated wines such as Nicolas's French mass-market range, the many acidic Muscadets now appearing from the Loire, Hungarian Bull's Blood, oaked Australian Chardonnays and, most notoriously, fizzy, sweet Italian Lambrusco.

–

Peter Sichel saw the way the wind was blowing and in 1995 sold the venerable firm of Sichel Söhne to a rival Rhenish winemaker, Langguth Erben. Freed from the need to devote his energies to promoting an over-sweetened popular wine to the Anglo-Saxons, Herr Sichel then astutely reinvented himself as an eminent wine expert. He founded the German Wine Society and the Society of Wine Educators, bought a prestigious Bordeaux vineyard and won a slew of awards from the international wine industry. All of this consigned Blue Nun to the distant past – at least in his own mind.

Meanwhile, in 2001 Blue Nun's new owner, Langguth, astonished everyone by attempting to revive a waning brand whose best days were clearly behind it. Instead of adapting the existing wine to contemporary palates, though, Langguth turned the clock back to the 1930s, applying the 'Blue Nun' trademark to products from a range of grape varieties – from a Spanish rosé to a Languedoc Merlot. Given the weight of unhelpful 1970s baggage with which the 'Blue Nun' name was freighted, this seemed to many, both then and now, to be an overly ambitious strategy. But Langguth stuck to it. Eight years after its acquisition of the brand, they even introduced a premium, sparkling 'Blue Nun': a wine that contained genuine flakes of 22-carat gold in a bid to entice young women drinkers. (Unsurprisingly, they weren't enticed.) Today, Langguth's Blue Nun range includes a Pinot Grigio from Germany and, in line with recent trends, a low-alcohol 0.5 per cent 'Blue Nun Light'. Peter Sichel would be turning in his grave.

Peter Sichel's apotheosis from mass-market product packager to international wine connoisseur notwithstanding, much of the German wine trade has always been highly critical of the success of Blue Nun. In 2020 the celebrated wine writer Hugh Johnson recalled that, fifty years before, 'no great dinner could begin without its Mosel… or Rhine Spätlese', since Germany had up until then been regarded as one of the finest white wine producers in the world. But Blue Nun and its imitators had, he alleged, managed to ruin the country's reputation as a producer of high-quality wines. Similarly, Rüdesheim winemaker Tom Drieseberg recently recalled that 'my first trip to the US, in the late 1990s, was a disaster. We were selling well here, but the perception out there was that German wine was "sweet, cheap and stinky".' It was a setback from which the German wine trade has never really recovered.

Nevertheless, today Blue Nun is the product most often quoted by the British media when they wish to conjure the ghosts of the 1970s. It remains an icon of bad taste, one joyously cited by celebrities ranging from Heston Blumenthal to Jeremy Clarkson to Alan Partridge, the fictional, over-the-hill British television and radio presenter for whom it was, inevitably, the drink of choice. For the satirists, it is the gift that keeps on giving.

Chapter 6

GREED IS GOOD FOR YOU

GUINNESS

1990 was a momentous year for Britain – and for the world. The Cold War ended as the Soviet Union collapsed. Many of Soviet Russia's constituent republics declared independence, while Soviet armies were withdrawn from the Eastern Bloc. Czechoslovakia staged its first free elections since 1946. Lech was elected president of a free Poland. Germany was reunified and restored to its 1945 boundaries, and the Berlin Wall was demolished. Elsewhere in the world, Yugoslavia fragmented into its constituent republics, which were soon to be engulfed by a bitter and vicious war. Nelson Mandela was released from prison in South Africa after serving twenty-seven years behind bars. America invaded the tiny Central American nation of Panama and deposed its rogue, unelected, drug-trafficking dictator, General Manuel Noriega.

In Britain, the Poll Tax Riots convulsed the nation's city centres after Margaret Thatcher's Conservative government introduced its highly unpopular 'Community Charge'. A brutal succession of IRA bombs killed police officers, members of the armed forces, a nun, numerous bystanders and Ian Gow MP. The fatal cattle disease bovine spongiform encephalopathy (BSE) continued to spread, resulting in the widespread culling of valuable herds, while agriculture minister John Gummer publicly fed a burger to his four-year-old daughter in a bizarre attempt to demonstrate that BSE was not transferable to humans. More encouragingly, Tim Berners-Lee began work on the World Wide Web and devised the world's first-ever webpage.

In politics, following former deputy prime minister Geoffrey Howe's withering parliamentary attack on her conduct and policies, Margaret Thatcher failed to win an outright victory in the ensuing Conservative Party leadership contest and stood down as prime minister after eleven years at the summit of British politics. And in August, in what was widely interpreted as a dishearteningly typical sign of the times, four leading businessmen were found guilty of share-trading fraud in the notorious and internationally publicised Guinness trial.

Guinness, a dark, creamy stout porter that had originated in Ireland, is one of the world's best known and most instantly recognisable drinks. It had (at least until 1990) a historic reputation as a much-loved Irish icon – despite the fact that most of the pints of Guinness then sold in Britain were produced at the firm's massive brewery in London's Park Royal.[40] While its stout was popularly associated with jovial bars, comical advertising and lighthearted whimsy, Guinness the company was, by the 1960s, a vast and deadly serious worldwide business, one whose big marketing budgets and aggressive business tactics had enabled it to elbow aside all other stout parties in the market.

Guinness beer was first brewed in Dublin in 1759 and first shipped to Britain a decade later. Porter (also known as 'plain') was introduced in 1778, and twenty-one years later the decision was taken to become a porter-only brewery. As we'll see, 'stout' porter was only added to their growing portfolio in the 1820s.

Since the firm owned no pubs, Guinness was not materially affected by the brewing recession of 1900, and by 1914 accounted for over 10 per cent of the British beer market. Impressively, the company pioneered corporate welfare schemes during the Edwardian era – while at the same time refusing to employ Catholics in any significant numbers until the 1960s. (The Guinness family were all staunchly pro-Union, Anglo-Irish Protestants.)

As a British brewing giant, Guinness decided to move its headquarters to London in 1932 and, the following year, to build a massive new brewery at the periphery of the Park Royal Trading Estate in west London. Designed by architects Sir Giles Gilbert Scott and Alexander Gibb, the vast, impressive art deco brewery complex embraced gardens and sports facilities, including an excellent football pitch once used by Queen's Park Rangers football club for training. Although the brewery has now gone, Guinness still have a foothold nearby: since 1997 Guinness has been an autonomous part of the British drinks conglomerate Diageo, whose headquarters lies just east of the former Park Royal brewery site.

The company's principal product was, and is, stout porter. 'Stout' effectively just means 'strong' (even though today's draught Guinness is only brewed to a strength of around 4.2 per cent ABV, roughly the same as an average bitter beer) and was not a term necessarily associated just with porter. Guinness's Bottled Extra Stout, however, *is* 'stout': brewed at a strength of 5.6 per cent for the North American market and 6 per cent for Australia and Japan, with Guinness's premium Foreign Extra Stout weighing in at a hefty 7.5 per cent. Ironically, today Guinness's delicious bottled West Indies Porter, at 6 per cent, is stronger than its flagship draught 'stout porter'.

–

Porter had dominated the British beer trade since the early years of the eighteenth century, being first mentioned in print in 1721.[41] By 1758 Henry Jackson's *An Essay on Bread* was noting that 'Beer, commonly call'd Porter, is almost become the universal cordial of the populace.' The beer's name came from some of its most enthusiastic customers: market porters, 'fellowship porters' (stevedores) and 'ticket porters' (couriers). In 1821, though, Guinness invented a 'stouter' kind of porter, 'Superior Porter' (later renamed 'Extra Stout'), and the name stuck. 'Mild' was just a weaker version of porter – though not necessarily as weak as its modern-day image would suggest: Herbert's *Art of Brewing* of 1871 put the strength of a typical mild at a formidable 7 per cent.

Stout's deep red-brown, almost black hue comes from the well-roasted malted barley that is one of its principal ingredients. Dark-brown or black malts with few fermentable sugars, called 'patent malts', proved ideal for brewing porter and stout. However, from the 1820s pubgoers turned increasingly to the new 'India Pale Ales' now entering the market. Bright, strong and amber-coloured, they appeared far better suited to the newly introduced glass tankards than murky old porter, whose dark depths could, notoriously, hide a multitude of sins and into which less fastidious publicans were apt to pour slops and leftovers. With the new, clear IPAs, any adulteration would be swiftly detected.

By the end of the nineteenth century pale ales and 'bitter' (effectively the same thing) had largely replaced porter in cities such as London and Manchester. Although in 1863 porter still accounted for 75 per cent of beer sales in London – porter's birthplace and its traditional stronghold – by 1900 porter's market share had diminished to only 25 per cent. London's last porter-only brewery, Meux's in Tottenham Court Road (where the Dominion Theatre now stands), converted to pale ales in 1872. By 1900 the only big name left in the stout porter market was Guinness.

A lot of guff has been spoken and a lot of ink spilled about how the taste of draught Guinness varies from place to place, and how it needs to be poured in a certain manner in order to unleash its special taste. Basically, since the 1960s draught Guinness has been a standardised, pasteurised, filtered keg beer – although one that mostly uses nitrogen as its dispensing agent, rather than the customary carbon dioxide, so as to produce a creamier, less fizzy beer (nitrogen bubbles being far smaller than those of CO2).[42] Keg Guinness was introduced in 1958; the 'live', cask-conditioned version lingered in Britain and Ireland until the early 1970s, while the last 'live' bottle-conditioned Guinness was brewed in 1994. With the end of active, cask-conditioned Guinness, there was no need for the traditional, ceremonial 'two-stage pour'. This dated from the days when the live beer had been served from two barrels, and involved aged stout being added to a fresher brew to produce a highly distinctive flavour. However, Guinness have always advised pubs and bars that the two-stage ritual be retained as, essentially, a crafty marketing ploy. While it has no effect whatsoever on the beer's taste, the time-consuming sacrament of the two-part pour metamorphoses the simple delivery of beer from bar counter to customer into a sacred rite.

One of John Gilroy's classic Guinness print ads of the 1930s. As well as being an outstanding graphic artist, whose many talents were shrewdly harnessed by the Ministry of Information during the Second World War,

Gilroy (1898–1985) was also a successful society portrait painter.

Guinness's singular reputation, enduring visibility and impressive sales throughout the twentieth century – an era when sales of porter and stout in general were declining – can be confidently attributed not just to the mystique surrounding the beer but also to the brewer's consistently outstanding advertising and marketing campaigns. In 1929, a young copywriter at the London advertising agency S. H. Benson, one Dorothy L. Sayers, coined the immortal phrase 'Guinness is Good for You' for their client – while writing her early novels in her spare time. (Today the firm is quick to assert that 'We never make any medical claims for our drinks.') The following year, Benson's creative director and part-time Royal College of Art lecturer John Gilroy created the first in a long line of delightful poster and print ads for Guinness. Gilroy's timeless compositions included the famous girder-carrying workman ('Guinness for Strength') and cartoon-like tableaux of various zoo animals drinking Guinness, allegedly inspired by his visit to the circus. The most successful of Gilroy's menagerie, the toucan of 1935, became so popular that the firm deployed it as an unofficial mascot for their Extra Stout brand until the end of the 1960s.[43] Gilroy's animals were so appealing that the artist was even offered a job by Walt Disney. (He turned him down.)

While most British Guinness was actually brewed in west London until 2000, a crucial element of the brand's identity and appeal was its perceived Irishness. Guinness's harp logo of 1862 was adapted from the celebrated medieval harp on display at Trinity College Dublin ('Brian

Boru's harp'), and registered as a trademark as early as 1876. Guinness's harp was even purloined by the newly created Irish Free State as a national symbol after 1922, although the Irish government have always been careful to face their instrument the other way. (The official harp faces left, while Guinness's faces right.) Social historian Brenda Murphy has argued that Guinness still 'carries Irishness embedded in the essence of the artefact', citing the St James's Gate's marketing director's declared ambition to associate the drink with 'the spirit of Ireland' and to persuade local drinkers 'that the core values that were Guinness were also the perceived core values of Ireland.' As one reviewer of Murphy's 2014 book, Aidan Beatty, commented in the *New Hibernia Review* of winter 2016:

> *Murphy addresses the ubiquity of Guinness in Irish life and in the rituals of Irish life: funerals, weddings, homecomings, and baptisms. She quotes a marketing manager at Guinness, who saw fit to claim his company was one of the 'guardians of the spirit of the nation', on a par with Fianna Fáil, the GAA, and the Catholic church. Murphy ascribes this perception to four interlocking factors: the role the Guinness family played in the lives of its employees and to a broader Dublin and nationwide audience; the symbolism of the Guinness harp logo; the use of advertising that continuously linked Guinness to Irishness; and, finally, the social and cultural predilection of pub culture in Ireland, in which Guinness as a product played a conspicuous part.*

The reviewer did, though, question whether this carefully manufactured 'Irishness' could be equally attributed to

Guinness's notoriously aggressive approach to its market rivals, and noted that there was little discussion in the book of 'how thoroughly they erased almost all their competitors'.

-

After 1977, however, the scaling up of the IRA's horrific bombing campaigns across Britain meant this Irishness was no longer perceived by Guinness as a benign and beneficial asset. In that year the IRA (more properly, the Provisional Irish Republican Army)[44] launched a new strategy that they called the 'Long War', by which they would export the conflict across the Irish Sea to Britain. Well-armed thanks to the money and weapons provided by Irish-Americans in the US and by Libya's maverick president, Colonel Gaddafi, the Provisionals swiftly turned what had originated as a defensive campaign against the Protestant majority in Ulster into a bombing campaign across the whole of the United Kingdom aimed at military, political and so-called 'economic' targets. The bombing of Chelsea Barracks in October 1981 killed two civilians and injured twenty-three soldiers, while, in July 1982, eleven Guardsmen and seven horses were killed when bombs were detonated in two central London parks. Two years later a massive bomb exploded at the Grand Hotel in Brighton, where the prime minister and senior party colleagues were staying while attending the Conservative Party Conference. This killed five people, including MP Anthony Berry, and almost claimed the life of Margaret Thatcher herself. By the end of the 1980s rubbish bins had disappeared from stations and streets and emergency checkpoints had appeared at the entrance to high-risk city areas in response to the heightened fear of explosive devices.

Faced with this campaign of terror, Guinness's management wondered if their continued use of the famous 'Irish harp' logo was such a wise move, and actually considered banishing it altogether. From the perspective of an era when Diageo's marketing of St Patrick's Day as an essentially Guinness-themed promotion of ersatz Oirishness has become accepted without demur or protest, the near-trashing of the Guinness harp clearly reflected the tensions of the time. While the harp was ultimately reprieved, Guinness stout was, nevertheless, marketed for some years as an international brand rather than a cornerstone of Ireland's cultural identity – at least until the Good Friday Agreement of 1997 ostensibly brought the bombing campaign to an end. The 'Pure Genius' campaign of 1987–94, fronted by Dutch actor Rutger Hauer (no stage Irishman he) and created by S. H. Benson's heirs, the advertising agency Ogilvy & Mather, contained not one molecule of Irish whimsy or wisdom.

Sadly, by the time the award-winning 'Pure Genius' advertisements were appearing on British TV and in British magazines, the Guinness board had needlessly squandered the firm's hard-won reputation. Decades of finely crafted and highly successful marketing campaigns were ruined as Guinness's CEO indulged in an unapologetic display of blatant corporate gluttony so disappointingly typical of the 'get rich quick' era of Thatcher's Britain.

The fraud trial that resulted from illegal insider trading during Guinness's acquisition of the Distillers Company in 1986 was an exemplary tale of greed and arrogance, a moral message straight out of a blockbuster film or novel. Many at the time were indeed quick to associate the narrative of the Guinness trial with the rock-bottom morality and naked self-indulgence of the protagonists of two of the most successful and talked-about fictional creations of 1987, both of which appeared just as the Guinness trial was gathering steam and starting to attract worldwide publicity: Tom Wolfe's novel *The Bonfire of the Vanities* and Oliver Stone's movie *Wall Street.* The trial's four principal defendants were compared to '*The Bonfire of the Vanities*' arrogant, self-styled 'Masters of the Universe' and in particular to the repellent *Wall Street* character of Gordon Gekko who Michael Douglas memorably incarnated for the film (winning himself an Academy Award for Best Actor in the process). *Wall Street* was hailed by critics and audiences alike as a masterly distillation of the excesses of the corporate culture of the 1980s. Gekko's assertion that 'greed, for lack of a better word, is good', contracted to a simpler 'greed is good', became a household phrase and a knowing business mantra almost overnight. (Disappointingly, it also encouraged aspirant bankers to apply for jobs on Wall Street.) In the film, Gekko was eventually arrested for insider trading; in real life, so were the so-called 'Guinness Four'.

The Guinness hearing, which ended on 28 August 1990, was acclaimed as Britain's 'trial of the century'. Lasting 113 days and costing upwards of £20 million, the most ever spent on a British trial to date, it had brought to the dock four of the biggest names in the City of London: Guinness chief executive Ernest Saunders, the enormously wealthy businessman Gerald Ronson, the well-known financier and philanthropist Sir Jack Lyons and the rapacious stockbroker Anthony Parnes. To many outside the commercial world, the trial laid bare the casual approach to legality and ethics adopted by the 'greed is good' generation of corporate captains. At the same time, its outcome – all four were found guilty – seemed to suggest that the end was nigh for the pin-striped Masters of the Universe of the City of London, men who believed that they were immune to laws and controls and that they had a divine right to grab as much money as they could.

–

It all began so innocently. In 1985 Guinness acquired Arthur Bell and Sons, a relatively small whisky firm but one that made the UK's best-selling blend, Bell's. This move encouraged John Connell, then chairman of the Distillers Company, to approach Guinness for help. Distillers was a large Scottish gin and whisky operation that was being dragged down by its under-performing flagship brand, Haig, a blend whose classy advertising image belied its growing reputation as a distinctly downmarket tipple. Distillers was also tainted by the legacy of Thalidomide, a drug used to treat morning sickness in pregnancy that had been made by the group's biochemical subsidiary between 1958 and 1961 but which had resulted in the birth of thousands of severely deformed babies. (The UK government was still paying compensation to Thalidomide victims as late as 2009, while in 2021 the UK government made a lifetime Health Grant pledge for the survivors.)

Connell's Distillers was currently being targeted for a hostile takeover by the Argyll Group, a Scottish supermarket and foods business built by the abrasive entrepreneur Jimmy Gulliver (who later bought the Safeway chain of supermarkets). The modest and honourable Connell saw Guinness chief executive Ernest Saunders as the white knight who could provide a more amenable and appropriate home for Distillers' brands than the ruthless Gulliver. He was clearly unaware that Saunders could be just as cold-blooded and aggressive as Gulliver; not for nothing had he been nicknamed 'Deadly Ernest' for his ruthless cost-cutting and pitiless business tactics.

Inevitably, it wasn't all as simple as Connell had imagined. To outbid Gulliver's Argyll and secure what became a £2.7 billion takeover, Saunders had to ensure that Guinness's stock price was higher than that of its intended victim. As it currently wasn't, Saunders, without telling any of his fellow board directors, illegally invited financier friends to buy Guinness shares so as to artificially boost the firm's ostensible value, paying them many millions of pounds to do so. One of these contacts was the notorious American stock dealer Ivan Boesky, the supposed model for Michael Douglas' egregious Gordon Gekko and a man who had cheerfully admitted in public that 'I think greed is healthy. You can be greedy and still feel good about yourself.' Saunders gave Boesky $100 million dollars (effectively most of Guinness's profits) to help inflate Guinness's share price – again, without the Guinness board's knowledge.

Meanwhile, Saunders reneged on his earlier assurances to Connell about the new company, keeping the chairmanship as well as the chief executive role for himself. Saunders later claimed that Connell 'had been massacred by the press' over the Argyll bid and, as a result, 'had no credibility and [so] we needed someone else as chairman of the new group.' Connell was instead left with the meaningless title of company president, and was soon shunted aside even from that. Saunders also scrapped the promised joint-holding company and sacked most of Distillers' senior staff and board members, privately dismissing them as just 'a lot of Scots backwoodsmen'.[45] A shaken Connell retired hurt from the fray with his wife for a holiday in Marbella, only to find that the despised Jimmy Gulliver of Argyll was staying at the same hotel.

Saunders' seemingly successful ploy began to unravel when Boesky was arrested by the US government's Securities and Exchange Commission (SEC). While plea bargaining with SEC officials, Boesky tipped them off about an illegal share dealing arrangement organised to underpin Guinness's stock price when it was pursuing Distillers. In turn the SEC in December 1986 informed the British government, who a month later charged Saunders with a range of serious financial offences. Saunders' partners-in-crime Sir Jack Lyons and Gerald Ronson were charged in October 1987 and the stock trader Anthony Parnes, who had assembled a colourful cast of supporters for the scheme, the following March. Subsequent trials involved other bankers implicated in the trading, notably the high-profile traders Lord Spens and Roger Seelig, while Saunders' Guinness henchman Tom Ward was prosecuted for paying an illegal 'success fee' of £5.2 million to an American lawyer, which the House of Lords later declared was invalid.

The case's prosecution pulled no punches. In their view, the whole price-rigging saga had been 'a disgraceful episode': Saunders and his allies had exhibited 'a shocking example of dishonest conduct' and had demonstrated 'how ambition and greed can cause men to behave dishonestly and dishonourably'. To make matters worse, 'When it looked as if his activities were about to be uncovered, he destroyed, or caused to be destroyed, some of Guinness' documents to try to protect himself.' Ronson, meanwhile, was described as the 'eager recipient' of a success fee of over £5 million, paid through two false invoices that disguised the support he had given to Saunders. Parnes, too, was denounced in similar terms for having submitted false invoices and creating bogus documents to earn his £3.35 million for intelligence gathering and share support activities, while Lyons received £3 million for actually doing very little except for lending his formerly prestigious name.

The jury's verdict and Lord Justice Henry's sentencing of September 1990 were brutally uncompromising. Saunders was sentenced to five years in prison. Lyons was fined £4 million for theft and false accounting and was subsequently stripped of his knighthood – and only escaped prison because of his poor health. Parnes was jailed for thirty months (reduced on appeal to twenty-one months) for false accounting and theft, while Ronson faced a year in prison and a fine of £5 million for false accounting, conspiracy and theft. Ronson, Parnes and Lyons were each also ordered to pay £440,000 in costs. The later trials of Spens and Seelig, however, collapsed, while Ward was eventually acquitted.

Famously, a year after the verdict, Saunders – who, noted an attendant reporter, 'cut a sorry, shambling figure, all the trappings of his past long gone' – had his five-year sentence halved on appeal, and was released from prison after serving only ten months after consultant psychiatrist Dr Patrick Gallwey told the Court of Appeal that Saunders was suffering from incipient Alzheimer's. The former Guinness CEO, Gallwey testified, 'was unable to recall three numbers backwards. He forgot the subject of a sentence almost before he had started. He could not even remember who was the president of the United States.'

Less than a year after his release, though, Ernest Saunders had apparently made a miraculous and inexplicable recovery from a disease that has no cure. By 1992 he was happily rebuilding his business career and had already become a consultant to Carphone Warehouse, a London-based business phone group. As journalist Jeremy Warner later wrote:

> *Dr Perkin, consultant neurologist to the Crown and one of three expert witnesses, maintained during the appeal that Mr Saunders was suffering from depression and not the degenerative brain disease. He reiterated his diagnosis in the June edition of the British Medical Journal in 1992… Questioned about his 'miraculous' recovery, Mr Saunders said yesterday: 'I was never diagnosed as having Alzheimer's. I was very unwell at the time of the appeal, perhaps hardly surprising with all the stresses and strains that I had been under. The symptoms that I was suffering from could have well been confused. I don't know. I'm not a doctor.'*

Saunders' lawyers echoed this claim, declaring that 'The features of pre-senile dementia which Mr Saunders exhibited are difficult to distinguish from those of depressive illness/neurotic depression and stress-related conditions.' They also added that 'This doctor's misdiagnosis is a matter for him. He is not the first doctor to be wrong [and] Mr Saunders is not a crook', inviting unwelcome comparisons with President Nixon's famous defence of 1974. Dr Gallwey, the forensic pathologist who had been the key expert witness at the appeal, argued that it was 'very difficult' to diagnose an Alzheimer's-related condition and 'so we did not make one; we expressed worries about it.' So that was all right then.

After emerging from prison following his successful appeal, Saunders went from strength to strength. By 1995 he was a flourishing corporate consultant who charged £16,000 a month for his services. The following year he attempted to publicly rehabilitate himself with a bid for Queen's Park Rangers football club, the west London team who trained at Guinness's sports ground and who had at one time been sponsored by the brewery. That particular scheme failed, but Saunders continued to loudly protest his innocence. He had been, he declared, made a 'convenient scapegoat [for] the culture of the market that existed in the City' during the 1980s – rather than being, as most observers saw him, one of the most emblematic products of that toxic culture. 'It is now clear that the Government of the day,' he proclaimed, 'were determined to have a high-profile "City" prosecution', and he told anyone who cared to listen that he regarded his career at Guinness as having been an unqualified success:

> *I helped rebuild a company that was in severe difficulties, to the considerable benefit of the Guinness family and shareholders. The company was worth £90 million in 1981. Today it is capitalised at £10 billion. It is ironic that flawed City tactics, which were completely unnecessary, should have tarnished this achievement.*

Just like the fictional Gordon Gekko, Saunders never admitted or even recognised that he had done anything wrong. The only Guinness defendant to concede that he might actually have been somewhat 'foolish' was disgraced financier Jack Lyons. From his Swiss retreat he told *The Times* in 2000 that

> *Not a day has passed in the past 10 years when I have not asked myself the question 'Why?' Why did I allow myself to become involved? Why did I fail to confirm whether these actions were lawful. Why did the Guinness lawyers not tell us that they weren't?*

The official government report into the whole Guinness affair was only finally published eleven years later. It condemned Saunders' 'enterprise of deception' behind his illegal share support scheme and, despite 'scapegoat' Saunders' constant bleatings to the media, firmly concluded that

> *We can see no reason why an operation with such deceptive purpose should be regarded as acceptable... In the most fundamental sense, it aims at the creation of a false market [which involved] Firstly, the cynical disregard of laws and regulations; secondly, the cavalier misuse of company monies; thirdly, a contempt for truth and common honesty. All these in a part of the City which was thought respectable.*

The case had tarnished the reputation of London's booming financial district, prompted calls for tighter regulation of the securities market and, some suggested, even helped to undermine Margaret Thatcher's position as prime minister. Rightly or wrongly, Thatcher will always be associated with the arrogant, 'greed is good' mindset of a loud minority of executives in the UK financial sector during the 1980s, and the Guinness debacle did nothing to help the Conservatives' reputation for probity and decency in public and commercial life. Just two months after the Guinness trial verdict, Margaet Thatcher was unseated as premier and replaced by John Major – who, though a former chief Secretary to the treasury and, briefly, chancellor of the exchequer, was an avowed fiscal moderate and no great friend to City of London bankers.

To many both inside and outside the great City institutions, the Guinness judgement of 1990 came as a welcome relief. Robin Leigh-Pemberton, the governor of the Bank of England, declared that the convicted defendants' actions had posed a 'threat to the entire basis of trust which still predominates in our business life.' The *New York Times*, less apocalyptically, linked it not to the *Wall Street* movie but to an enduring television soap opera, dubbing it an 'alcoholic *Dallas*' after the long-running saga[46] of corruption in the oil trade, with Ernest Saunders cast as the series' egocentric, manipulative and amoral villain J. R. Ewing. The paper also noted with dismay that, since the start of the trial, 'the faces of Mr Saunders and other leading characters in the Guinness saga have become as instantly recognizable to the public as Britain's leading entertainers and sports figures.'

The Guinness beer brands themselves, however, sailed serenely on. The firm's advertising of the 1990s continued to eschew Irish imagery and, understandably, any mention of business probity or competence. Instead, Guinness's agency, Abbott Mead Vickers BBDO, produced a series of award-winning films that needed no translation to fascinate global markets. Abbott Mead Vickers' new campaign, 'Good things come to those who wait', won international plaudits for their 60-second TV and cinema ad of 1995, 'Dancing Man'. The film was set to a soundtrack as far removed from folksy Irish music as you could get: Cuban bandleader Pérez Prado's rollicking, sax-heavy 1958 mambo hit 'Guaglione'.

What came next was even more widely acclaimed. Director Jonathan Glazer's 'Surfer' film of 1999 had no ostensible connection with the brewery nor with the concept of Irishness; but its astonishing CGI effects won it a slew of advertising awards and, the year after it was shown, the accolade of 'Best Ad of All Time' in a poll conducted by the UK's Channel Four and *The Times*. Diageo's purchase of the Guinness group in 1997 had not only staunched the wound of 1990's trial verdict; the highly experienced multinational was also sensible enough not to interfere in Guinness's prize-winning and highly successful advertising campaigns.

-

Today Guinness is, like the protagonists of 1999's 'Surfer' ad, riding the crest of a wave. In April 2024 the trade media announced that stout had become so popular that it was now the fastest-growing beer variety in the UK. At the same time, supermarket giant Tesco revealed that, over the past year, the demand by volume for porters and stouts across their stores had risen by 35 per cent.

Guinness was, of course, not the only producer of Irish stout to benefit from this trend. Having enjoyed a near monopoly position in the Irish stout market at the time of the trial, forty years later it saw its former supremacy being gradually eroded by Irish rivals Beamish and Murphy's (both brewed in Cork but owned by Heineken of Amsterdam).

However, given the overall growth in the global stout market – which caught both brewers and retailers by delighted surprise – Diageo had no reason to be unduly worried. By 2023 Guinness had grown to become the most popular draught beer in the UK, accounting for 11 per cent of all pub beer sales; by Christmas 2024 demand significantly exceeded supply in the UK, especially in London. The famous stout may not be as good for you as was once claimed, but it certainly makes for healthy returns.

Chapter 7

AFORE YE GO

MALT WHISKY

Whisky is inextricably intertwined not just with Scottish history; it has also been a continuous (though at times barely distinguishable) thread running through the narrative fabric of Britain during the last two centuries. Scotch has become the UK's biggest food and drink export, valued at £6.2 billion in 2022 and worth more than £5.5 billion to the UK economy. As the Scotch Whisky Association proudly proclaims, 'More Scotch Whisky is sold worldwide than Irish, US and Japanese whiskies combined.' The Scotch whisky industry also employs more than 11,000 people within Scotland and supports over 42,000 more across the UK.

As exactly the right drink to keep out these islands' pervasive cold and damp, Scotch whisky has been a defining feature of British social life for two centuries. A stimulating inspiration to poets and novelists, a medicinal recourse for the old and infirm (or simply the thirsty), liquid courage for those facing impending battle, a portal for those eager for self-discovery, an economic lifeline for the UK Treasury and, to Scotland's Gaelic-speaking population, the 'water of life' (*uisge beatha*), Robert Louis

Stevenson's 'king o' drinks' has helped us to shape and respond to personal and external challenges since the modern whisky industry was created in the 1820s. As the late, kilt-wearing Scots MP Bill Walker (quoted here by business historian Julie Bower) declaimed in his parliamentary paean to the Scots spirit:[47]

> *Scotch whisky is more than a whisky. It is part of Scotland's heritage and folklore. It is used as a medicine to cure many ills. As a toddy, it can dispel colds and 'flu. In porridge, it can drive out the freezing cold of Scotland's winters. It lubricates the larynx and helps parties go with a swing.*

Whisky[48] has been a stimulus and a prop for politicians and celebrities on both sides of the Atlantic over the last century. Winston Churchill drank Johnnie Walker Red Label throughout the day. Sean Connery always preferred Laphroaig. (In the film *Spectre*, though, Daniel Craig's James Bond drank Macallan.) Harrison Ford apparently adores Bruichladdich. Dean Martin always swore by the venerable blend J&B Rare, while Stephen King is happy to endorse its former Berry Bros & Rudd stablemate, Cutty Sark. *Carry On* comedian Sid James was an inveterate Cutty Sark drinker. *Mad Men*'s fabulous Christina Hendricks drinks Johnnie Walker Blue Label – and even promotes it as the brand's US ambassador. Brian Cox and Amy Schumer are the latest in a long line of A-list film stars who have admitted their enthusiasm for the peat-heavy 16-year-old Lagavulin from Islay. The American writer and journalist Hunter S. Thompson and evergreen singing legend Frank Sinatra both drank prodigious quantities of premium blend Chivas Regal, which has also been namechecked over the years by celebrity compatriots ranging from singers Stevie Wonder, Tom Waits and Kelly Clarkson to fictional characters played on the screen by Jack Lemmon (in 1975's *The Prisoner of Second Avenue*), Melanie Griffith (as Tess in 1988's film *Working Girl*), Robin Williams (as the eponymous Mrs Doubtfire) and Robin Wright's Claire Underwood in the US *House of Cards*. And the queue of celebrities eager to endorse whisky brands shows no sign of shrinking.

The allure of Scotch has always exerted a fascination for British royalty, too. Royal Lochnagar was Queen Victoria and Prince Albert's favourite tipple, earning its regal appellation in the year of the Great Exhibition, 1851. The peaty island malt Laphroaig is a firm favourite of King Charles III and has enjoyed his Royal Warrant since 1994. In a similar vein, the gruff and fiercely private monarch King George V happily awarded *his* Royal Warrant to the firm of John Walker & Sons for their White, Red and Black label whiskies – brands that his dutiful second son and eventual heir, George VI, also patronised. In dramatic contrast, the favourite drink of George VI's elder brother, the Duke of Windsor, who had abdicated in the former's favour after a brief eleven-month reign as King Edward VIII in 1936, was a cocktail called the Wallis: named (of course) after his wife, it was made with Cointreau, peppermint gin, lemon juice and soda. A good thing he abdicated, I say. Though, to be fair, he was apparently also partial to a glass of J&B.

Famously, the late Queen Elizabeth II's sister, HRH Princess Margaret, was an avid fan not just of Scotch whisky but of one particular brand. Margaret always insisted that a bottle of Famous Grouse follow her wherever she went, whatever the occasion. Grouse was an independently owned blend, created and owned by Matthew Gloag from 1896 until September 2024, when it was bought by the whisky colossus William Grant. It is also currently the UK's best-selling whisky brand. Biographer Noel Botham noted that a decanter of Famous Grouse was always present on the drinks tray at Margaret's apartment in Clarence House: HRH would have a glass or two from the decanter, diluted with a splash of Malvern Water, before setting off for an event. 'It was', Botham concluded, 'the only drink she really enjoyed in the evening.' The outspoken American socialite Solange Batsell-Herter, in her unapologetically flowery memoir *No More Tiaras* of 2011, remembered Princess Margaret visiting a friend in Vermont in 1965 and drinking 'nothing but Famous Grouse whisky. She sent a case of it before her arrival and [the hostess] was very grateful when the case showed up, because the whisky disappeared at a fast rate.' Twenty years later, when visiting the celebrated Macallan distillery in Moray, HRH ostentatiously refused a glass of the firm's finest in front of all the assembled dignitaries and rudely insisted on a glass of Grouse instead.

With age, and particularly following her divorce from the Earl of Snowdon of 1978 and her subsequent break-up with boyfriend Roddy Llewellyn in 1981, HRH's whisky consumption began to get out of hand. Restaurateur and broadcaster Gordon Ramsay recounts the princess visiting his former restaurant: 'She started with Scotch and went on drinking for three hours.' And it was while drinking whisky at her retreat in Mustique in the Caribbean in 1998 that Princess Margaret suffered her first stroke. Four years later she was dead.

Another famous Margaret of Britain's post-war years, Conservative party leader and prime minister Margaret

Thatcher, was also a loyal and evangelical whisky drinker. Thatcher had been brought up a Methodist, and very little alcohol was drunk in her childhood home; but in later years she sought to keep pace with her husband Denis's prodigious consumption. While Denis drank gin and tonics, Margaret's preferred tipple was blended whisky – ideally Bell's, Britain's second-favourite whisky brand[49] (owned, as we have seen, by Diageo since 1985), served with soda. However, she happily drank the official House of Commons and House of Lords blends when in the respective parliamentary bars. Mrs Thatcher was also partial to a dram of Macallan, the venerable malt that can trace its ancestry back to 1824 – Year One of the modern whisky age – and which is currently still owned by the independent, Glasgow-based spirits distiller and retailer Edrington. She was indeed known to give away signed bottles of Macallan malt as presents. For example, in 1999, nine years after she had been removed as party leader and premier, she despatched a bottle of Macallan to the former Chilean military dictator Augusto Pinochet, then under house arrest in Surrey on the orders of the then Labour government, accompanied by a note that read, pointedly: 'Scotch is one British institution that will never let you down'. Today bottles of Macallan and the two parliamentary blends personally autographed by the former prime minister frequently pop up in whisky auctions.

'You must have whisky to give you energy' was one of Margaret Thatcher's forcefully expressed sayings – though it is not perhaps one whose medical basis bears much examination. Yet while, during her eleven years as prime minister, she liked nothing more than relaxing with a glass of Bell's at the end of the day, at least while in office she recognised that she did not possess her husband's legendary capacity for what Denis called a 'snorter' or four. It was only after Thatcher was ousted as party leader and prime minister in November 1990 that her whisky drinking became excessive. As whisky writer Iain Russell has remarked, in retirement she was suddenly left without her accustomed parliamentary aides and 'now Denis was left in charge of pouring the drinks – and that was the one area in which he was decidedly liberal.' Given the established links between heavy drinking and dementia, it is possible that Margaret's rising whisky consumption during these years might have hastened the onset of her Alzheimer's disease, which was a major cause of her death in 2013.

Whisky has not just been the stimulus and support of politicians and royalty. Writers and artists, too, have enthusiastically embraced its charms. Welsh poet Dylan Thomas's last words, blurted out to his lover following a mammoth 1953 drinking session in a New York bar, were 'I've had eighteen straight whiskies – I think that's a record!' Thomas then collapsed into a coma and died, aged only thirty-nine, four days later. Whisky may have proved to be the water of life for many; but for some it could hasten the end, too.

-

Scotch whisky has, then, has been a continuous presence in British life, and death, over the last two centuries. Strangely, though, the history of whisky in its purest form – as a single (or, as the Americans say, straight) malt, created at a single distillery and bottled in Scotland – is surprisingly recent.

The Scotch whisky industry we know today was effectively created in the early years of George IV's reign, in the wake of the king's extravagantly planned official visit to Edinburgh of 1822. The Disneyesque pageant that the novelist Sir Walter Scott had devised for his monarch's progress through the Scots capital – a lavish and colourful spectacle that many genuine Highlanders, at the time being forced from their ancestral homes to make way for more profitable sheep farming, found distastefully offensive – was preceded by a royal toast conducted in none other than Glenlivet single malt whisky, which George IV cheerfully knocked back even before he disembarked from his ship in Leith harbour. Thereafter the smitten sovereign insisted on drinking Glenlivet throughout his stay, even though the distilling of the drink was technically illegal at the time. The obsequious Walter Scott, impressed by his king's sterling example, later declared that Glenlivet was 'the only liquor fit for a gentleman to drink in the morning.'

The king's support for whisky helped to create the right atmosphere for the following year's legislation. The 1823 Excise Act was designed to end illicit distilling and, at the same time, to create a new, legitimate and financially viable whisky industry that could revive the economic fortunes of the Highlands – as well as swell the coffers of one of the Act's principal sponsors, Speyside landowner the 4th Duke of Gordon. Building on George IV's unanticipated promotion of Glenlivet, its terms allowed anyone who could afford £10 for a licence to set up a distillery, thus enabling many small-scale whisky makers to emerge from the shadows after centuries of virtual prohibition. Its regulations were designed, in the words of the Scotch Whisky Association, 'to create a level playing field for distillers, generate a source of income for grain farmers in Scotland, and ultimately ensure a supply of consistent, quality spirit for consumers to enjoy.' Of course, those who could not afford the new licence fee were essentially ruined; or, if they continued to distil outside the provisions of the act, they could be arrested and either imprisoned or transported.

Significantly, one of the first whisky producers to set up shop in the wake of the Excise Act was George Smith of Glenlivet, the maker of George IV's preferred Edinburgh tipple, Smith ran his business from the hamlet of Upper Drumin in Moray, near to the River Spey – an area rich in whisky distillers both then and now. Smith had previously been an illicit distiller, but now he took advantage of the Excise Act to make his business entirely legitimate. After registering his newly lawful firm, however, he was warned that those rival Speyside farmers who were still distilling their surplus grain illegally, in secret, might take umbrage at his apparent desertion of their ranks – for his decision to turn from poacher into gamekeeper. The advice was astute: Smith received a series of death threats and, as a result, placed a 24-hour armed guard around his distillery. He later recalled that 'I was warned by my civil neighbours that they meant to burn the new distillery to the ground and me in the heart of it. The laird of Aberlour had presented me with a pair of hair trigger pistols worth ten guineas, and they were never out of my belt for years.' Smith had made the right decision, though, as the decades that followed comprehensively transformed his company's fortunes. Since 2001 Glenlivet's hard-to-find Ballindalloch distillery, now owned by Pernod Ricard, has been the world's best-selling malt whisky.

The rise of Glenlivet notwithstanding, by the end of the nineteenth century the UK whisky market was dominated not by single-origin malts such as Glenlivet and Macallan but by blended whiskies. Blends were, and still are, comprised not of blended single malts; this is actually quite a modern concept. Instead, they are made by combining a range of single malts, selected for the character they will bring to the finished blend, with between 40 per cent and 60 per cent of nondescript, cheap grain whisky. Malt whisky is made only from malted barley and fashioned by the 'pot still' method, by which a fermented alcoholic liquid – in this case, a fermented mash of malted barley, water and yeast – is distilled in a big copper vessel. This is heated to allow the concentrated alcoholic vapours to boil off and to be collected, cooled and then condensed in a separate vessel. Grain whisky, on the other hand, is distilled continuously from a mixture of malted barley, wheat or maize. It is far more cost-effective than malt whisky to make; hence the growth of blended whisky, bolstered by malts but bulked out with cheap and cheerful grain liquor.

While the majority of malt distilleries were and are located in the Highlands and Islands of Scotland, grain distilleries – the largest of which are Diageo's (formerly Haig's) Cameronbridge plant in Fife and William Grant's Girvan factory in Ayrshire – are concentrated in the Lowlands. Grain whisky does not need ageing, and is thus far cheaper to make than its malt cousin. It can be made into an appealing drink, however. Quite a few 'single grain' whiskies do exist today: pale and (sometimes) interesting, they range from the refined, such as Compass Box, Cambus and Cameronbridge, to mass-market products such as Haig Club, launched in 2014 by Diageo in a distinctive blue, rectangular bottle and backed by celebrities David Beckham and Simon Fuller. Haig Club has clearly been designed to appeal to fans of mixed drinks, consumers for whom traditional whiskies are too assertive. Suffice to say that it has not been entirely welcomed by whisky aficionados: online reviews have ranged from 'approachable' and 'hidden gem' to 'very disappointing', 'thin and watery' and 'the worst whisky I have ever tasted'.

Since the 1870s, the energetically marketed, internationally exported blend brands have dominated the Scotch whisky market, both at home and abroad. Sales of blended whiskies exploded during the last decades of the nineteenth century, helped by Britain's constantly expanding railway network, which could carry the whisky not just across Britain but to the eastern Scottish ports for export to Europe, America or the far-flung territories of the British Empire, by the late-Victorian fashion for all things Scottish, prompted by the publication in 1868 of Queen Victoria's surprise bestseller *Leaves from the Journal of Our Life in the Highlands*, and, perhaps crucially, by the dreaded phylloxera louse. The continental spread of phylloxera after 1858, as we have already seen, devastated France's vineyards and almost wiped out the French brandy industry. This disaster may have ruined many cognac and Armagnac producers in France; but for their former auld alliance partners in Scotland it was an unexpected blessing. The virtual disappearance of brandy from British dinner tables and bars not only enabled the English gin and tonic to ascend the social scale but also promoted blended whisky and soda to the status of the fashionable drink of choice for late-Victorian and Edwardian Britain.

It was not until the 1988 Whisky Act, though – 165 years after the Excise Act created the industry – that a definitive, legally binding definition of 'Scotch whisky' appeared on the UK statute books. Not only did the 1988 legislation (enthusiastically promoted by the newly created drinks conglomerate Diageo as well as by the Scotch Whisky Association) characterise 'Scotch' only as whisky that had been produced and matured in Scotland in oak casks for a minimum of three years; it also prohibited the sale of Scotch whisky of a strength lower than 40 per cent ABV. This neatly obliterated the bargain-basement, low-strength end of the whisky trade at a stroke – and also did for Diageo's own, recently launched discount blend Claymore, which the company offloaded as soon as they could. (Today Claymore is made by Whyte & Mackay – the Buckfast-to-Vladivar drinks division of the giant, Manila-based Global Alliance Group.)

In recent years, blended whiskies have continued to dominate the Scotch market, accounting for 65 per cent of whisky exports in terms of both volume and value in 2018. However, during the 1980s and 1990s, as Margaret Thatcher was championing Macallan malt, British drinkers as a whole were also becoming better acquainted with single-origin whiskies: refined and characterful products that invariably boasted a long and distinguished provenance from picturesque, remote distilleries. The malt revolution had begun.

-

Until the later years of the twentieth century, single malts were generally known just as 'fillings' – that is, ingredients – for blended whisky. There were, however, honourable exceptions. William Grant continue to insist that their flagship malt, Glenfiddich, was the first properly marketed malt whisky, having been relaunched with considerable fanfare in 1963 in an unusual triangular ('t'round') bottle. However, whisky writers have since challenged Glenfiddich's claims to be both the first to advertise their unblended (straight) malt whisky and the first to offer visitor tours of the distillery, which they did in 1969. Whisky writer Fletcher Finlay has observed that 'other distilleries such as Macallan, Glendronach, Brora, and Glenlivet had also been selling malt whiskies produced at a single distillery since the early 1800s', while Ian Buxton notes that Tobermory distillery on the Isle of Mull 'was actively welcoming visitors from the early 1920s' and Speyside's Glenfarclas distillery 'opened their doors at much the same time as Glenfiddich – so closely in fact that they could hardly be accused of "copying" their Speyside rivals.' Buxton also cites 'Macallan's then chairman George Harbinson, [who] was able to assure his presumably happy shareholders in 1963 that "the sale of Macallan in bottle is gaining momentum with a steadily increasing demand for the over 15 year old from the south of England".' Buxton's researchers have revealed that Glenfiddich Pure Malt[50] was being promoted in the market as early as 1903 and that 'Bowmore were even advertising in Canada in the late nineteenth century.' Indeed, as long ago as 1887 the renowned Scots novelist, poet and travel writer Robert Louis Stevenson was hymning three obviously well-known single malts in his poem 'The Scotsman's Return From Abroad':

But maistly thee, the bluid o' Scots,
Frae Maidenkirk to John o' Grots,
The king o' drinks, as I conceive it,
Talisker, Isla, or Glenlivet!

By 1970, around thirty single malts were available to buy in the UK. But their time had not yet come. Instead, the 1970s and early 1980s saw the rapidly growing whisky conglomerates promoting their blander, more profitable global blend brands rather than their more characterful single malts. The success of William Grant's Glenfiddich notwithstanding, malts were still generally seen as a niche market in their own right, better treated simply as ingredients to beef up the big whisky producers' most popular, internationally advertised blends. For example, in the 1970s Distillers Company Ltd (DCL) refused point-blank to promote their superb, peaty Hebridean single malts Talisker (from the Isle of Skye), Lagavulin and Laphroaig (both from Islay). At the same time, Ian Buxton cites Neil McKerrow of the long-established but notoriously sleepy Edinburgh-based wine and spirits retailers Macdonald & Muir, owners of the Glenmorangie distillery in Ross-shire, happily boasting that 'we have never advertised [Glenmorangie] to the consumer' and that 'Glenmorangie has achieved a strong following purely on the basis of word of mouth.' Who would have thought these distilleries were actually supposed to be in business?

DCL did gingerly dip their toe in the malt mash by agreeing in 1983 that their Johnnie Walker subsidiary could promote its Speyside whisky Cardhu as a standalone single malt. Cardhu enjoyed an impressive pedigree: another of the Excise Act whiskies born in 1824, it was sold as a single malt until 1893, when it was acquired by John Walker & Sons simply to serve as a 'filling' for Walker's national brand 'Old Highland Whisky' – a marque that later metamorphosed into Johnnie Walker Red and Black Labels. Yet this move was not enthusiastically greeted by the risk-averse DCL board (most of whom were later swept away as a result of the Guinness 'merger'). The DCL sceptics pointed a finger at Cardhu's marketing copy, which declared the malt to be of a 'higher proof than usual whiskies and considerably richer in flavour' and which suggested that 'It compares with ordinary whiskies as cognac compares to brandy.' The board members were worried that this bald statement implicitly denigrated the Distillers blends that had made the firm so much money – vigorously promoted brands such as Dewars, White Horse and Johnnie Walker itself.

In general, though, the emphasis in Scottish whisky production during these years was heavily skewed towards blends. These blander drinks could, prevailing wisdom had it, earn the big distillers far more per bottle than their more cultivated, single-distillery malt cousins. Or could they? Over-excited by the prospect of unlimited growth, during the later 1970s Britain's whisky magnates (the whiskerage, perhaps? the mashups? the maltesers?) forgot to factor in the variability of demand. And as it turned out, the major whisky combines – and in particular the giant DCL, which apart from Cardhu had (to mangle a metaphor) put all their eggs in the blended basket – discovered to their horror by 1985 that they had vastly over-estimated the market growth for their international blends. No amount of unpaid promotion of their products by the two Margarets could help to soak up what was being described in the trade media as both a 'spirit lake' and a 'whisky loch'.

The big boys' first reaction was sheer panic. In this DCL, as ever, took the lead. In 1983 – the year of Margaret Thatcher's landslide election victory – the firm had controlled five of Scotland's fourteen grain distilleries and 45 of the country's 118 malt distilleries. However, due to their complacency and apathy – over the past ten years DCL had failed to develop any major new products except for the pallid, low-priced Claymore – the firm had seen its UK market share plummet from 75 per cent in 1960 to a crushing 15 per cent in 1983. Faced now with a massive glut of Scotch, a problem entirely of their own making, the DCL Board responded by axing twenty-one malt distilleries as a thoughtless short-term palliative.

In the years that followed, all that DCL and their major rivals could devise in an attempt to halt the UK's declining consumption of Scotch was a race to the bottom, in the form of a frenzied promotion of cheap, mass-market blends and increasingly desperate discount offers. As with so much of British industry at the time, the big whisky manufacturers were obsessed with the goal of high volume at the expense of brand integrity. The result, predictably, was no improvement in Scotch whisky sales whatsoever. Except, that was, for the niche malt market. During the early 1980s sales of Glenfiddich soared way above William Grant's business forecasts and even beyond the availability of sufficiently aged stock.

Fittingly, the turnaround for Scotch whisky coincided with the climax of Margaet Thatcher's premiership in the year of her second landslide election victory. In March 1987, in the wake of the Guinness shares scandal and Ernest Saunders' arrest, the newly created drinks multinational, Diageo, which had by now fully absorbed the old DCL operation, appointed the patrician Anthony Tennant (Eton, Cambridge and the Guards, if you remember) to become the new chief executive of the troubled leviathan. We have already seen how Tennant steadied the ship at the IDV drinks division of Grand Metropolitan, quietly but determinedly putting Watney's out of its misery and reintroducing real ale into its tied estate. Now Tennant applied the same resolution and common sense to Diageo's whisky portfolio. Given that the firm had vast untapped stocks of fine malt whiskies, he reasoned, why not make the most of products that could command a premium price and at the same time improve the image of the company's entire whisky portfolio?

As a result of his dramatic change of direction, Tennant put malt whisky firmly in the spotlight for the first time ever in DCL's long and chequered history. While he did launch new super-deluxe blends such as Johnnie Walker Blue Label, Tennant also unveiled a new, groundbreaking single malt range, marketed under the banner of 'Classic Malts' and comprising Lagavulin, Cragganmore, Talisker, Oban, Glenkinchie, and Dalwhinnie. DCL's new malt-focused marketing campaign lingered lovingly on the history of each brand's distillery and location (particularly if it was a charmingly romantic one) and even provided consumers with individual tasting notes. The result was an astonishing u-turn from DCL's condescending marginalisation of malt whiskies of just a few years earlier. To those critics who claimed that Scotch had been losing its authenticity and sense of place, the proud and well-documented heritage of single malts provided the ideal riposte. And Anthony Tennant had finally harnessed that heritage.

Just as Margaret Thatcher was being ushered out of the door of 10 Downing Street, so malt whisky had finally ascended to its place in the sun. No more were malt whiskies seen just as supporting cast members, the Rosencrantz and Guildenstern to blended whisky's Hamlet. DCL's Classic Malts campaign helped to justify the premium price of single malts and to establish this growing sector as a distinct category in the whisky market, rather than just as a source of character for their mass-market blends.

Ironically, Thatcher's favourite Macallan malt whisky brand did particularly well in this brave new single-malt world. An independent, family-run business since 1824 (that year again), despite its relatively tiny promotional budget Macallan punched well above its weight in the marketplace. In 1996 its marketing resources were given a fillip when the firm was bought by Highland Distillers. Three years later Highland Distillers were themselves absorbed into the Edrington group, backed by minority shareholder William Grant.

Edrington was (and is), though, hardly in the same league as the giant Diageo. All of Edrington's shares were owned by the Robertson Trust, a charity founded in 1961 by the three Robertson sisters, Elspeth, Agnes and Ethel. Today the Robertson Trust is Scotland's largest independent charitable trust, having since 1961 given £322 million to Scottish causes, particularly to those which benefit young people from deprived backgrounds. Yet this family-run organisation still managed to propel Macallan to the number three spot in the world's sales league of malt whiskies, behind brands backed by two of the industry's biggest players: Pernod Ricard's Glenlivet and William Grant's Glenfiddich. As an additional bonus, in 2001 the Speaker of the House of Commons at Westminster, Michael Martin MP, selected The Macallan 10 Year Old as the official Scotch of the Speaker's Office – even though Martin himself had long forsworn alcohol. (He declared that he had merely savoured the aromas of the prospective candidates instead.) Even though we have no record of her actual reaction to this honour, it is to be hoped that Margaret Thatcher, by that point Baroness Thatcher of Kesteven, would have been pleased.[51]

This is not to say that, in modern Britain at least, blends are out and malts are in. The blended Scotch whisky industry still remains substantially larger than its single malt equivalent. In 2022 the largest grain whisky distilleries, Diageo's Cameronbridge and William Grant's Girvan, boasted annual capacities of around 110 million litres each; in contrast, the largest malt whisky distillery, Pernod Ricard's Glenlivet, registered an annual capacity of only 21 million litres, while Edrington's Macallan was only 15 million litres.

But the prospects for malt whisky undoubtedly look encouraging. In the period 2008–21 – between the global banking crisis and the worldwide Covid pandemic – blended whisky's UK sales dropped from 263 million litres a year to 256 million, while single malt sales leaped from 23 million litres to 44 million. In 2018 bottled blended whisky accounted for 65 per cent of the UK Scotch whisky market while bottled single malts comprised only 10 per cent of the total in terms of volume. (In case you are wondering about my maths, the remaining 25 per cent was accounted for by bulk, unbottled exports.) However, the value of the UK malt whisky sales in that year represented 28 per cent of the whole market – almost a third. And that proportion is rising. Historian Julie Bower has recently highlighted this 'changing landscape' for whisky, concluding that 'we are living in a period where malt whisky production is matching grain whisky production for the first time since grain whisky was introduced.'

Everyone, as we have seen, is now getting in on the act. The latest celebrity to endorse premium Scottish malt whiskies is the peerless *Parks and Recreation* star and accomplished carpenter Nick Offerman, who recently lent his name to special issues of eleven-year-old Lagavulin ('I am giggling with delight at the notion of people enjoying this limited-edition Scotch').

Even Suntory, the global Japanese drinks behemoth, now buys substantial supplies of Scotch malt whisky each year for its own Japanese whisky blends. To that end, in 1994 it acquired the whisky retailer Morrison Bowmore, owners of three classic malt whiskies: Auchentoshan (a delightful and rare Lowland whisky), Glen Garioch (from Aberdeenshire) and Bowmore (from Islay). Three years earlier it had even bought a 25 per cent stake in Macallan. What would Margaret Thatcher have said about that?

Chapter 8

LOADSAMONEY

BEAUJOLAIS NOUVEAU

While Beaujolais Nouveau had been known in the eponymous wine-growing region for decades, the peculiarly British phenomenon of competing to import the first Beaujolais Nouveau into the country, which had begun in the 1970s as a harmless bit of fun, evolved during the 1980s into a frenetic, over-hyped and disturbingly competitive contest that seemed to reflect the me-first culture of Margaret Thatcher's Britain. What made the fashion for the Beaujolais Nouveau race even more inexplicable was that the wine at its heart was poorly regarded by French growers. Beaujolais *vignerons* were initially bewildered at Britons' passion for this acidic and immature varietal – though they were more than happy to take their money.

The 1980s had transformed what had originated as a wine critics' flippant and drunken dare into a national obsession. The dash to be the first to bring home a case of newly bottled, undeveloped and anaemic Beaujolais wine in the back seat or boot of a swift and classic British sports car in the hours following the wine's unveiling seized the imagination of a nation – or at least some of its wealthier representatives. In 1985, in response to British demand, the

Beaujolais growers even changed the wine's release date in order to boost the marketing of the subsequent 'race'. However, like so much from the 1980s, while the wine itself is still just about with us, and a more civilised version of the race is still being staged, the Beaujolais Nouveau craze is now but fading memory.

The Beaujolais Nouveau phenomenon was created by four entrepreneurial and colourful writers and vinophiles: broadcaster and politician Clement Freud, the *Sunday Times* wine correspondent Allan Hall, Austrian-born wine critic Joseph Berkmann and Beaujolais winemaker Georges Duboeuf. The background of this diverse quartet amply demonstrates, however, why any analysis of Britain's social history of the 1970s is, these days, so fraught and complex.

Clement Freud, for one, remains a highly controversial character, even many years after his death. Understandably feted as something of a Renaissance man and a household name during his lifetime, in retrospect his career illustrates the outrageous and even criminal liberties taken by influential celebrities of the 1970s – men who were then regarded as media darlings but are now rightly seen as toxic predators.

The grandson of the world-famous neurologist Sigmund Freud and brother of the artist Lucian Freud, Clement Freud was born in Berlin. Aged nine, he fled with his family in 1933 following the appointment of Adolf Hitler as Chancellor of Germany. After the war he served as a liaison officer at the Nuremberg war crimes trials of 1946, presumably due to his faultless German, and then entered the hotel catering business. From there, he found his way into sports journalism and food writing. His honorary and paid posts were hugely varied, ranging from being the occasional wine correspondent of the *Sun* newspaper (both before and after its purchase and conversion into a tabloid by Rupert Murdoch in 1969), columnist for the horse-racing bible the *Racing Post*, rector of Dundee University, and, more revealingly, director of and catering consultant to London's questionable Playboy Club.[52] After 1967 he also became a nationwide media celebrity, firstly through his appearances as the lugubrious front man (partnering the unforgettable Henry the bloodhound) in television ads for Quaker Pet Foods' Chunky Meat dog food, and then as a longstanding fixture on BBC Radio 4's comedy panel show *Just a Minute* – despite his frequently-expressed loathing of the show's even more enduring chairman, Nicholas Parsons. In 1973 Freud unexpectedly won the Isle of Ely constituency for the Liberal Party at a byelection – one of two byelection victories for the Liberals on the same day. His victory heralded a revival in the party's fortunes that was to lead to them holding the balance of power after Edward Heath's narrow defeat in the general election of February 1974. Freud held on to his seat until the Conservatives' landslide general election win of 1987, when a knighthood was offered to him as compensation.

Seven years after Clement Freud's death in 2009, however, an ITV documentary accused Freud of multiple cases of child sex abuse dating back as far as the 1940s. One anonymous woman announced that Freud had groomed her from the age of eleven in 1971 and had violently raped her at eighteen; while Sylvia Woosley, who had lived with the Freuds for years, declared that she had been abused from the age of ten until she left their home at nineteen. On the same day as the documentary, *Exposure: Abused and Betrayed – A Life Sentence*, was broadcast on 15 June 2016, Freud's widow issued a full and contrite apology.

Like Clement Freud, Joseph Berkmann's native tongue was German. Born and bred in the Austrian Tyrol, his early career, like Freud's, was enormously wide-ranging. The biography he outlined to wine critic Jancis Robinson noted that he had been 'Sent to various boarding schools run first by Jesuits and then by Nazis; began work at 14 breaking stones at a river irrigation project; then as a miner drilling holes at 3,000m altitude; became a waiter to get the girls and never looked back' and that he had 'Lived in Germany, Switzerland, Libya, Rome, New York, Caracas, Istanbul [and] Invaded UK on 20 May 1956.'

A successful restaurateur almost from the moment of his arrival in London, by the mid-1960s Berkmann had also made himself into a wine expert. (His first publication on wine, of 1964, was subtitled 'May God and My Wine Merchants Forgive Me!') A pioneer of popular wine journalism – 'We made ourselves very unpopular with the wine trade by writing about fraudulent wines, which then made up 60 per cent of UK sales,' he later said of his *Sunday Times* articles of the mid-1970s – his Clerkenwell-based consumer wine importing business prominently showcased his friend Georges Duboeuf's Beaujolais wines. As a good Austrian he was also a proficient skier, in which capacity he first met *Sunday Times* editor Harold Evans – and, through Evans, wine journalists Allan Hall and Clement Freud. Together with Hall, Berkmann published *The Good Wine Guide* in 1976 and 1977; however, as he told Robinson, he then 'gave up because Allan wouldn't sober up.' Married four times and now living, aged ninety-four, in St Tropez and Mexico (he moved to Mexico ostensibly to write his memoirs, which he subsequently destroyed), Berkmann has been celebrated, like Freud and Hall, as one of the era's great raconteurs and *bon viveurs*.

The third and possibly the most significant of the quartet who created the vogue for Beaujolais Nouveau, Georges Duboeuf, was also no stranger to controversy. Born into a Burgundian winemaking family, in his teens Georges was delivering bottles by bicycle to customers in neighbouring villages. Then in 1964 the aspirant winemaker launched his own Beaujolais brand, Les Vins Georges Duboeuf, whose bottles wore the distinctive floral labels that still adorn their descendants today. From then on he never looked back.

'Beaujolais Nouveau', a fresh, juvenile *en primeur* Beaujolais wine, comes from the historic province originally named after the town of Beaujeu. The small Beaujolais wine region around Beaujeu lies roughly between the rivers Azergues and Saône in the Rhône *département* north of Lyon. Its wine had been famous, at least in Burgundy, for centuries. Traditionally, to celebrate the harvest, immature Beaujolais wine – which had not had the time to develop the complexity and maturity that the Gamay grape, the main constituent of Beaujolais, could potentially offer – was offered for free to the *domaine*'s labourers as a reward for all their hard work. This distribution of young wine in time metamorphosed into a local festival, in which winemakers, locals and the odd curious visitor would be served from pitchers of the tart, adolescent wine. It was only in 1951 that the official body that oversaw the Beaujolais wine industry, the Union Interprofessional des Vins de Beaujolais (UVB), permitted the public sale of this Beaujolais Nouveau, decreeing an official launch date for the release of the wine of 15 November. (In later years this was moved to the third

Thursday in November to give enough time for international media outlets to meet the deadlines for their weekend editions.)

While bottles of Beaujolais Nouveau had been appearing on local shelves since 1951, it was Georges Duboeuf who made the product into a global phenomenon. Beaujolais seemed to be an excellent candidate for such treatment. Its principal grape, Gamay, had long been regarded as somewhat inferior to its cultured cousin, Pinot Noir, which formed the basis of all of the historically esteemed Burgundian reds. Even top-end Beaujolais wines were (and, partly thanks to the Beaujolais Nouveau effect, continue to be) frequently underrated and overlooked. Beaujolais Nouveau was, considered Duboeuf, ripe for promotion and promulgation. He forecast that increased sales of Beaujolais Nouveau could help tide the local growers over in the traditionally lean weeks before Christmas, and indeed that the relatively characterless young Beaujolais wine could additionally be marketed abroad as the ideal Christmas wine, since its lack of definition theoretically enabled it to be partnered with anything.

To attract the attention of the media, Duboeuf hit upon the novel idea of staging a race, with a prize being awarded to the first person to deliver the new wine to Paris. He was inspired, the story goes, by glimpsing a painted sign in the window of a Paris bistro announcing that *le beaujolais nouveau est arrivé*. The concept just needed a far bigger stage on which to thrive.

Once it was launched, other Beaujolais producers were more than happy to take part in Duboeuf's contest, recognising that the predicted growth in wine sales during the difficult winter months would help them all. However, the canny *vigneron* always ensured that it was he who was featured most prominently in all the newspaper reports and television pictures publicising the event. As a result, by 1970 Duboeuf was being dubbed (mostly by himself) 'the king of Beaujolais', or alternatively as the wine region's 'Pope'.

Duboeuf's predictions proved to be right. The publicity generated by his gimmicky challenge helped all of the local growers to make record profits for November and early December, normally a very quiet time for the winemakers. Duboeuf's own firm, naturally, did very well, and was soon producing 20 per cent of all of the wine made in Beaujolais country. Duboeuf even shipped Beaujolais Nouveau to America: here its arrival neatly coincided with the Thanksgiving festival and, as Duboeuf had anticipated, its easy-going and light, inoffensive style made it an ideal accompaniment to Thanksgiving's traditional turkey dinners. He even created a wine theme park, Hameau des Vins, in the small Beaujolais town of Romanèche-Thorins. Today, immodestly renamed the Hameau Duboeuf Park, it continues to thrive, having been nominated for the Parc World Experience Awards 2019.

Then in 2006 the king was dramatically deposed. The wine world was aghast to learn that Duboeuf had been fined €30,000 for fraud, for having illegally blended different types of grape rather than a single source of Gamay to make his wine. As the *Guardian*'s Angelique Chrisafis reported at the time:

> *In a trial that has shocked the French wine world, Duboeuf, who is one of France's best-known producers, was accused of fiddling the country's strict grading and labelling system and mixing cheap, average and high-quality grapes from different vineyards to conceal a bad harvest in 2004. During checks conducted at Duboeuf's*

> *Lancié winery last year, the national wine 'fraud squad' found that a series of barrels – equivalent to about 300,000 bottles – had been mixed. Under France's appellation controlée system, blending is forbidden in order to ensure the exact geographical origin of each bottle of wine.*

Duboeuf predictably blamed his staff for the 'mistake', asserting that he had known nothing of this practice. Anyway, he pointed out, none of the 'fraudulent' wine in question had yet been sold. Heads had to roll – but Duboeuf made sure that they belonged to other people. His production manager at Lancié, Sylvain Dory, promptly 'resigned', and was later given a three-month suspended sentence and fined €3,000. Duboeuf, meanwhile, remained at the summit of his Beaujolais empire. However, his aura of invincibility and omniscience had evaporated. When Duboeuf died in 2020, few of the critics' obituaries deigned to mention the 2006 scandal. But the well-publicised episode had severely damaged the reputation not just of Duboeuf's own company but also of Beaujolais as a serious wine.

The fourth musketeer in the creation of the British obsession with Beaujolais Nouveau was the bibulous *Sunday Times* lifestyle and wine writer Allan Hall. On 18 November 1970, Clement Freud and Joseph Berkmann, dining lavishly at the Hotel Maritonnes in Romanèche-Thorins, had challenged each other to be the first to arrive in London with a case of Duboeuf's *en primeur* Beaujolais. Despite having drunk prodigiously, they duly set off in their respective Rolls-Royces (as you do). The *bon-vivant* duo then repeated the feat the following year. (Berkmann won both times.) Then in 1972 Yorkshire-born Hall, who had already convinced *Sunday Times* editor Harold Evans to launch the *Sunday Times* Wine Club, persuaded Evans to get *The Sunday Times* to back a public version of the Freud-Berkmann contest, 'Bring Back the Beaujolais', with a bottle of champagne to be awarded to the first to arrive at *The Sunday Times*' Fleet Street offices.

Enthusiastically supported by Georges Duboeuf – and subsequently, when they saw how much media attention it generated, by his fellow *vignerons* – the British 'Beaujolais Run' swiftly passed into legend. Following the wine's release at midnight on the third Thursday of November, a legion of well-heeled Britons in their various sports cars grabbed a case or two and drove hell-for-leather for the Channel ports. It soon became a crazy motor race, with established checkpoints along the way, as well as a big-money charity fundraiser – originally for the Great Ormond Street Children's Hospital. It attracted sponsors, including the Ford Motor Company in 1976. And by the 1980s the varied means of transport were becoming increasingly bizarre. The lists included two barristers on motorbikes, who won the 1980 race in just nine hours and seventeen minutes; the British Army's Red Devils parachute display team, who dropped a consignment by parachute into the River Thames by London's Savoy Hotel in a record two-hour time; an RAF Harrier jump jet, which set the surely unbeatable time of thirty-two minutes; and even a man riding an elephant – who surprisingly failed to win.

By 1985 a thousand participants were setting off from Beaujeu for Britain on that third Thursday in November. What the French daily newspaper *Le Figaro* subsequently called 'the greatest marketing stroke since the end of World War II' had captivated Britain's, and soon also the world's, media. A large part of the attraction of the event for global journalists was seeing archetypal products of Thatcher's Britain – those bankers, lawyers and hedge fund managers who had done very well out of the mass-privatisation of British industries and institutions – careering along French roads in their Aston Martins and Jaguars. In many senses the race encapsulated the confidence and bravado of the newly enriched professionals of 1980s Britain. City of London wine bars in the run-up to Christmas were full of braying bankers toasting each other in Beaujolais Nouveau. The wine's thin, sallow taste didn't really matter; it was the race, and indeed winning the race, that counted. For those who won, the rewards could be substantial; but for those who couldn't even afford to enter, it was a mystifying spectacle – a case of, to paraphrase Oscar Wilde, the unspeakable in pursuit of the undrinkable.

The cult of Beaujolais Nouveau helped to create the phenomenon known as the 'yuppie'. The term first appeared in Britain in 1984, having been first used by political commentators reporting on the US presidential election of that year, and stood for 'young urban professionals'. As historian Amy Edwards has observed:

> *The advent of the term yuppie in British culture almost perfectly aligned with the deregulation of the stock market, the height of privatization mania, and a boom in the numbers of people employed by financial institutions.*

There was even a book about yuppies: 1984's *The Official British Yuppie Handbook*, an adaption of an original American publication. Its only real definition of a yuppie was a job that was 'highly paid [and] high powered'. In Britain, yuppies inhabited trendy wine bars, voted Tory and participated in the annual Beaujolais Nouveau race. Finance-sector yuppies were a ubiquitous presence across the popular culture of the 1980s, from Martin Amis's 1984 novel *Money: A Suicide Note* to Caryl Churchill's 1987 West End hit *Serious Money*, starring a young Gary Oldman as corporate raider Billy Corman, to American films *Trading Places* (1983), *Working Girl* (1988) and, most famously, *Wall Street* (1987).

On British television, while the yuppie remained a figure of fun, the get-rich-quick ethos of Thatcher's Britain – an attitude that permeated both work and leisure and which was enshrined in the Beaujolais Nouveau race – was best expressed in the ambitious market trader Derek Trotter of *Only Fools and Horses*, a legendary British sitcom that ran for a decade from 1981, and in comedian

Harry Enfield's timeless 'Loadsamoney' character, the Essex plasterer-made-good who had done very well out of the booming property market and the consequent demand for home improvements. The novelty comic song Enfield adapted from the character, 'Loadsamoney (Doin' Up the House)', actually reached number 4 in the UK pop charts in April 1988. The following month the leader of the Labour Party, Neil Kinnock, recycled Enfield's term 'loadsamoney' as a cudgel with which to attack the creation by the Thatcher government of a 'loadsamoney economy' that only benefited the yuppie traders who populated the Beaujolais Nouveau race. As Amy Edwards has noted of Enfield's inspired creation, 'The character's premise was based on a new cohort of tradesmen. Less investor, more small business owner, Loadsamoney's riches were no less tied to the movements of financial market transactions than his barrow boy counterparts in the City.' To Enfield's horror, though, Loadsamoney soon became a folk hero to those rapacious young bankers his comic concept had been meant to satirise. Accompanied by the character's trademark gesture of waving an imaginary, thick bundle of cash in the air, 'loadsamoney' became the most popular catchphrase in the country.

By the time that Loadsamoney was waving his wad on stage, however, the writing was already on the wall for many of Britain's financial traders. The Thatcher government's deregulation of the banking system, starting with the so-called 'Big Bang' of 1986, led in turn to a massive increase in loans to households, many of which subsequently turned toxic, as well as a lowering of underwriting standards as banks competed over-aggressively for business. The Thatcherite revolution in British banking had also encouraged numerous American firms to gobble up long-established City of London institutions at seemingly insane prices. These new owners then began to exchange the clubby, cliquey atmosphere of the Square Mile with an avaricious, bonus-focused culture normally associated with American investment banks, modernising banks' computer technologies and office working practices. The Americans even, horror of horrors, started to clamp down on that traditional City perk, the long, boozy lunch.

The over-heating of the market and the rashly bellicose policies adopted by some of the newly reconstituted banks, many of whose young and ruthlessly ambitious staff had never experienced either a bear market or a serious slump, eventually helped to plunge Britain into a serious recession towards the end of 1990. Margaret Thatcher herself, now at odds with increasing numbers of her own MPs and increasingly remote from those ordinary Britons who had not profited from the great race to achieve deregulation and privatisation, was ousted by the Tory party as prime minister and replaced by her former chancellor, John Major. Yet this act alone did nothing to halt the incoming tide. In the subsequent economic downturn, many smaller banks went under, while the Bank of England was forced to prop up many more, including that mighty pillar of the British high street, the Midland Bank.

In this context of economic gloom, the high-spirited hilarity of the Beaujolais Nouveau event, in which some of the nation's most affluent individuals competed in costly supercars to bring back a case of mediocre wine from France, suddenly seemed out of place and out of date. By the 1990s, the novelty of the race had worn as thin as the wine. Consumption of Beaujolais Nouveau fell dramatically, while colourful accounts of the hijinks of the wine race disappeared from the pages of the national newspapers.

Suddenly Britons turned on the former fad with the zeal of the newly converted. Beaujolais Nouveau, like the proverbial emperor, was suddenly found to have no clothes. Writer Peter Viney was not alone in admitting that it was 'an ideal light red for people who didn't like red wine.' By the turn of the millennium, Britain was importing less than one sixtieth of the quantity of Beaujolais Nouveau being bought by the Japanese.

It wasn't just the British who were turning against Beaujolais Nouveau. To many wine critics both in France and abroad, Beaujolais Nouveau had played a large part in undermining the reputation of the region's viticulture. In 2003 the region's producers had actually sued a magazine after it carried an interview with François Mauss, the Luxembourgeois president of the prestigious Grand Jury of European Tasters. In the piece, Mauss had loftily declared that Beaujolais wine was 'not proper wine' and that Beaujolais Nouveau was nothing but a '*vin de merde*'. To make things worse, the Beaujolais growers, having alerted the world's media to Mauss's caustic comments by their legal action, actually lost the case.

By that time, though, the race to import *vin de merde* into Britain had become a mere sideshow.

As wine journalist Ian Mansfield recalls, there were already clouds on the horizon of the Beaujolais Nouveau race as early as 1985:

> *That year probably triggered a change... as there were road accidents and fatalities. I have vague memories during my wine-selling days of being told*

that in addition to awful weather, some drivers got more than a bit merry before the race, with the inevitable consequences on the road, and it wasn't too many years later that French decided they had enough of the crazy Brits racing through their dark streets.

By the year of the Mauss case, the Great Race was no longer featuring either in the Sunday supplements or in TV's magazine programmes. It had been largely forgotten, consigned to the spittoon of history along with the yuppies, the 'loadsamoney' bankers of the 1980s and, indeed, Beaujolais Nouveau itself.

-

Today Allan Hall's competition is still with us, rebranded as 'The Beaujolais Run'. But it is now a completely different animal. No longer a race but 'an enjoyable navigational shootout', its emphasis is far more on driving the cars than on winning the competition or delivering (or even drinking) the wine. These days it is a gentle, five-day drive 'through a cryptic checkpoint course' to Maçon and back – a 'quintessentially British charity lifestyle event... to repatriate France's first harvest and bring back the Beaujolais.' Revealingly, the term 'Beaujolais Nouveau' is never used on its promotional website, presumably owing to the wine's unhelpful historic 'loadsamoney' baggage.

The event is no longer based in London, either. Instead, it operates from the famous Goodwood estate in Sussex, a location that in recent years has become a prestigious and upmarket motorsport venue. Home both to the Duke of Richmond and, since 1993, the Goodwood Festival of Speed, since 2003 the estate has also hosted the stylish, BMW-owned plant that builds Rolls-Royce cars. It is not a destination that welcomes the poor and needy.

The Beaujolais Run event may appeal to some of the descendants of the ultra-wealthy financial-sector types who populated the Beaujolais Nouveau race during the 1980s. But thankfully today the emphasis is the cars, not their drivers. Recent Beaujolais Runs have featured an impressively wide range of classic British and international sports cars, from Austins to Astons and from Fords to Ferraris. Journalist Ed Foster recorded that the entrants for the 2008 race included a Jaguar XKR and a Mercedes CLS 63 AMG, 'while the rest of the field was made up of 4x4s, Elises, DB9s and the odd classic in the shape of a Morris Minor (which arrived at and left each checkpoint to rapturous applause) and an MGB (which broke down).' Three years later the lineup 'saw a diverse selection of vehicles ranging from a 1964 Mini Cooper S to Jaguar's latest XKR-S, with modern gems including a rare Ferrari 360 Challenge Stradale, an Aston Martin DB9 and a banana-yellow Corvette, and the classics including three Jaguar E-Types.'

The Beaujolais Run's charitable partner is now the Royal Air Force Benevolent Fund. Ties with the RAF are clearly strong: the 2018 Run was specifically themed to commemorate both the centenary of the Royal Air Force and the 75th anniversary of Operation Chastise – the 1943 sortie that saw the Lancaster bombers of the famed 617 Squadron attacking the supposedly impregnable German dams – with participants being encouraged to attempt to follow part of the bombers' original route.

-

Beaujolais Nouveau is still alive and kicking, too. Perhaps not, though, in the UK, where consumers have turned away from the wine in droves since the 1990s, understandably preferring Mediterranean and New World reds with far more flavour and body. Nor have the British been tempted back to appropriately aged Beaujolais, either. In a tasting report for Berry Bros & Rudd of 26 May 2010, the highly experienced wine critic and renowned Burgundy expert Jasper Morris MW[53] directly linked the old Beaujolais Nouveau phenomenon with the persistent reluctance of British drinkers to take real Beaujolais seriously:

> *...the wretched nouveau, such a brilliant marketing idea at the outset, has ended up as a form of homeopathic inoculation against beaujolais – one small dose in November and you don't have to touch the stuff for the rest of the year. This is a tragedy for those still making exciting wine of quality and durability.*

Peter Viney concurs: in a widely publicised blog of 22 November 2014, he alleged that 'Beaujolais Nouveau certainly damaged the general reputation of the appellation' and noted that, from the 1990s onwards, more and more properly matured wine was sold under individual village names rather than a generic 'Beaujolais' designation. Today, for many Britons, the raffish image of Beaujolais Nouveau still dissuades them from choosing older wines from this region, which are all too often regarded as underpriced, inadequately developed and simplistic.

The rest of the world, however, remains untainted by British associations of Beaujolais Nouveau with the bankers' bonuses and yuppie sports cars of the Thatcher years. Instead, much of the globe still seems, oddly enough, to be mesmerised by the Beaujolais Nouveau promotional razzmatazz. Four years after Georges Duboeuf's death, Nouveau still accounts for half of the Beaujolais area's wine production, while its export sales now exceed all of the aged vintages of both its venerable Burgundian neighbours and its esteemed Bordelais rivals. It has thus become the proverbial tail that wags the Beaujolais dog. Celebrations are still held all over the United States every November to welcome the wine. In New York, for example, the famed motorcycle gang the Gotham City Riders (motto: 'financially stable, mentally questionable') process on their Harley-Davidsons to greet the wine at the quayside and then proceed to dine in style at a suitable Manhattan restaurant on a menu specifically matched to the *en primeur* wine. Well might France's Communist daily newspaper *L'Humanité* have claimed that Beaujolais 'irrigates the entire world'.

Today it is the Japanese who are by far the biggest consumers of this light, bright and easy-drinking red. After a decade of falling demand due to high transport costs and the Covid-19 pandemic, in 2023 key Japanese importers sought to exploit the renewed interest in Beaujolais Nouveau by launching a major media campaign, while at the same time lowering the wine's price. The Suntory corporation, which predictably commands much of the Beaujolais Nouveau market there, even repackaged the wine in 500-milllitre plastic bottles 'to respond to rising environmental awareness among consumers' and simultaneously cut the carbon dioxide emissions during transportation by 40 per cent. Wine connoisseurs in Britain and France were doubtless appalled at this news, yet Suntory astutely and correctly guessed that the fresh, fruity and innocuous taste of their *en primeur* would, packaged in its small plastic containers, appeal to a younger generation of drinkers who, perhaps, had never sampled French wine before.

While international wine critics continue to disparage its appeal, Beaujolais producers are understandably happy with the revenue that Beaujolais Nouveau generates. 2023 saw a record 50 million bottles of the stuff produced, almost entirely for an export trade driven by an aggressive promotional strategy that continues to violate many of the sacrosanct traditions of the long-established French wine industry. The annual *Fête du Beaujolais Nouveau* may have become a media circus, but it is one that keeps the Beaujolais wine industry in business.

Nor has Britain remained wholly immune to the lure of *nouveau*, either. Since 1999, for example, Sharpham Wine on the Dart estuary in Devon has been issuing a 'New Release' wine that is essentially a white version of Beaujolais Nouveau. The estate's Bacchus and Madeleine Angevine grapes are picked, pressed and fermented in only six weeks to create what the vineyard calls 'a fast, fun, fruity wine which is ready to drink immediately' and which, they say, is 'packed with vibrant fruit characters of peach melba, lemon sherbet and elderflower, with a mouth-watering acidity and gentle spritz on the finish.' Duboeuf's concept seemingly lives on, shorn of the investment bankers and the media hullabaloo. Beaujolais Nouveau is dead: long live the New Release!

Chapter 9

BLAME IT ON THE BUCKY

BUCKFAST TONIC WINE

'Tonic wine' has a puzzlingly long history in Britain. Essentially it is potent, complex and occasionally (but not always) fortified red wine. Usually made at a strength of 15 per cent ABV or higher, making it stronger than most table wines, tonic wine is invariably formulated from wine concentrate or even grape juice. The embryonic wine then has a variety of vitamins, fruits or minerals added – whatever the specific recipe dictates. And there's always a good deal of added sugar. But tonic wine's historic selling proposition was always that it provided wide-ranging if rather vaguely defined health benefits. While this claim inevitably turned out to be largely spurious, and is one that cannot legally be made today, the aura of promoting health and wellbeing is still one that lingers about today's tonic wine brands.

The fad for tonic wine developed in the late nineteenth century, when it was promoted first and foremost as a medicinal aid. It was, effectively, the descendant of all those catch-all elixirs of previous centuries that were said to have cured everything from colds to cholera. Sometimes there *was* a genuine medical benefit or effect. The addition of hedgerow fruits to some brands, for example, introduced a rigorous antioxidant into the mix that could help treat cardiovascular diseases, while in the 1860s a product called Vin Mariani was developed in Corsica that, it was claimed, could 'restore health, energy and vitality' through its magic ingredient: coca leaves, steeped in wine in order to extract their cocaine content.

The overnight success of Angelo Mariani's cocaine-fuelled Vin Mariani 'restorative' encouraged other global manufacturers to concoct their own, highly lucrative 'tonic wines'. Sanatogen was invented by the Bauer corporation in Germany in 1898 as a 'brain tonic'; in Britain after the Second World War it was added to wine concentrate (or rather 'Ruby British Wine') to create a tonic wine that is still the market leader in the UK today. (There's also a variant 'with added iron'.) During the 1950s, Sanatogen Tonic Wine was controversially claimed to have been 'endorsed by over 20,000 Physicians', a boast that seemed to have little basis in truth and which seems incredible today. Currently, though, the Sanatogen wine label dispassionately notes that 'The name *Tonic Wine* does not imply health giving or medicinal properties.'

Tonic wines had their first British heyday in the 1950s and 60s, when they were primarily targeted at tired and disconsolate British working-class housewives. ('And your husband wonders what's wrong with you!'). Advertisements for Sanatogen suggested that 'a glass or two' would make you feel better when engaged in tiring, repetitious housework while your husband was out at work all day ('In no time at all you should feel your old self again'), while a 1960s ad for Buckfast promised to help lonely and exhausted housewives cope with 'life's little ups and downs'. The British tonic wine Wincarnis,[54] first devised in 1881 by William Coleman of Norwich as a drink fortified with the magic ingredient of meat (its name derived from the word *carnis*, from the Latin for meat) and originally branded, somewhat less enticingly, as Coleman's Liebig's Extract of Meat and Malt Wine, was particularly keen to stress its medicinal qualities. The late-Victorian labels on Coleman's wine stated, in the same vein as Sanatogen, that the product had been 'recommended by 10,000 medical men [sic]' – when, in truth, the 'recommendations' of these '10,000 medical men' were actually the return coupons sent by doctors requesting their promised free samples.

An Edwardian print as for Wincarnis which audaciously links Coleman & Co's product with direct medical benefits. Note the detachable coupon to enable doctors to get their free samples.

Other health associations were promoted in a more insidious manner. As historian Thora Hands observes,

Wincarnis could allegedly 'not only treat winter illnesses but could also be used to prevent them [while] the medicinal qualities of Wincarnis were further supported by claims that it was used in nursing homes, hospitals and by the royal Army Medical Corps.'[55] Hands notes one particular 1890s print advertisement for Wincarnis, in which

> *a man is pictured sitting working at his desk while a woman (presumably his wife) brings him a glass of Wincarnis 'by doctor's orders'. The caption claimed that: 'a man who spends his energies recklessly will quickly overdraw his account at the Bank of Health. A man as he manages himself may die old at thirty or young at eighty; brain fag is the foster parent of disease.' In other words, overwork meant an early demise for professional middle-class men and an early widowhood for their wives, unless it was kept in check by a glass or two of Wincarnis.*

Until the creation of the UK's National Health Service in 1948, tonic wine was an easy solution for people who could not afford (or simply did not want) to see a doctor, for real or imagined conditions. Self-medicating at home with tonic wine instead was both cheaper and easier. As such, tonic wine was very much directed at working-class audiences who could not afford complex healthcare or were simply not in the habit of consulting doctors. (Harold Wilson, the Labour prime minister from 1964 to 1970, was dubbed 'Wincarnis man' by his critics on account of his humble background and commonplace tastes.)

By the 1940s tonic wines were rather more restrained in overtly claiming medicinal properties. This ad, however, still implies that they should be seen as health-giving drinks.

Tonic wine's promotion of alleged health benefits was intended to mask the strength of the drink. Indeed, rarely was the alcoholic nature of such products mentioned at all in their marketing – even though Wincarnis, a typical example, came in at 17 per cent ABV, the strength of a sherry. Thora Hands, again:

> *It is hardly surprising that the drink trade capitalised on this and marketed products accordingly. As a tonic, alcohol could be drunk moderately and respectably to alleviate a myriad of psychological and physiological problems. This was an attractive*

idea – particularly for certain groups of consumers who could not otherwise drink without incurring social and moral disapproval.

Even in today's supposedly more informed society, tonic wine sales are booming. Currently the tonic wine market is growing at just over 6 per cent a year, and sales are expected to reach 3.4 billion US dollars globally by 2032. The product is particularly popular in the Caribbean, where it is alleged to have aphrodisiac and energising properties. Famous traditional brands there include Magnum, Baba Roots, Ragga and even Rude Boy. Wincarnis sells well in the West Indies, too – particularly in Jamaica, where it is often mixed with stout or milk. Wincarnis even sell a ginger wine version.

-

There is one British tonic wine, though, that carries a special social resonance, at least for UK consumers. And it is a brand owned and promoted not by an established distiller, nor a big drink combine, but by Benedictine monks.

Buckfast Abbey was founded as a Benedictine religious house by one Aethelweard of Devon in 1018. After 1134 the abbey was rebuilt as what eventually became a Cistercian institution, the white-cowled Cistercians being a more austere offshoot of the black-cowled Benedictines. Like all British abbeys, Buckfast was forced to submit to dissolution and dismemberment by the Crown during the English Reformation – a shameful episode in British history that remains the nation's most notorious instance of self-imposed cultural vandalism. On 25 February 1539 Buckfast Abbey was formally surrendered to Henry VIII's agent and forcibly 'dissolved'. The monks were dismissed (though by then there were only ten left: the institution had been declining for years), the abbot was pensioned off, and the abbey's one and a half tons of gold and silver was transported to the Tower of London 'for safekeeping'. The site's new proprietor, the well-connected local landowner Sir Thomas Denys, stripped the abbey buildings for stone and other useful building materials and 'reduced them to ruins'. What structures that remained were razed by a local mill owner in 1800 to make way for a Tudor-style mansion and a wool mill.

In 1882 a subsequent owner of the abbey site, Dr James Gale, decided to sell the property once more. Gale was a local celebrity: a blind inventor who had devised a safe manner for storing gunpowder, had founded the South Devon and Cornwall Institution for the Instruction and Employment of the Blind, and who had been chosen as the subject of a hagiographical biography as early as 1868. Gale was also a Catholic; as such, he was keen to offer the old abbey site to a Catholic religious community. (The time was right: British Roman Catholics had seen their civil rights fully restored in 1829, while in 1850 a Catholic diocesan regime had been re-established across the country.) To that end, Gale placed an advertisement in the Catholic review *The Tablet*, citing the abbey site as 'a grand acquisition could it be restored to its original purpose.' Within six weeks, a group of French Benedictine monks who had been ejected from their own, suppressed French abbey had bought the property at a knock-down price and were soon living on site.

Buckfast was formally reinstated as the Abbey of St Mary in 1902, though its new church was not completed until 1938.[56] The church's architect was a Catholic, too:

ecclesiastical specialist Frederick Walters, who had studied as a pupil under the Catholic church architect George Goldie, who in turn had been a close friend of the celebrated British Gothic pioneer A. W. N. Pugin. Walters' design was ambitious: essentially a variant of the magnificent Anglican cathedral at Worcester, it was clothed not in Worcester's Gothic fenestration but instead in the round-arched Romanesque idiom of the twelfth century – although provided with a noble central tower phrased in a transitional Gothic style.

The new monks farmed and kept bees. In 1897 they also launched a tonic wine, using a recipe their French founders had brought with them, and which they were soon promoting with the slogan 'Three small glasses a day, for good health and lively blood.' The wine was only sold locally, though, and, while it proved a rewarding line for the abbey, the income it generated was hardly transformative.

This all changed in 1927. A chance visit to the abbey by a Mr Robert Joyce, the owner of the London-based wine merchant J. Chandler and Company, encouraged the monks to think big. Joyce offered to distribute and sell the wine across the British Isles for the monks, initiating a partnership that survives to this day. He also suggested that the monks reformulate and rebrand the product as a sweeter, generic tonic wine, along the lines of Wincarnis, rather than as the medicinal cure it had previously been. However, Chandler's cannily continued to distribute Buckfast Tonic Wine through chemists' shops in order to preserve the brand's time-honoured if spurious medicinal associations, leading to particularly strong sales of the brand during winter time, when it was seen as a preventative against colds and flu.

Over the years the partnership has continued to prove highly lucrative both for the monks of Buckfast and for the staff of J. Chandler. Neither the syrupy, reddish-brown wine nor the product's oddly amateurish label design seem to have been changed for decades. Buckfast Tonic Wine is mixed at 15 per cent ABV, a little higher than most table wine. Its base fortified wine concentrate from Spain is supercharged by a hefty dose of caffeine, making one glass of the resulting drink roughly equivalent to around eight cans of Coke, and softened by a generous shot of vanillin. The resulting if unorthodox recipe has nevertheless proved a runaway success.

The wine's flavour is in itself a contentious subject. Some present-day drinkers have hymned Buckfast's 'aromatic fragrances' and its 'smooth', 'rounded' and 'mature' nature. One British reviewer, though, has described it as tasting 'a bit like undiluted Ribena mixed with Benylin' – while to another critic this unlikely taste combination worked surprisingly well. In January 2023, however, an American wine critic publicly recorded his utter incredulity after tasting 'something I've never experienced before'. Unsurprisingly, his colourful online review echoed round UK online media outlets for some months. In sampling Buckfast Wine, 'Acceptable West' detected

> *Barnyardy funk (in a bad way) almost like a dead animal in a bird's nest. A mix of flat Coca-Cola and caramel with a whiff of gun metal. On the palate, overwhelming sweetness and sugar. Cherry Cola mixed with Benadryl. Unlike anything I've tasted. I'm not sure what this liquid is but it is not wine…*

The critic concluded flatly that 'I've drunk a lot of wines in my life and will never forget this one.'[57]

Given the drink's low price and its weighty dollop of caffeine, Buckfast Tonic Wine has proved popular with students and other young people across Britain and Ireland. (The Irish version of Bucky Wine is slightly less alcoholic than its British sibling, at 14.8 per cent ABV. It omits the vanilla taste but carries more of a caffeine kick.) Buckfast Wine's low price and substantial caffeine hit also account for its historic appeal to those working in physically demanding industries.

Buckfast Wine has, as a result, sold particularly well in the areas of Northern Ireland (particularly in and around Lurgan) and those districts of Central Scotland formerly dominated by heavy industry. Today, indeed, the economically depressed Scottish Central Lowland areas east and west of Glasgow – specifically Coatbridge, Airdrie, Cumbernauld and the neighbouring districts of North Lanarkshire – have earned the unwelcome nickname of 'the Buckfast Triangle'. Similar social problems resulting in the over-consumption of alcohol have also been witnessed west of Glasgow, in the rustbelt of Renfrewshire. In 1980 there were over 750,000 people working in industrial manufacturing in Renfrewshire alone; by 1996, thanks to foreign competition, changing habits and new technologies, this had declined to 343,000, while the most recent figures record only 178,000. In 2023 a Glasgow Caledonian University report observed that 'deindustrialisation, the declining importance of industrial activities to employment and production has had a long-term economic and social impact in Lanarkshire' and, moreover, that 'the long reach of deindustrialisation was intensified by [post-2010] austerity.' The long-term effect of the resulting long-term unemployment on individuals and communities in these areas was, predictably, shattering and corrosive.

Unsurprisingly, cheap, strong alcoholic drinks have long been adopted as a physical and psychological comfort blanket by many of those who see little hope and no future. Buckfast Wine, in particular, has controversially won widespread brand loyalty. As a result, it has become known by a variety of ironic, affectionate and belligerent nicknames. In the depressed former industrial areas west of Belfast the wine is called 'Lurgan champagne'. In Scotland's Central Belt it has earned a plethora of witty sobriquets, from 'Commotion Lotion', 'Cumbernauld Rocket Fuel' and 'The Dark Destroyer' to 'Stab-yer-Pal', 'What the Hell are you Looking At?' and 'Wreck-the-Hoose Juice'. There is also the rather ominous alias of 'A bottle of 30 days', referring to the length of the custodial sentence that drinkers can reportedly expect following an alcohol-fuelled offence.

Following the economic devastation of the Lowlands' economic heartlands in the 1980s, Buckfast Wine became increasingly associated with public binge drinking across the blighted Bucky Triangle, east of Glasgow, as well as elsewhere in the Midland Valley and post-industrial Ayrshire. Buckfast Tonic Wine has become inexorably linked with public intoxication, under-age drinking and anti-social behaviour, while its sale and consumption have accordingly caused great controversy in Scotland since the 1990s. As writer David Leishman has observed, 'Six of the eight Scottish constituencies with the highest levels of alcohol-related mortality [in Britain] are to be found within North Lanarkshire, with the constituency of Coatbridge, Chryston & Bellshill being the worst in the UK.'

Bucky consumption during the 1990s was famously reflected in Gregor Fisher's popular and enduring television character Rab C. Nesbitt, the focus of the eponymous BBC Scotland comedy that enjoyed a run of seven series between 1988 and 1999. Nesbitt, instantly recognisable by his distinctive sartorial choice of filthy headband, frayed jacket and string vest, was unapologetically portrayed as a reformed alcoholic. And while Bucky Wine was never specifically mentioned on screen, for obvious reasons, its spectre haunted the programme. When, for example, Nesbitt attempts to excuse his lack of achievement in life, he alleges that if his neighbours in Govan (a strongly working-class district in western Glasgow) spotted any emerging local talent they were liable to 'try tae batter it tae death wi' empty wine bottles'. By the end of the 1990s, Nesbitt and Buckfast Wine were virtually synonymous.

Inevitably, there are two sides to this story: the legislators' and the manufacturer's. Both have merit to them, and, while the first may prompt outrage, the producers have common-sense arguments on their side too. What has continued to make the tale of Bucky Wine such an appealing media story, of course, is the fact that this supposed 'Wreck-the-Hoose Juice', which has seemingly wrought such havoc on working class drinkers in the de-industrialised Central Belt of Lowland Scotland, is produced by monks at a civilised Romanesque abbey nestling far away in the Devon hills.

-

The case against Buckfast Wine does seem fairly damning at face value. Its whopping caffeine kick and strong alcohol content, it has been suggested, may cause the wine to act as a stimulant that could dispel inhibitions and self-control. In addition, its glass bottle has all too often provided drunks with a handy weapon, as well as having become a litter nuisance when carelessly discarded.

Accordingly, since the Scottish Parliament reconvened in 1999, a large number of Scottish politicians and social activists have singled out Buckfast Tonic Wine as being directly or indirectly responsible for crime, disorder and, more controversially, the social deprivation of the post-industrial towns to the east and west of Glasgow. Although Buckfast Wine accounts for only 0.5 per cent of alcohol sales in Scotland, it has been alleged to have been responsible for 80 per cent of public intoxication incidents. As a result, there have been numerous calls for the drink to be banned, either throughout Scotland or in certain areas or shops in the Central Belt; or, alternatively, to be made prohibitively expensive.

Unsurprisingly, Buckfast Abbey and its distributors, J. Chandler, have fiercely resisted such attempts. They have also opposed suggestions that the wine be sold in plastic bottles in order to reduce incidents of glassing, arguing that hundreds of discarded plastic bottles would prove an environmental disaster.

Since 1992 arguments have swung both ways, with fans of Bucky Wine sometimes making their voices heard as loudly as the legislators. In 2005 the Scottish justice minister, Cathy Jamieson MSP – whose own constituency, Kilmarnock, had been heavily impacted by the retreat of industry – suggested that retailers should stop selling the wine. On a subsequent visit to her constituency, though, she was greeted by teenagers chanting 'Don't ban Buckie.' At the same time, Bucky sales in

Scotland increased substantially as a result of her well-publicised comments.

A year later, in September 2006, the Scottish Executive's health minister described Buckfast Wine as 'irresponsible' and a contributor to anti-social behaviour, an opinion that Scotland's first minister, Jack McConnell, subsequently echoed when he claimed that Bucky had become 'a badge of pride amongst those who are involved in antisocial behaviour'. Buckfast's distributors vehemently denied the claims, deriding Bucky's critics as demonstrating 'a complete lack of judgement.' Talks between J. Chandler & Co and the Scottish government got nowhere, with Chandler accusing the latter of distracting attention from the government's failed social policy by blaming the Scottish rustbelt's ills on the drinks industry – a claim that has some justification.

Tempers frayed again four years later, when a BBC investigation into the Bucky phenomenon revealed that Buckfast had been mentioned in an astonishing 5,638 crime reports in the Strathclyde police region of west-central Scotland between 2006 and 2009. That meant an average of three Bucky-fuelled incidents per day. In 2017, Scottish Police reported that 6,500 crimes over the past two years could be associated with the effects of Bucky Wine. A subsequent survey at a young offenders' institution showed that, of the 117 people who had drunk alcohol excessively before committing their crimes, 43 per cent per said they had drunk Buckfast.

When, in 2013, Strathclyde Police proposed marking Buckfast bottles in order to trace where they were retailed, Chandler's replied, 'This is discrimination at the highest level' and that 'Buckfast is no more involved in crime than any other brand of alcohol'. A former head of the Scottish

Police Federation did not attempt to hide his frustration and told the *Scotsman* that

> *Buckfast, the distributors and the lawyers who act on behalf of the monks refuse, point blank, to take any responsibility for the antisocial behaviour that's caused by the distribution and the consumption of Buckfast. They even refuse to change the glass bottles to plastic bottles despite overwhelming evidence that large areas in play parks and certain areas in Scotland are littered with this green glass.*

Chandler's applied to the courts to stop the scheme, and in the event the case was settled out of court, with the police agreeing to drop their putative scheme.

Much media attention naturally focused on the Devon monks' role in producing a drink abused by Scottish alcoholics at the other end of Britain. As the popular media headline had it, Buckfast was 'Made by Monks, Drunk by Drunks'. Aside from Abbot Charlesworth's interview of 2013, though, the monks of Buckfast have wisely refrained from direct comment on this controversy. David Leishman has noted

> *The lack of response from the monks as regards the social repercussions of their commercial activities could seem to be the natural corollary of their discretion and monastic retreat. We can note, however, that a problematics of silence and absence is also central to the commercial positioning of the wine as its distributors attempt to navigate between the contradictory poles of acceptability and transgression.*

While the monks and their distributor remain understandably eager to minimise Buckfast Wine sales in Lanarkshire and Renfrewshire, Leishman notes that 'the firm is reluctant to acknowledge the volume of Buckfast consumed in this area' – even though drinks trade studies of 1994 'regularly stated that 80 per cent of Buckfast's worldwide sales were achieved in this part of Central Scotland'.

As legendary broadcaster and journalist Derek Cooper noted over fifty years ago, Buckfast's advertising of the time emphasised the product's 'goodness', which Cooper suggested was 'not an unwise line to stress considering its impeccable religious connections.'[58] In 1994 Devon journalist Wailim Wong quoted an Abbey spokesman who declared that 'We believe Buckfast is unfairly attacked by the media since it has a monastic background' – a claim that is not without foundation. Helen Liddell – former MP for the North Lanarkshire constituency of Monklands East, once secretary of state for Scotland and now Baroness Liddell of Coatdyke – at one point attempted to exploit a sense of spiritual obligation among the monks by providing them with a video that illustrated the alleged social impact of their wine. As Baroness Liddell wrote in 2012: 'There is no doubt that the monks here are compassionate men. And I believe that no one with any compassion could watch this video and not be affected.' Liddell even threatened to write to the Pope if the monks did not take action. In a similar vein, one Glasgow newspaper article of 1992 invited readers to pray for the soul of the prior of Buckfast Abbey, who was likened to Pontius Pilate.

In 2010 the influential *Economist* magazine weighed in on the issue. An anonymous editorial of 23 February, while rehearsing the spectacular commercial success of the brand as well as social problems associated with its consumption, particularly in Scotland (where, the magazine alleged, the inhabitants drank '25% more per head than people in England and Wales'), did suggest that 'it seems a little odd that a particular target of political ire is a Benedictine abbey in Devon and not Scotland's big distillers.' While pointing out that each bottle of Bucky contained as much caffeine as eight cans of Coke, and that 'alcohol and caffeine combined apparently make the imbiber particularly anxious and aggressive', the *Economist* ultimately came down on the side of the producers. The magazine interviewed Chandler's Jim Wilson, who candidly admitted that some of the company's success may be 'because it has become excitingly off-limits to teenagers who, for example, view speed consumption of the stuff on YouTube as a badge of honour.' But Wilson cautioned against singling out Bucky without addressing the drinks industry as a whole – or, of course, tackling the problem of alcohol-related crimes at their source. The editorial's rather glib conclusion was that, while 'drink is said to be the curse of the working class... worrying about the specific drinks imbibed by the working class is evidently the curse of the bourgeoisie.'

The monks' commercial partners have continued to mount a robust defence of their position. In 2001 Chandler's managing director, Anthony Joyce, opined that the alcohol content of Buckfast Wine was, at 15 per cent by volume, 'only slightly stronger' than other table wines, noting in passing that Scotch whisky, a product that is hardly unknown in Central Scotland, is three times stronger. He also reaffirmed that 'The overwhelming majority of consumers worldwide drink Buckfast responsibly.' Chandler's have additionally contested that any proposed ban on Bucky sales would contravene the Human Rights Act of 1998, which forbids any restrictive commercial measure that singles out a brand rather than a category of drink. It is also difficult to argue with Chandler director Jim Wilson's 2010 argument that the problems may lie with the economic dislocation of Central Scotland rather than with their wine, given that it has been sold 'for more than 80 years in several different countries and nowhere else is anybody linking it to health or crime'. ('If a reckless driver crashes a fast car,' Wilson added, 'do you ban the car or the driver?') In 2003 Joyce reiterated that the issue should not be the nature of his wine but the challenges inherent in post-industrial Scottish society: 'The problem is essentially a social one and that is where the Scottish Executive should be directing its time, effort and money – as my company has in support of numerous community-led initiatives in Scotland.' This claim was backed up by academic sociologists, who suggested that simply banning Buckfast would have little effect on the underlying social crisis in Central Scotland.

Buckfast's high caffeine content is a trickier subject to defend. In citing the many other popular alcoholic alternatives available in Scotland, Chandler's consistently fail to address this undeniable product trait. In contrast, they constantly reiterate the fact that, as Joyce has repeatedly declared to reporters, 'The monks of Buckfast take a very responsible attitude and this is reflected in the marketing policy of J. Chandler & Co' and that 'The product is not promoted or advertised.' (Chandler's constantly if controversially maintain that they are 'the most responsible drinks manufacturer in Britain'.) Even the absence of marketing, however, has been ably deconstructed by some critics. As Leishman observes,

> *Rather than helping to minimize the abuse of Buckfast, it has been argued that this absence helps to position the drink as a product on the fringes of the alcohol market. Going further, it has been noted that Buckfast's mode of communication – notoriety garnered through word of mouth in the absence of any official advertising – creates an analogy with illicit drugs...*

–

The heated debate on Bucky Wine's role as hero or villain shows no sign of being resolved. Some commentators have suggested that the wine return to its 'craft roots' in Devon, using the monks as brand spokesmen. However, this is to miss the point. Buckfast Abbey and Chandler's both make an enormous amount of money from Buckfast Tonic Wine. A locally marketed artisanal drink would in all probability earn a mere fraction of the profits that Bucky currently does.

Buckfast Abbey and its commercial partners have instead turned to more subtle ways of improving the wine's image. Some, though, have been more successful than others. From 2013 to 2015, British TV chef Martin Blunos was enlisted to promote Bucky Wine by, somewhat incredibly, including the drink as a principal element in a series of new recipes. A press release of 2014 quoted Blunos's improbable claim that 'Buckfast is an amazing ingredient for both sweet and savoury dishes' such as 'the Buckie burger, the Triple B (Buckfast beef bourguignon), mulled pears and Buckfast fruit loaf.' Unsurprisingly, this cookery experiment was not repeated – nor do these weird, Bucky-based dishes feature anywhere on Blunos's online profile.

Yet despite the bitter war of words regarding the drink's connection with alcohol abuse in some of the most depressed areas of the UK – a heated dispute that has gone on since the 1990s and which still shows no signs of abating – sales of Buckfast Tonic Wine continue to soar. In 2016 sales of Bucky attained record yearly profits for the abbey and its distributors of £8.8 million; the following year, Chandler's reported record sales of £43.2 million; while during the post-Covid financial year of 2022–3 Buckfast grew its sales by 4.9 per cent to £41.8 million.

Interestingly, Chandler's review of 2017's sales performance, which noted that sales of Buckfast bottles had increased by an astonishing 2 million year-on-year, also observed that sales were strengthening in England, and particularly in the wealthy south-east counties – areas that are as far removed from Coatbridge in terms of distance, geography and demography as you can imagine. Reacting to this news, the venerable and respected British trade magazine *The Grocer*, first published in 1862, reported that the increased sales of Buckfast in south-eastern England had promoted the contentious drink up to 91st place in the league table of the UK's hundred best-selling alcohol brands.

The sales trend has remained upward-looking ever since – even during (or perhaps assisted by) the Covid epidemic of 2020–1. As we have seen, tonic wine sales globally are booming, and Buckfast Wine is riding high on this wave of success. The numerous accusations made over the years by the Scottish Executive, the bitter media dispute that has raged on since 1990 regarding the drink's fraught relationship with issues of social responsibility and crime prevention, even the unsightly string vest of Rab C Nesbitt… all these factors appear to have little effect on the mounting sales of Buckfast Wine. Perhaps, to quote that time-worn adage, *any* publicity is good publicity.

Chapter 10

THE FOUNTAIN OF YOUTH

WKD

Torquay was once a small fishing village, which in turn evolved into a genteel Victorian resort on the South Devon coast. The Torquay we see today was effectively created by the arrival at nearby Torre of Isambard Kingdom Brunel's South Devon Railway in 1848, which opened up this comfortable coastline to national tourism. By the time Queen Victoria died in 1901 it was now a thriving borough which had been promoting itself for the past decade as the capital of the 'English Riviera' on account of its mild climate (for Britain, anyway). Lured by lush posters created for the Southern Railway during the interwar years by leading graphic artists such as Walter Spradbery, Kenneth Shoesmith, Frank Newbould and Martine, visitors flocked to Torquay's waving palm trees, calm seas (protected by the sheltered anchorage of Torbay), sandy beaches, electric trams, Victorian villas, the historic complex of Torre Abbey and Edward Richards' delightful art nouveau Pavilion Theatre.

However, during the 1960s and 1970s, as British holidaymakers chose to fly abroad on cheap package deals, the town began its long decline. Infamous during this period for the inexplicable demolition of Agatha Christie's childhood home (in 1961) and the Marine Spa (in 1971), by the mid-1970s Torquay was best known across the country as the setting for the tawdry hotel of the now-legendary TV comedy *Fawlty Towers* (first aired on the BBC in 1975). The town soon became renowned more for drug abuse and knife crime than for lazing in the sun under the palm trees. The much-vaunted Coral Island leisure complex closed in 1988, the delightful Living Coasts – Britain's first (and to date only) coastal zoo – closed in 2020, while the Pavilion Theatre has been shut since 2013 and is currently in a seriously dilapidated condition.

By 2023 Torquay was being cited in the national press as one of the nation's worst seaside towns. In a survey commissioned by the *Daily Telegraph*, Torquay earned only 33 points out of a possible 100, planting it firmly in the bottom ten of Britain's crap towns. (The winner, St Ives in Cornwall, scored 98 per cent.) While formerly failing resorts such Margate and Hastings were witnessing a welcome gentrification based on arts provision and faster trains, Torquay continued to slide downwards. No longer marketed as the capital of the 'English Riviera', an optimistic promotional label attached to the Torbay towns as early as the 1890s, Torquay was instead regularly dubbed Devon's crime capital. By 2022 its once-bustling high street featured so many empty shops that, the regional media reported, locals were actually apologising to visitors in the street for the shabby and semi-derelict state of this once-proud resort.

It is perhaps, then, fitting that Torquay should have been the birthplace of an alcoholic drink that social commentators of the last thirty years have accused of hastening the breakdown and dysfunctionality of British society. To many academics and journalists, the teenage culture of these years was only tangentially related to the so-called phenomenon 'Cool Britannia' of the years following Tony Blair's New Labour landslide election victory of 1997. In hindsight, what evolved at this time was a morally compromised Britain in which style and marketing triumphed over content and value, and commercialism increasingly won out over professed principle.

The disheartening trajectory of Blair's Britain was neatly reflected in the huge success of WKD, the Torquay 'alcopop' that not only helped to create a whole new bargain-basement drinks sector in the UK but which had, by 2006, become the best-selling beverage of its kind across the nation.[59]

An 'alcopop' was exactly what its name suggested: a brightly coloured and tooth-wrenchingly sweet fizzy drink. It looked innocuous, but it wasn't, since it was stealthily fortified by a major dose of alcohol – usually that relatively tasteless spirit, vodka. In the rest of the world 'alcopops' had generally been categorised using a far more sophisticated and adult-oriented designation; in the US, for example, they were referred to as 'coolers' or 'spirit coolers'. The semi-comical, *Carry On*, end-of-the-pier British name 'alcopop', however, instantly conjured a picture of giggling teen drinkers at the bus stop. Which was exactly who its key audience was, whatever the drink's manufacturers may have professed. It was in truth a cynical vodka vehicle that was unambiguously aimed at, let's face it, the younger and less affluent drinker.

Did WKD create a generation of alcoholic teenagers and fuel the descent of what David Cameron in 2010 memorably called 'Broken Britain'? Or was it all a storm in a plastic bottle? Given that, at the time of writing, the latest addition to the WKD stable is a non-alcoholic variety, the theory that the effect of alcopops was a tad exaggerated sounds more plausible.

WKD – generally pronounced 'wicked' – was predictably reviled by industry critics on its launch in 1996. But in the ensuing years it proved a massive hit both with the 18–25 audience at which it was ostensibly targeted and with under-18s, too – an audience who should obviously not have been consuming alcohol at all. WKD was brightly coloured, it was fizzy, it was jarringly sweet: what was not to like for the average teenager? Its kick came from its hidden alcohol. Initially freighted with a hefty alcohol content of 5.5 per cent ABV, derived partly from 'triple-distilled' vodka, partly from the mysterious 'alternative alcohol base' (which didn't mean wine, either), WKD's strength was gradually reduced in stages to the 4 per cent

ABV it has been since 2022, not so much to placate its critics as to minimise the tax burden on its manufacturers.

–

Interestingly, the UK's first home-grown alcopop did not originate with any of the established drinks giants. Most of these quailed before the moral implications of an alcoholic drink aimed squarely if clandestinely at the under-age market – although they were happy to jump on the alcopop bandwagon once WKD had proved a success. Instead, WKD was invented and first produced in downbeat Torquay by a new company that few in the drinks trade had heard of: Beverage Brands. And behind Beverage Brands was its outspoken and charismatic founder, Joe Woods.

Joseph Gerard Woods was born in Greenock, Scotland, but moved to Torquay when he was eleven years old. As a young businessman he was always looking to break into the drinks trade by offering something different. In 1985 he started a Guernsey-based company producing Baileys-type concoctions made with cream from the famous Guernsey cows, which he marketed under the unwieldy name of The Original Tipples Channel Island Cream Liqueurs. These were sold both in glass bottles and in small plastic pots as coffee additives. Woods then turned to Scottish whisky giant William Grant to help him exploit this market, but soon, in 1991, found himself being strongarmed out of his own company by his new masters. He later admitted to journalist Tim Palmer that 'I thought I had joined with a company with huge resources, distribution and technical expertise, but I found it restricted rather than helped our development.' Ironically, Grants turfed Woods out, only to then lose interest in the product altogether.

Shaking off this disillusionment, Woods now began searching for gaps in other drinks sectors. Having analysed the phenomenal growth of the US soda industry, and prevented by his agreement with Grants from any involvement in alcoholic products for five years, he started exploring the burgeoning market for fruit-flavoured spring waters – or 'new age beverages', as they were now being popularly tagged. In 1992 Woods founded a new company in Torquay, the aforementioned Beverage Brands, and launched a range of four sparkling, flavoured spring waters under the brand name Caledonian Clear (so called because they were bottled at a plant in Cumnock in Ayrshire). Success soon followed, as the Zenith Guide to UK Adult Soft Drinks gave Caledonian Clear the award for 'Most Stylish Newcomer'. Yet the market was already populated with far too many competitors for Woods' small, Torquay-based operation to make much of an impact. Woods instead looked about for a UK market in which he could be a big player; and in 1996 he found it. That year Beverage Brands unveiled a far more blatantly controversial and unapologetically downmarket brand than Caledonian Clear: WKD Original Vodka.

With WKD, Joe Woods quickly realised that he had finally struck gold. In order to give his small, Torquay-based outfit more weight in the marketplace, he again sold a majority share in his company to a well-connected outside interest. But this time he didn't make the same mistake that he had with William Grant. Instead of selecting a far bigger business partner, Woods picked the SHS Group, a little-known firelighter-to-cordials manufacturer whose headquarters was incongruously perched at the edge of Belfast Airport. SHS, then best known for its Shloer brand, the long-established, grape juice-based alternative to table wine, was hardly Pernod Ricard or Diageo – or even William Grant. But Woods realised that, with SHS as Beverage Brands' protection, he could now be a bigger fish in a smaller pond while he and his WKD brand were, at the same time, safe from corporate predators. Most importantly, Woods could rely on the marketing and distribution muscle of SHS to prise the brand into both the on and off trades, to pubs and supermarkets. He even felt secure enough to agree to shut the Beverage Brands operation in his home town of Torquay in 2011, although he remained a prominent figure in the Torbay sailing and philanthropic worlds until his untimely death, aged only sixty, in 2015.

–

Right from the start, WKD was unambiguously aimed at the youth market – whereas the existing market leader, Bacardi Breezer, launched in 1993, was pitched at a more urbane adult audience. WKD's first marketing campaign posed the question, 'Have you got a WKD side?' And yes, they had. The original Blue version – supposedly a 'mixed fruit' flavour, whatever that meant, and coloured a luminous shade of electric-blue rarely found in nature – was soon supplemented by a dazzlingly orange 'Iron Brew' flavour created specifically for the Scottish market as an alcoholic version of Cumbernauld-based A. G. Barr's venerable soda Irn-Bru, which had first been made way back in 1901.[60]

As Beverage Brands expanded the WKD range, they still ensured that the drinks continued to be perceived as subversive and iconoclastic. The subliminal message of this ad jars somewhat with the obligatory government warning at bottom right.

Additions to the WKD lineup followed thick and fast after 1996. In 2021 a raspberry-flavour Pink Gin variant was introduced. In 2022 came Berry Blast; in 2023 Orange and Passionfruit; and in 2024 a lurid purple, grape-tasting 'Love Island' variant hit the shelves.

WKD's promotion took its cue from these adolescent-friendly flavours. Unlike its more grown-up and internationally focused ready-to-drink rivals such as Diageo's Smirnoff Ice and Bacardi Breezer (relaunched in the UK in 2019 without either its Bacardi name or the distinctive Bacardi bat logo), WKD Original Vodka's extensive advertising and promotional campaigns were targeted at a down-to-earth, working-class and juvenile market. The drink was advertised at football clubs, distributed at student bars and sold at nightclubs. The common millennial terms 'lad' and 'laddish' – along with their feminine counterpart, the noun 'ladette'[61] ('a young woman who behaves in a noisy way, uses rude language, and drinks a lot of alcohol') – seemed an ideal fit for WKD's marketing strategy, which boldly went where no one had gone before. The defiantly downmarket drink was appropriately paired as the sponsor of the 'WKD Shed Sports Show', which shared its billing on the short-lived and brazenly laddish channel Nuts TV with such televisual delights as 'Rude News' and 'Overexposed', a guide to glamour shoots. WKD even sponsored the same station's 'WKD Nuts Football Awards' before the channel folded in January 2009 after only twenty-eight months on air. SHS's sponsorship money then moved to the Professional Darts Corporation's World Matchplay, Grand Slam of Darts and the World Darts Championships. The image that WKD Vodka liked to project through such sponsorship was about as far from the aspirational, high-end vodkas promoted by Bacardi, Diageo and the like as you could get. As SHS's marketing department proudly proclaimed of their darts tie-ins:

> *The three PDC tournaments run across 38 days and will be screened live on Sky Sports. WKD logos will appear on players' shirts and on venue branding. Sampling activity and on-site promotions will also run at the tournaments. In the lead up to each tournament, tickets to sold-out sessions will be offered as prizes via social networking sites. Online promotions will also give consumers the*

chance to win darts shirts signed by players, and other darts-related merchandise. Away from the tournaments, WKD will be the subject of darts-themed activities in selected on-trade outlets around the UK.

This press release revealed the hidden secret of WKD's success. Unlike the big spirit, wine and beer brands, which spent hundreds of thousands of pounds on television and poster advertising, SHS targeted its young market directly through social media and, physically, at places where young people were likely to gather. Social media not only enabled the marketing department to reach the youth market quickly and efficiently; they also didn't have to spend much, as social media marketing was notoriously cheap. As a result, SHS did not need a Diageo-sized marketing war-chest to achieve its aim of sector domination. Teenagers and students could be targeted rapidly and frequently through a medium that they regarded as their own, and which they believed they could control. 'Students are a really important audience for WKD,' admitted SHS's marketing director Amanda Grabham in 2011, announcing that the brand's planned social media campaign would be 'in collaboration with students across the UK' and would, as a result, 'ensure WKD is front of mind this summer.' That's *in collaboration with*, not *targeted at*. WKD and its cunning parent were helping to expand the boundaries of social media marketing with only a modest financial outlay.

The match made in heaven arrived in 2024, when SHS signed an agreement by which its WKD brand would become the 'official alcohol partner' of the ITV2 reality television series *Love Island*. This iconic show was the most watched programme of the day by 18–35s – and of course was highly popular with under-18s, too. It attracted what was, in 2024 terms, an enviable average audience – 5.9 million. WKD's Pink variety was pushed to the front of the marketing stage – from where, said SHS's head of brand marketing, Alison Gray, 'in the "always on" world of young adults, linking with the show gives WKD the opportunity to drive relevant messaging to our target audience 24/7.' Gray's colleague Marcus Freer even dragged his family into it: 'I knew I'd got it right when we told our 18-year-old daughter a couple of weeks ago and she was so excited. She just thought it was great.' The SHS press release explained that '[Freer's] daughter in many ways embodies the *Love Island* audience, which is perceived as primarily female. But Freer is adamant this doesn't represent a move away from the laddish marketing that has characterised its "winning formula".'

WKD's highly successful exploitation of the barely legal teen market inevitably attracted heavy criticism. In 2016 Emily Robinson, deputy chief executive of the charity Alcohol Concern (now Alcohol Change UK), said what everyone else was thinking but were too afraid to say:

> *We think that the creation of alcopops was a pretty cynical attempt to recruit young drinkers who don't naturally like the taste of alcohol by tempting them with flavours more likely to be found in soft drinks. Marketing and branding these drinks in a style that appealed to young people was key to the success.*

During the early years of the alcopop revolution some supermarkets, notably the Co-op and the frozen-food retail chain Iceland, initially withdrew alcopops from their shelves – though within a year or two most had put them back. In the autumn of 1996 John Major's chancellor of the exchequer, Kenneth Clarke, increased the tax on alcopops by a whopping 40 per cent in an attempt to increase their price beyond the reach of teenage purses. (The attempt failed.) At the same time, the Portman Group, the 'drink responsibly' watchdog and regulator formed and funded by the alcohol producers themselves, issued its first code of practice in response to the launch of WKD.

None of these actions, though, seemed to stem the alcopop tide. In 2002, a report from Tony Blair's shiny new Prime Minister's Strategy Unit found that the consumption of alcohol by 11- to 15-year-olds had risen by 63 per cent since 1992, much of which was fuelled by the new fad for alcopops. As journalist Jonathan Duffy subsequently noted in the online *BBC News Magazine* of 9 November 2005:

> *Alcopops were widely seen as a gateway drink, priming teenage taste buds, more normally accustomed to sweet fizzy drinks, for something with a boozy kick. And what a kick – typically, they boasted alcohol levels of 5%, similar to a premium lager, and stronger than the ciders and beers that mischievous teenagers had traditionally turned to when looking to spice up an evening.*

As national concern about under-age drinking and associated anti-social behaviour rose, pressure was put on the manufacturers to dilute both the drinks and their heavily promoted, teen-friendly allure. At Beverage Brands, Joe Woods thought it was better to be seen to help the regulators rather than simply deny what was happening, and helped the Portman Group to craft their alcopop-aware code of practice. This did not, however, prevent the Advertising Standards Authority from subsequently banning some of WKD's television ads as 'advertising likely to appeal to under-18s'.

Looking back in 2016 on the first twenty-odd years of alcopops in the UK, however, Emily Robinson believed that, even with the admirable self-regulation advocated and established by the Portman Group and others, the damage to British society by targeting ready-to-drink alcoholic products at teens had already been done:

> *We're seeing the effects of the alcopops culture now among people in their 30s and 40s – those from the 'alcopops generation'. Admissions to hospital for alcoholic liver disease for the under-30s has increased by 112% over the past 10 years. We're seeing people dying from liver disease now in their twenties and thirties, which used to be completely unheard of.*

–

The social challenge became even more acute with SHS's 2022 launch of WKD varieties that combined the appeal of alcopops with the lure of caffeine-rich energy drinks, whose UK and global sales were now riding high. As the demand for the alcopops of the 1990s faded, SHS astutely sought to appropriate the opportunity presented by an adjacent market sector in order to return their brand to the centre of the stage. 'WKD X', as it was called, came in two 'flavours': Blue and Gold (these were *flavours*?). But the kicker – literally and metaphorically – was X's thumping caffeine content, at 30mg of caffeine per 10cl. As a contrast, the proportion of caffeine in Buckfast Wine, an unmistakeably adult beverage, was not much more, at 37.5 per cent.[62] And that caffeine content was far more than in the established 'energy drink' market leader, the Austrian phenomenon that was Red Bull. At the same time, the alcohol content of WKD X was racked up to a lofty 7 per cent, higher than nearly all standard beers and lagers. This hopped-up WKD, said its manufacturers, would be 'perfectly placed to bring a nationally recognised brand to the fledgling enhanced RTD category' – if 'enhanced' meant dizzyingly high levels of caffeine and alcohol. WKD X was a high-octane Red Bull, a starter-pack Bucky Wine for the young. SHS's marketeers insisted that 'Consumers are already well versed in mixing alcoholic drinks with energy drinks' – invoking visions of fourteen-year-olds pouring vodka into their cans of Red Bull on the park bench – and that 'what WKD X delivers is the convenience of a pre-mixed format from a respected brand that consumers know and love.'

The trade's media and consumer watchdogs were not so sure. Under predictable headlines along the lines of 'Something wicked this way comes',[63] the food and drink press questioned the decision to make WKD X so formidably strong, given that the contemporary drinks trend was for *less* alcoholic content. Commentators also wondered if the creation of a booze-boosted 'enhanced RTD' sector might not reawaken popular fears of an epidemic of out-of-control teenagers, anti-social behaviour and petty crime. Already, similarly packaged brands such as Phusion Projects of Chicago's 'Four Loko' and the St Helier Beverage Company's 'Dragon Soop', the latter first launched in Scotland with a more-than-robust

ABV of 7.5 per cent, had been accused of acting irresponsibly and had been forced – or, in the UK, politely encouraged – to moderate their formulae. In the US, the Federal Trade Commission's consumer protection director David Vladeck declared on record that 'there is good reason to believe that these caffeinated alcohol drinks pose significant risks to consumer health and safety.' He also observed that 'The very high levels of caffeine in energy drinks work against the drowsiness effects of alcohol in what researchers describe as "wide awake drunk" [and that] consumers might mistakenly assume that these beverages are safe because they are widely sold.' However, as British journalist Jimmy Nicholls remarked, the equivalent authorities in the UK were reluctant to act in a similar vein.

A 2012 report by the Committee on Toxicity, which advised the Food Standards Agency, was inconclusive on the effects of mixing caffeine and alcohol. While declaring that the existing evidence did not 'support a harmful toxicological or behavioural interaction between caffeine and alcohol', it merely concluded that there was a 'substantial uncertainty' around the issue. Instead, it was left to independent charitable watchdogs to warn consumers about the dangers inherent in unexpectedly alcoholic 'enhanced RTDs'. In its guidance, the Drinkaware Trust noted that 'Energy drinks can mask the sedative effects of alcohol, making people less aware of how much they've had to drink.' Similarly, the Portman Group reminded both manufacturers and drinkers that 'Alcohol is a depressant, and it is therefore irresponsible and misleading to market an alcoholic drink in a way which implies it will make the consumer feel more energetic, even if the stimulation effect is attributed to the energy component.'

Dame Jackie Baillie, Scottish Labour MSP for Dumbarton since 1999, campaigned long and hard for a caffeine limit on alcoholic drinks of 15mg per 100ml – half the amount present in WKD X, and under half of that in Buckfast Wine. SHS was quick to respond to such implied criticism, asserting that 'WKD X packaging prominently displays that the product contains both alcohol and caffeine' and that, being sold only in single 500ml cans, it was not suitable for session drinking. However, British journalist Jimmy Nicholls found many independent voices who found this line of defence somewhat disingenuous. Amongst his more cynical interviewees was Matt Rees of UK marketing agency Fiora, who agreed that the packaging of caffeinated alcohol in a manner designed to appeal to the young 'just doesn't sound very healthy, and it doesn't sound very safe' and, moreover, went 'against the grain of both regulatory and media attitude towards the food and drink industry'. Of course, Rees added, that could be exactly what SHS were after: 'I can see the combination of alcohol and caffeine acquiring a notoriety that attracts the typical WKD consumer to knock it back in quantities.'

Increasingly, those who knocked WKD back in quantities were women. The 2002 Prime Minister's Strategy Unit report cited recent research by the Home Office that had found that, of fourteen-year-old girls who were experienced drinkers, over 75 per cent regularly drank alcopops. Andrew McNeil of the Institute of Alcohol Studieswent further, declaring that 'Alcopops have clearly been influential in switching women on to alcohol.'

Alcopops in general, and WKD in particular, certainly helped to generate one of the most memorable and pejorative social caricatures of the 1990s, one that continued to flourish throughout the alcopop-fuelled Blair years. The stereotypical Essex Girl was neatly defined in Maria Ferguson's 2019 play of the same name, in which Maria herself played the title role. Not only was WKD specifically mentioned in the play's prologue; a full bottle of WKD Blue was also specified as one of the key stage props. WKD was now a cultural icon.

In 2001, at the summit of the Blair's Britain, before the Iraq War took the shine off Tony Blair's suit, Germaine Greer identified the typical Essex Girl as someone who

> *is tough, loud, vulgar and unashamed. Her hair is badly dyed not because she can't afford a hairdresser, but because she wants it to look brassy... Nobody laughs harder at an Essex girl joke than she does: she is not ashamed to admit what she puts behind her ears to make her more attractive is her ankles. She is anarchy on stilts; when she and her mates descend upon Southend for a rave, even the bouncers grow pale.*

By 2007 even America's *Time* magazine had heard of Essex Girl, 'a lady from London's eastern suburbs who dresses in white strappy sandals and suntan oil, streaks her hair blond, has a command of Spanish that runs only to the word Ibiza, and perfects an air of tarty prettiness.' Three years later the distasteful cliché was celebrated on prime-time television by the launch of the Brentwood-based reality show *The Only Way is Essex* – swiftly abbreviated in popular culture to its catchy acronym *TOWIE*. Once *TOWIE* had established itself as a ratings success (surviving the 'utter car crash' of the one live episode of December 2012) and its runtime had been extended, SHS grabbed the opportunity to embrace its archetypal audience and duly sponsored the 2014 series. In stating the obvious, that *TOWIE* was 'a really important programme' for its young consumers, SHS's marketeers were implicitly recognising WKD's critical contribution towards creating the enduring stereotype of the Essex Girl.

Somewhat inevitably, the media's eager promotion of the much-parodied Essex Girl provoked a strong backlash. Academic consultant Dr Terri Simpkin identified gender discrimination in the media caricature, 'because so-called Essex girls weren't wilting wallflowers – they were more overt as sexual beings, they took control of their own sexuality', while the Essex Women's Advisory Group (EWAG) was set up as a charitable foundation to 'challenge negative stereotypes by promoting the confidence and achievements of Essex women and girls' – although this did not stop them from issuing a book called *Essex Limericks* in 2010, 'a celebration of Essex Girls and some of the lovely-named places where we live.' As celebrated author and chancellor of Essex University Sarah Perry wrote in 2023, 'The Essex girl has become a useful repository for a score of social anxieties: an irredeemably vulgar, plump, sexually threatening, feckless and indolent woman, an affront to morality, and a threat to the values of sobriety, industry and obedience that prop up the ruling class.'

Its close association with so-called Essex Girls has, though, hardly harmed WKD. Indeed, the drink, so often forecast as on its way out by trade 'experts', has over the last twenty years made more comebacks than Frank Sinatra. In 2021, at the time of the brand's 25th anniversary, SHS's Marcus Freer told *The Grocer* that WKD had been 'written off so many times but keeps coming back.' Indeed, as early as 2005 WKD and its alcopop rivals were being repeatedly dismissed in the drinks trade as yesterday's trend. A spokesman for market researchers Mintel confidently claimed that 'The target audience is incredibly fickle... The problem with a category like this that's so fashionable is that new drinkers will say, "that's what adults are drinking. I want something else"'.

Laddishness was over, declared the trade media, hopefully, and the Essex Girl and her trademark accessory WKD Blue were yesterday's news. Moderate, responsible consumption was in, and binge drinking was out. But all of these predictions proved to be horribly wrong. What the nation's new prime minister, David Cameron,[64] had in 2011 christened 'Broken Britain', a land characterised by 'irresponsibility, selfishness, behaving as if your choices have no consequences, children without fathers, schools without discipline, reward without effort, crime without punishment, rights without responsibilities', was still very much with us. WKD X, *TOWIE*, *Love Island* and Essex Girl have not gone away, and today still remain prominent and popular props of today's fractured society.

-

During the years after the 1996 launch, WKD had stayed ahead of the game by refining and adapting its offer to changing trends and tastes. Neither Beverage Brands nor its parent, SHS, possessed deep enough pockets to achieve what Bacardi had managed with WKD's upmarket rival Breezer – namely, simply take the product off the shelves, reformulate and repackage it, and then thrust it at a changing market through a well-funded relaunch four years later. SHS had to bob and weave as the UK market shifted; its constant stream of innovations, some of which were accused of being morally questionable and all of which cynically exploited the predilections of the young, helped it to survive the lean years. As SHS's Marcus Freer admitted, 'We've stayed relevant by listening and keeping up with the times and recognising what 18- to 24-year-olds do, which does change.'

The WKD brand, along with the whole alcopop sector, did incredibly well during the Covid pandemic: its appeal to housebound teenagers enabled its sales to grow an astonishing 37.9 per cent in 2020, to take its annual earnings to a whopping £42 million and its annual profits to an impressive £11.7 million. Today the WKD brand has already colonised Canada, Hong Kong, Japan and the Irish Republic, and is even eyeing up the lucrative but highly competitive US market. Yesterday Torquay, today Tilbury… tomorrow Tacoma?

Chapter 11

LOST IN A FANTASY

THE MARGARITA

In 1983 legendary British rock band Status Quo's classic though much-derided hit single 'Marguerita Time'[65] reached number three in the UK charts. Its unexpected success not only demonstrated the British public's appetite for anodyne, inoffensive yet forgettable rock tunes; it also showed how the Anglo-American cocktail after which it was named had become a familiar trope of Thatcher's Britain – recognisable enough to help propel even the most lacklustre of pop singles to the heady heights of the top ten.

The Margarita's heritage was a complex – and, as we'll discover, often quite confusing – mixture of both British and American influences. As such, this most definitive of cocktails could be considered not just as a timely example of the constant cross-pollination of the two cultures; it could even, from the standpoint of 1983, be perceived as a resonant symbol of the much-vaunted 'Special Relationship' between the UK and the US – a relationship that had recently been comprehensively rejuvenated and invigorated. For by 1983 the British and American premiers, Ronald Reagan and Margaret Thatcher, had brought their two nations closer together than they had ever been since 1945.

On the global stage in the early 1980s, the principal aim of both Thatcher and Reagan was to work together to frustrate the ambitions of what the American president memorably labelled the 'evil empire' of Soviet Russia. The two premiers certainly had much in common. Both leaders were strong advocates of the unfettered market and of tax reductions; both aimed to dismantle a public sector built in the post-war decades through cross-party consensus; both believed that big government was a principal cause of their mutual economic problems, including high inflation and slow economic growth; and both Reagan and Thatcher had been politically embattled during the unsteady early years of their administrations. By 1983, however, after Reagan had gone out of his way to offer ostentatious support for Britain during the Falklands War of the previous year, both seemed to be settled in their posts and confident in the depth of their support.

The close political collaboration between the British and American administrations of the 1980s spilled over into the cultural world, too. British 'New Romantic' bands rode high in the US charts as British high streets were invaded by American-themed bars and American-styled cocktails – first and foremost of which was the Margarita. At the same time, however, the Britain of these years, thanks to its perceived willingness to follow an American lead, stood closer to nuclear Armageddon than at any time since the Cuban Missile Crisis of 1962. The Margarita was, in essence, the Reagan–Thatcher axis of the 1980s in a cocktail glass: sweet yet sour – and all too easily unbalanced. Yet by the time of Thatcher's second election victory in 1983, the tequila-based Margarita –

strong, classless and delicious – had been enthusiastically adopted by the very same young British men and women whose changing political tastes were to help Margaret Thatcher and her Conservative Party to successive electoral majorities as the decade progressed.

The Margarita cocktail's glamorous Mexican-American appeal, together with its perfect combination of relatively exotic ingredients – none of which could be found growing in the windswept British Isles – brought a touch of transatlantic sun and Hollywood glitz to even the most cheerless British high street. Unlike many other iconic drinks of the era, however, the Margarita's popularity has endured beyond the Thatcher years. The famous cocktail survived the fall of Margaret Thatcher herself in 1990 and the subsequent erosion of the so-called 'Special Relationship' during John Major's seven-year premiership. While other, faddish cocktails fell by the wayside, the Margarita survived long enough to become a bar-counter staple during the 'cocktail renaissance' of the early years of the twenty-first century.

Perhaps not uncoincidentally, the revival of the Margarita in the early years of the new century concurred with (or possibly was a sort of by-product of) another Anglo-American political rapprochement. UK prime minister Tony Blair's complicity in the American-led invasion of Iraq in 2003, which again risked Britain being seen as a willing poodle to the mighty US superpower, came just as the hand-made Margarita was reclaiming its stylish niche on cocktail bar menus. While Blair's wartime collaboration with the Americans, which many saw as both unnecessary and unsanctioned, ultimately caused long-lasting damage to his public reputation, the

Margarita remains a cocktail favourite right across the nation.

Francis Rossi, who had been one of the two founders of Status Quo back in 1962, was a huge fan of the Margarita cocktail. Hence the 1983 song, which he co-wrote with fellow band member Bernie Frost. Rossi later recalled to music journalist Dave Ling that 'I'd never been a drinker until then, but they were delicious and really got you pissed. I used to order them six at a time. For a while I got out of control on tequila.' The embarrassingly lacklustre lyrics they penned for 'Marguerita Time', though, hardly suggested that the drink had sparked any inspirational light-bulb moments for Rossi or Ling. Rather, they suggested that the pair had imbibed one too many already: '*You and me a mystery, Lost in a dream. Lost in a fantasy.*'

Rossi's enthusiasm for the cocktail was to have serious repercussions for the future of Status Quo, however. His fellow band founder, bassist Alan Lancaster, couldn't stand the song, believing it to be trite and over-Americanised. He refused to appear on BBC TV's *Top of the Pops*, or indeed anywhere else, to perform it publicly. Even though the distinctly middle-of-the-road song became one of the band's greatest hits, and was the first of their tracks to be playlisted by both BBC Radio 1 and Radio 2, 'Marguerita Time' divided not only Status Quo's audiences but also the band itself. Lancaster left the group in a huff after they continued to argue about the song; as a direct consequence, the band split up in 1984, just a year after 'Marguerita Time' had been issued. Rossi re-formed Status Quo in a wholly different guise the following year, but still remembers that

> *A lot of our fans absolutely hated 'Marguerita Time'. The guy that drives us around these days keeps on at me for us to put it back into the set. He's got no fucking chance... [but] our hard-core fans were up in arms... Personally, I still love 'Marguerita Time', but finding a balance is hard. Whatever we do, we seem to ostracise one side or the other.*

–

The Margarita cocktail itself seemed an unlikely hit for an innately conservative audience of British drinkers barely aware, in 1983 at least, of the provenance of the drink's principal spirit. Tequila is distinct from all other types of mezcal – that is, spirits made from the agave succulent – as it can only be made from the superior blue agave, also known as the blue Weber agave and whose Latin name is, appropriately *Agave tequilana*.

Yet very few Britons of the 1980s could tell you that tequila was distilled from the blue agave plant, nor that Tequila was the name of the central Mexican town (and future UNESCO World Heritage Site) around which that particular species of plant grew.

Thatcher's Britain, though, knew what a 'cocktail' was, since the mixed-drink sector was enjoying its biggest resurgence since the 1930s. Not many, however, could confidently state when or where the term 'cocktail' had originated, nor even if it was invented in Britain or America. The debate on how the term 'cocktail' arose has raged for decades. Now, though, we do seem to have a definitive answer.

Everyone agrees, at least, that the word 'cocktail' is many centuries old. One etymological school of thought, recently endorsed by University of Minnesota linguist Professor Anatoly Liberman, claims it originated from the habit of docking the tails of horses that were not purebred. The docking of horses' tails, which the theory suggests was designed to prevent the tail interfering with the harness gear, was a cruel, painful and now thankfully abandoned practice that involved removing part of the poor animal's tailbone. This resulted in short, neat, perky tails: 'cocktailed' horses, if you like. And, as the docked tail signified that the horse was not purebred, so was the 'cocktail' drink christened: a mixture of flavours that did not come from one, purebred single origin.

However, the problem with this theory is that it is based on a fallacy. Docking wasn't just applied to the tails of everyday working horses: during the eighteenth and early nineteenth centuries, *all* horses' tails were docked, including those of thoroughbred racehorses. The aim of docking was merely to produce a neat, uniform tail, not to designate the horse's function or its purebred status.

There are, though, countless other theories about where the term 'cocktail' might have originated. One story tells how an ancient Aztec king ordered his daughter, one Princess Xochitl, to serve a mixed drink to a guest, and her name subsequently inspired the generic term for this sort of concoction. Alternatively, the 'cocktail' was named directly after the Aztec goddess Xochiquetzal (and try saying that name after three Margaritas). Some claim that it derived from the seventeenth-century British drink 'cock ale', which the *Oxford English Dictionary* enticingly defines as 'ale mixed with the jelly or minced meat of a boiled cock, besides other ingredients.' (My guess is that this is one historic recipe that won't be revived any time soon.) Others have suggested that the term arose in New Orleans, where pharmacist Antoine Peychaud was known to serve his proprietary bitters (still available today, and distinguished by its pronounced aniseed flavour) mixed with brandy in an egg cup, which in French was called a 'coquetier'.

An alternative hypothesis involves an oft-told story about a late-eighteenth-century innkeeper in Yorktown, Virginia, one Betsy or Betty Flanagan. In 1779, at the height of the American Revolution, Betsy allegedly offered the American officers who were taking time off from the front at her tavern a dinner of chicken, made from fowl she had stolen from her loyalist neighbours, followed by a traditional drink called a 'bracer', a brandy bolstered by bitters and an egg white. Betsy audaciously served these drinks in glasses decorated by tail-feathers plucked from the abducted hens. And these impressively festooned libations were, of course, acclaimed by her military clientele as 'cocktails'.

There is also a rather less flamboyant story that suggests that 'cocktail' was simply derived from the French word *coquetel*, meaning a mixture. The problem is, the French term *coquetel* most likely came from the English term 'cocktail', and not the other way round. So we are back to square one.

Cocktail historian David Wondrich, though, seems to have finally found the most credible answer. He has discovered that the first published citation of the word 'cocktail' occurred in London's *Morning Post and Gazetteer* of 20 March 1798, in a verse that runs as follows:

Mr Pitt,

two petit vers of 'L'huile de Venus'
Ditto, one of 'perfeit amour'
Ditto, 'cock-tail' (vulgarly called ginger)

Wondrich suggests that 'cocktail' was employed here as a synonym for 'gingering', as in 'ginger up': a practice by which an old horse would be invigorated by means of a ginger suppository that would cause it to hold (or cock) its tail erect. The *Morning Post*'s verse was most likely a none-too-subtle dig at the current prime minister, William Pitt, who was widely rumoured to be wholly uninterested in women – and thus was clearly in need of 'gingering up.' (In truth, it seems probable that the unfathomable Mr Pitt was actually homosexual.)

Wondrich also cites a Suffolk satire of roughly the same time, published in 1790, which alleged that a local clergyman 'hath been guilty of monopolizing all the ginger and pepper in the neighbourhood, to make the asses who vote for Sir Gerard Vanneck cock their tails' at the forthcoming election for the Suffolk rotten borough of Dunwich. It failed to work, though: Vanneck actually lost his supposedly safe seat and died the following year.

The word 'cocktail' was, then, apparently of British and not American origin, despite what many since have believed – including none other than British author Charles Dickens, who first experienced cocktails in the American bars he visited during his 1842 tour. Subsequently, though, the term was heartily adopted by Americans. Thus was the 'Special Relationship' forged in the bars of both nations a century before Churchill actually invented that particular phrase during his celebrated speech of 5 March 1946 at Fulton, Missouri.

Subsequent printed references to the word 'cocktail' in American publications, Wondrich has observed, seem to vindicate the 'gingering' theory. In 1803 the American periodical *The Farmer's Cabinet* described a cocktail as a pick-me-up – '11. [a.m.] Drank a glass of cocktail – excellent for the head… Call'd at the Doct's. found Burnham – he looked very wise – drank another glass of cocktail' – while three years later the term was defined by the *Balance and Columbian Repository* as a 'stimulating liquor' comprising a mixture of spirits, sugar, water and alcoholic bitters, the latter generally regarded, then as now, as a *digestif.* Wondrich concludes that 'this suggests that a cocktail was initially considered a medicinal drink, which accords with the use of bitters'. It also seems to have been a morning libation – a drinking tradition revived in both Britain and the US in the unsettled years between the two world wars.

The tradition of mixing bitters – made from the concentrated extract of roots, barks and peels steeped in alcohol – with wine or spirits dates back, Wondrich has found, at least to the late seventeenth century, when Southwark apothecary Richard Stoughton recommended that his proprietary brand of Stoughton's Bitters should be taken in brandy or wine as a hangover cure. The cocktail historian also observes that, in 1783,

> *British officers were meeting with George Washington and his staff to arrange the British surrender of New York, "Washington pulled out his watch," as the Loyalist William Smith recorded in his diary, "and observing that it was near Dinner Time, offered Wine and Bitters."'*

'Was the Father of His Country', Wondrich mused, 'the host of the first cocktail hour on record?' Interestingly, legendary American bartender Jerry Thomas, a man since hailed as 'The Father of American Mixology', defined cocktails in his groundbreaking book of 1862, *How to Mix Drinks; or, The Bon Vivant's Companion*, as blended beverages that included these stomach-settling bitters, as opposed to other mixed drinks that we would also call cocktails today, such as punches and cobblers.

-

The Margarita has a similarly murky and confused Anglo-American provenance. Claims for its origin also come from both sides of the pond. And there are certainly a lot of them.

The invention of a cocktail comprising three parts tequila to one part triple sec, a sweet, orange-flavoured liqueur from France, and one part (or a smaller measure) of lime juice has been attributed to a colourful and bewilderingly extensive cast of mid-century characters. This includes one Berta Estrada, who purportedly created the drink in 1930 at her eponymous bar in Taxco, Mexico; Danny Negrete, a bartender at the Garci Crespo Spa in the Mexican city of Tehuacán, who in 1936 crafted the cocktail as a wedding gift for his prospective sister-in-law, Margarita; John Durlesser of McHenry's Tail o' the Cock restaurant in Los Angeles, who allegedly invented the Margarita in 1937; William Tarling, who included a recipe for a Margarita in his *Café Royal Cocktail Book*, published by the United Kingdom Bartenders Guild in 1937; New York barman Charlie Connolly, who featured the cocktail in his 1939 book *The World Famous Cotton Club* (said to be the first publication to stipulate that the drink should be served in a glass rimmed with salt); Carlos Orozco, bartender at Hussong's in Ensenada in Mexico, who in 1941 reputedly named the new drink after Mexican-German patron Margarita Henkel Cesena, the daughter of a local rancher – or possibly even of the German ambassador to Mexico (although Hitler's ambassador in 1941 was one Heinrich Rüdt von Collenberg); Francisco 'Pancho' Morales, a bartender at Tommy's Place in Ciudad Juarez, Mexico, who in 1942 created the drink after an American customer asked for a 'magnolia' (a mix of gin, grenadine, lemon and cream… which is nothing like a Margarita); Carlos 'Danny' Herrera (this sagas is full of Dannys), who in 1938 (or was it 1947?) supposedly fashioned the cocktail at the Rancho La Gloria in Mexico's Rosarito Beach for a customer with a tequila allergy (a somewhat unlikely tale, given the Margarita's unavoidably high tequila content) – or, alternatively, for former Ziegfeld Follies showgirl Marjorie King, who was allergic to many spirits but not to tequila; Margarita Sames, a wealthy Dallas socialite who in 1948 allegedly created the drink at her Acapulco holiday home for her guests, who inevitably proceeded to name it after her; and Santos Cruz, a bartender at the Studio Lounge (or was it the Balinese Room?) in Galveston, Texas, who supposedly made the first Margarita for jazz singer Peggy (Margaret) Lee, again in 1948.

Confused? You will be. This is only a small selection of the disconcertingly wide range of creation myths that surround the Margarita. Yet they are all, to use a traditional academic phrase, fantastical bollocks. For the Margarita cocktail had already been included in Harry Craddock's *Savoy Cocktail Book* of 1930, a published volume that predates all of these fanciful anecdotes. Craddock's featured Margarita recipe[66] was a mixture of tequila (one and a half ounces), triple sec (half an ounce) and lemon or lime juice (one ounce). It even mentions the classic salt-rimmed glass.

Now, it is certainly possible that Craddock may have learned of the Margarita, or something like it, from his American experiences. Born in Gloucestershire, Harry moved to the US in 1897, when he was only twenty-one; he then worked in hotel bars in Cleveland and New York while also becoming an American citizen. With the advent of Prohibition in America in 1920, however, Craddock wisely returned to England. There he joined the American Bar at London's famous Savoy Hotel and authored the *Savoy Cocktail Book*, a collection of 750 cocktails that is still in print today.

But did Harry Craddock really discover the Margarita in America? His formidable cocktail encyclopedia also included recipes for what appears to have been the Margarita's ancestor: the 'Daisy'. The Daisy cocktail could be found on both sides of the Atlantic during the later nineteenth century: more often than not made with gin (Craddock's Gin Daisy was made from gin and lemon juice, with sugar and grenadine), but also available as a rum cocktail (the Craddock Rum Daisy included either maraschino or curaçao, an orange liqueur derived from triple sec), or even as a Whisky Daisy, the Daisy was a popular and versatile late-Victorian vehicle for spirits in both Britain and America that lasted into the 1930s. And as the Spanish for daisy is *margarita*, it seems likely that the tequila-based drink we now know by that name evolved from the 'tequila daisy'.

Wondrich has himself traced the Daisy cocktail back to Jerry Thomas's *Bartenders Guide* of 1876, which cites a brandy Daisy made from brandy, syrup, lemon juice and curaçao, served over ice and made into a long drink with a shot of soda water. Wondrich's speculation about the Daisy continues:

While its origin has not been definitively proven, a credible claim was advanced in 1883 that it was created ten years before at Fred Eberlin's popular bar, around the corner from the New York Stock Exchange, when one Billy Taylor imparted to bartender Frank Haas (1847–1924) the idea he had for a new drink… Haas's version, upon which he built a long career, was specifically a whisky drink, with lime juice, raspberry syrup, soda water, and at least one other ingredient, but the brandy version also enjoyed some popularity, while other sweeteners found in the drink's early years include yellow Chartreuse and orgeat.

Like most cocktails, the Daisy enjoyed a resurgence during the Prohibition era in America,[67] a trend that presumably in turn influenced the bartenders of 1920s Britain – hence the chain of daisies featured in Craddock's 1930 comprehensive guide. Wondrich even discovered a Tequila Daisy recipe of 1925, from the celebrated Turf Bar in Tijuana, Mexico. The story goes that the advertised tipple was a gin drink with lime, grenadine and soda water, but in his haste the bartender seized the wrong bottle and used tequila instead of gin. Yet another improbable tale… but at least we know that the Margarita's ancestor was alive and kicking in the mid-1920s.

–

Whatever its origin, the popularity of the Margarita cocktail soared in the US in the years after 1945, largely as a result of being energetically promoted by the best-selling brand of tequila in America, Jose Cuervo. (Today Jose Cuervo is still the market leader, accounting for a fifth of all global tequila sales. It is also, astonishingly, still an independent, family-run concern, having fended off Diageo's attempts to acquire it during 2011–12.) The imaginative advertising campaign that Jose Cuervo launched following the end of the Second World War tried to enhance the drink's visibility with the rather hesitant slogan 'Margarita: It's more than a girl's name.' What really helped tequila to take off in the US, though, was the firm's well-funded national advertising drive of 1956. Just two years later Danny Flores' catchy, bouncing ditty 'Tequila' was number one in the American pop charts. This ageless song has remained a party favourite on both sides of the Atlantic ever since.

During the 1960s, as Mexican restaurants multiplied across the US and as Victor 'Trader Vic' Bergeron started serving Margaritas in bulbous coupes across his 'Señor Pico' restaurant chain (which is still going strong today), the appeal of the Margarita soared. By the 1970s the Margarita craze had even reached Britain, too, just as the nation had completely forgotten that there had ever been a drink called the 'Daisy'. That troubled decade witnessed the appearance of the frozen Margarita, a variant of the original made by blending ice with lime juice and triple sec, or indeed whatever other fruit flavours you fancied. (Cocktail aficionados understandably deride this period of the drink's history as a time when the Margarita became little more than an alcoholic slushy.) While the frozen Margarita had proved plausibly popular in the sun-drenched American states of California, Arizona, Texas and Florida, it also came in handy during the UK's long, hot summer of 1976, when temperatures regularly topped 32 degrees[68] and the nation experienced its driest summer for two centuries – and its hottest for 350 years.

José Cuervo, a company which began making tequila (properly 'Vino Mezcal de Tequila') in 1795, almost singlehandedly created the demand for tequila, and for the Margarita, in the 1940s.

During the 1980s, however, the average drinking Briton turned increasingly to wines and lagers, and away from cocktails and other traditional aperitifs. Partly thanks to Status Quo's single, the Margarita, at least, remained in the public consciousness; yet many of its cocktail cousins fell into disuse, as pre-mixed concoctions that anyone could make replaced more complex, bartender-crafted creations. Few now remember the Blue Lagoon, the Fluffy Duck (an unlikely combination of advocaat, gin and triple sec), the Fuzzy Navel, the Harvey Wallbanger (created as part of a 1969 US marketing drive to shift more bottles of Galliano), the Freddy Fudpucker (a Harvey Wallbanger with tequila instead of vodka – and try saying that name after a few drinks), the Slippery Nipple (sambuca, Irish cream and grenadine: yuk) or the drink that only inebriated or shameless exhibitionists would dare to order: the Slow Comfortable Screw Against The Wall.

Of these 1980s favourites, only the Margarita, the Piña Colada and the Buck's Fizz have stood the test of time. Like the Margarita, the Piña Colada – a blend of rum, pineapple juice, coconut milk and lime juice – was also given a welcome impetus on both sides of the Atlantic by a chart-topping pop song of this period, in this case Rupert Holmes' singalong hit 'Escape (The Piña Colada Song)' of 1979. In contrast to Francis Rossi's enthusiasm for Margaritas, however, Holmes later insisted he had never touched even a glass of the eponymous cocktail. And even the Buck's Fizz has a pop song link. A combination of two parts champagne to one part orange juice said to have been invented at London's Buck's club in 1921, in 1980 the cocktail's name was famously borrowed by a British pop group that went on to win the Eurovision Song Contest with the song 'Making Your Mind Up' and its integral skirt-removal routine.

Only in the early years of the twenty-first century – a period of renewed Anglo-American amity, with British forces ostentatiously supporting the US invasion of Iraq in 2003 in search of those mythical weapons of mass destruction – did the cocktail, that evocative symbol of the cheery fusion of British and American cultural and drinking traditions, regain its former popularity. David Wondrich dates the advent of what he terms the 'cocktail renaissance' precisely to this time, suggesting sensibly that the phenomenon abruptly ended with the Covid pandemic of 2020. In the event, though, cocktail bars seem to be just as prevalent in Britain in the post-Covid era as they were before the spread of the virus.

–

Wondrich attributes the resurgence of the cocktail to the renewed interest in artisanal drinks, particularly to 'craft' beers, and to the exponential growth in Sir Tim Berners-Lee's World Wide Web, a resource that allowed anyone to look up the recipes for the sort of obscure cocktails previously only memorised by veteran bartenders. Without doubt, the so-called 'cocktail renaissance' certainly revitalised the spirits industry, both worldwide and in Britain. The new fashionability of cocktails such as the Margarita encouraged British shoppers of all backgrounds back to the spirits aisle, just when many of the shelves' pricier denizens were beginning to be dismissed as increasingly elitist or aimed at the older drinker. The result was a boom in the founding of British spirits distilleries, just in time to help beleaguered Britons weather the financial crisis of 2008 and the Cameron government's ill-advised austerity programme of 2010. The number of distilleries in the UK doubled between 2010 and 2016, with forty-nine new spirits companies being created in 2015 alone. In 2021 an astounding 110 were created – presumably as a result of the pandemic, as stay-at-home drinkers needed something strong and stimulating to get them through the lockdown. Nor did the expansion of the cottage British spirits industry ebb with the retreat of Covid: a further fifty British distilleries were opened during 2023, an 8.7 per cent increase on 2022.

Admittedly, locally made gins and vodkas were the principal British beneficiary of the renewed interest in the cocktail. By 2023, as small-scale craft gin-makers were establishing themselves in the most unlikely British locations, the CEO of the Wine and Spirit Trade Association exclaimed that this was 'a hugely exciting time for everyone involved in the UK gin industry'. However, the appeal of the Margarita made it an exciting time for tequila importers too. As the Margarita appeared on restaurant menus and pub drinks lists as well as on cocktail bar blackboards, tequila made significant inroads into the British supermarket and off-licence. In 2023 off-trade sales of tequila and sister-spirit mezcal grew 15 per cent, to £46.1 million; at the upmarket British supermarket chain Waitrose the increase was 18 per cent.

This upsurge in tequila sales, for which the Margarita is largely responsible, should not, however, be an excuse for too much merriment. Tequila sales in Britain still remain a small proportion of the whole £5.6 billion spirits market. To put tequila's British success in a broader context, in 2023 £870.4 million-worth of gin was sold, while UK sales of vodka earned almost £1.5 billion. As Nielsen analyst Andrew Eagle has commented, while 'tequila is of the few spirits to have achieved growth in the aftermath of lockdown, [its growth] comes from a very small base.'

There is, though, still much to be optimistic about. In a January 2024 interview with *The Grocer*'s drinks editor, James Beeson, Eagle observed that Waitrose had recently increased the presence of tequila and mezcal on its shelves by over 10 per cent, while Waitrose spirits buyer John Vine told Beeson that expanding its tequila range was a 'key focus' of Waitrose's recent refresh of its spirits portfolio – even though tequila and mezcal still only represented 5.3 per cent of all of the spirits on Waitrose's shelves. At the same time, drinks giant Pernod Ricard declared that it was prepared to devote 'huge financial resources' towards promoting tequila in the UK.

To create a buzz around tequila and the Margarita – drinks that immediately evoke breathtakingly empty, cactus-strewn landscapes bathed in sunshine – for potential customers living in congested, grey and rain-soaked Britain has taken some doing. To build awareness of their products, tequila producers have resorted to a time-worn ploy: the endorsement of celebrity brand ambassadors. Thus in June 2017 British drinks conglomerate Diageo acquired George Clooney's premium tequila, Casamigos, while eight years later Dwayne 'The Rock' Johnson's tequila brand, Teremana, was widely available across Britain, having been introduced into 550 Tesco stores.

The energetic promotion of tequila in these years even reached the heights of the British royal family. After dropping out of university and working as a barman and a nightclub manager, young Jack Brooksbank was hired as a brand ambassador by Clooney's Casamigos operation. While working in that capacity he started dating a young woman who just happened to be the Duke of York's younger daughter, Princess Eugenie, who is currently twelfth in line for the throne. Eight years later the couple were married at the royal venue of St George's Chapel in Windsor Castle and moved into a royal residence in Kensington Palace. Nevertheless, the outrageously satirical television sitcom *The Windsors* never let its audience forget the groom's past tequila connections: during series three, Tom Stourton's Jack Brooksbank character constantly explodes onto the screen swathed in bandoliers fitted with tequila bottles. At the time of writing, and despite his marriage into the House of Windsor, Brooksbank has yet to be elevated to the peerage.

Notwithstanding the valiant efforts of Jack Brooksbank, George Clooney, Dwayne Johnson and their fellow promoters, today the majority of British drinkers have yet to take to tequila as a neat drink, either as a bar-room shot or as an evening tipple. Instead, tequila's growing presence in the mass UK market is almost entirely due to its status as the principal ingredient of the Margarita.

By now most British adults have tried a Margarita. Its unapologetic fruit flavours and its combination of acidity (the lime juice), sweetness (the triple sec) and the shock of the salt manage to make it at the same time both daring and accessibly reassuring. It is, in essence, the model cocktail. In his indefatigable *Oxford Companion to Spirits and Cocktails*, David Wondrich observes that the cocktail revolution of the past twenty years has 'changed the way people drink, perhaps for good'. Let's hope he's right. Classic mixology is certainly back, as the Margarita and its siblings reintroduce the elegance, exuberance and creativity of the interwar bar into our hurried and hectic lives. The classic Daisy may have withered but the modern Margarita lives on.

Chapter 12

CONTINENTAL SHELF

APEROL SPRITZ

Aperol Spritz, *the* fashionable British tipple of the early 2020s, boasted three great qualities. It was easy on the eye, easy on the stomach, and easy on the wallet. In its classic form, of three parts prosecco to two of Aperol and one of soda water,[69] it has conquered not just the world but, to everyone's surprise, post-Brexit Britain, too.

Aperol itself was originally devised in Padua in 1919 by the brothers Luigi and Silvio Barbieri as a herb-based bitter aperitif. Its base wine was infused with orange oils, rhubarb, gentian and cinchona bark – the latter long known, as we have seen, as an anti-malarial agent owing to its significant quinine content (which accounts for the plant's popular name of 'fever tree') and for its high proportion of digestion-calming alkaloids. So Aperol was healthy, too.

Aperol's name was adapted by the Barbieris from the French colloquial diminutive for aperitif, *apéro*. It was deliberately framed as a far lighter, cheaper and weaker drink than its principal adversary in the marketplace, Campari, made by the eponymous Milanese manufacturer that casually absorbed the far smaller Aperol business in 2003. Unlike Aperol, Campari's recipe has been kept a closely-guarded secret since it was initially developed in 1860 by Gaspare Campari. All its makers will admit to is that the base wine is infused with 'bitter herbs, aromatic plants and fruit'. Some critics have suggested that the 'fruit' may include the bitter chinotto orange, found only near Mediterranean coasts. However, this is pure speculation. What we do know is that the bright red colour of Campari (which contrasts with the more orangey vermilion of Aperol) came for many years from carmine dye, made from the female cochineal beetle. In 2006, though, the company switched to an artificial dye. So those female *Dactylopius coccus* beetles once crushed by the millions to extract the valuable cochineal can breathe again.

Campari ranges in strength from 20.5 per cent to 28.5 per cent, depending on where it is sold; British Campari weighs in at 25 per cent ABV. Aperol, on the other hand, is less than half that alcoholic strength, at 11 per cent.[70] This has made it highly appealing at a time when health-conscious Britons are seeking to reduce their alcohol intake. And not only is Aperol far lower in alcohol than its principal rival; its unique, almost luminescent colour helps it to stand out prominently on the bar back and the pub table as well as on the advertising poster or the social media post. Like Campari, dilution barely dims its vermilion lustre, making the Aperol Spritz ideally suited to the Instagram age.

From the 1950s onwards, drinkers in the Veneto, the home of this distinctive aperitif, began to consume Aperol as a long summer drink, combining it with local white wine, most frequently Soave, and soda water. By the end of the 1970s, though, another local wine had replaced the Soave as the must-have mixer for Aperol: sparkling prosecco. Yet it was only after Aperol was bought in 2003 by Davide Campari-Milano (which now trades in the UK under the anglophone brand of Campari Group) that the Aperol Spritz, buoyed as it now was by Campari's marketing muscle and global distribution, began to take off as an international sensation. By 2015, thanks to Campari's massive marketing resources, the Aperol Spritz had become a common sight not just in Italy but all over continental Europe. And in a few years it had even colonised the bar counters and pub tables of soggy Britain, too.

The origin of the 'spritz' is yet another of those well-worn myths that abound in the drinks trade. The much-repeated story has the Germanic drink designation *spritz* – simply denoting wine that has had some soda water added to dilute it and create a long drink – was created during the century (1814–1918) when the Veneto was part of the Austro-Hungarian Empire. Visiting Austro-Hungarian troops, or in another version imperial tourists, would ask the locals to spray (*spritzen*) some water, ideally soda water, into Veneto wine since its alcohol content was higher than they were accustomed to in their native land. This story is clearly rubbish, and would have Austrians or Hungarians *spritz*-ing with rage at the very idea that their wines were somehow weaker than those of north-east Italy. If anything, the reverse is true: wines such as Soave and, yes, prosecco tend to be a little weaker than their Central European cousins. It seems likely that *spritz* was just a German term for the habit of diluting wine with soda water, which by the mid-nineteenth century was common across Mediterranean Europe, where a spritz was better for dealing with the heat than undiluted wine.

During the twentieth century Aperol had rarely been a man's drink; instead it was most popular with young female audiences on account of its attractive neon patina and low alcohol content. Campari was keen to change all that, and to make it a gender-neutral habit rather than a niche product for those women who were in the know. To that end, from 2010 Campari began to target male audiences head on, initially by making Aperol the official sponsor of motorcycling's Grand Prix calendar, MotoGP. This was a brave but logical step for the brand, since Italian riders and Italian teams have traditionally dominated this sport. (At the time of writing, five of the top ten riders and eight of the top ten MotoGP teams are Italian.) Even more ambitious – some said crazy – was Campari Group's foray into mainstream British football. For three years from January 2014 Aperol was, to widespread surprise, Manchester United football club's 'Official Global Spirits Partner'. This didn't mean, though, that Aperol branding appeared on the players' shirts. Aperol merely joined Chilean wine producer Concha y Toro, Thai brewer Boon Rawd and Pepsi as Manchester United's corporate drinks sponsors.

Raising Aperol's profile in the UK soon paid handsome dividends. At the close of 2014, Waitrose reported that Aperol sales were up a staggering 800 per cent for the year, exceeding a more modest but still very welcome 28.1 per cent growth in the aperitif's sales worldwide. By September 2018 Campari was reporting an astonishing 43 per cent leap in annual sales for Aperol globally, prompting some drinks trade analysts to cheekily suggest that its parent company, Gruppo Campari, should change its name to Gruppo Aperol. And as the Covid pandemic receded, Aperol's sales grew at over 20 per cent a year, prompting Gruppo Campari to build a new bottling line at its Novi Ligure plant in Piedmont in 2024.

Aperol's marketeers were keen, however, that the brand should, while taking the world by storm, not lose sight of its Paduan roots. Accordingly, in 2019 they instituted a whole series of centenary-themed events for Aperol, most of which were centred on the ancient city of Padua, where, one hundred years before, the Barbieri brothers had launched their new aperitif at the Padua International Fair.[71] Sergio Giordani, the mayor of Padova at the time, was understandably delighted, declaring that it was 'fantastic to have a brand that is so deeply rooted in our city and region's heritage being so eager to give back to its home town'. That same year, the Aperol Spritz cocktail was dubbed the ninth most popular aperitif in the world – although it was never precisely explained what data had been employed to justify this rather curious claim.

Aperol's high visibility, vivid colour and low alcohol content made it just the right drink at just the right time in Brexit Britain. Its engaging, Instagram-friendly and almost fluorescent orange-red hue suggested continental sophistication and a promise of sun-drenched terraces and carefree relaxation – all of which were thin on the ground in Britain after 2016. Its modest strength also chimed with the growing trend towards lessening alcohol consumption to prioritise personal health.

These were not the only reasons why the Aperol Spritz was so wildly popular in Britain by 2025, though. The cocktail's other principal ingredient was one of the least expected yet exceptional successes of Britain's post-war drinks story. Its inclusion in the Aperol Spritz made this new long highball a major attraction for British drinkers. The combination of two good-looking drinks made for a compelling popular cocktail that was easy to make and cheap to buy. One enjoyed an aura of chic refinement, while the other encapsulated exuberant yet inexpensive celebration. And both carried a relatively low alcoholic payload. The fusion of Aperol and prosecco, products from the same region of Italy, seemed an ideal marriage that was just the right medicine for the angst-ridden and tentative Britain that was stumbling its way out of Europe and towards the depths of uncertainty and isolation even before the Covid pandemic descended in early 2020. The Aperol Spritz was a drink that, perhaps uniquely in Britain during the last eighty years, appealed to all ages and all classes. And a good part of that allure could be attributed to the sparkling wine that, by 2016, had become an indispensable fixture in most British fridges.

Aperol Spritz: a splash of Italian colour in grey, post-Brexit Britain.

Prosecco was barely known in Britain before the millennium. Previously, those who could not afford pricey French champagnes resorted to Spanish cava, a Catalonian sparkler that had risen during the 1870s from the ashes of the devastating phylloxera epidemic. By the 1980s, cava was doing very well indeed in the UK. Too well, perhaps, as Britain became flooded with cheap, downmarket cava as greedy Spanish producers opted for a strategic goal of low prices, high volume and short-term profits. The turn of the twenty-first century, though, saw cava's cheap and cheerful bubbles displaced in the market almost overnight by a new, sparkling upstart: Italian prosecco. This Italian wine was as cheap as Spanish cava, yet was kinder to the palate than many of the rougher examples of its Spanish rival, being demonstrably fruitier and a little bit sweeter. Suddenly prosecco was in and cava was out – and Britain never looked back.[72]

The British love prosecco. Its popularity grew rapidly after 2000, with consumption actually doubling between 2013 and 2014. By 2024 the UK was prosecco's largest market in terms of both volume and per capita expenditure, consuming around 36 per cent of the world's supply. It was also, unsurprisingly, the nation's favourite sparkling wine. In 2022 the Prosecco DOC consortium imported 130 million bottles to the UK, a 3.5 per cent increase from 2021.

Prosecco's success can be attributed both to its flavour and to its price. It was still a dry wine but its prominent fruit flavours – among them lemon, apple and honeydew melon, or whatever else you can detect – lent it more easy appeal and drinkability than other similarly-priced

European sparklers. It was also relatively cheap to make: in 2023 it cost only around 3.70 euros per bottle to produce. Even with retailers' mark-ups this still made it a highly appealing supermarket offer. Prosecco was a special yet accessible wine that didn't have to be reserved just for birthdays, anniversaries and Christmases but could serve well as an after-work drink, as an accompaniment to the Sunday lunch or as an acceptable dinner-party gift. Prosecco's easy-drinking style also allowed it to be paired with virtually any food, even desserts. It was the ultimate affordable luxury wine: Babycham all grown up.

Prosecco, the nation's fizz drinkers will be cheered to learn, has also been found to have health benefits. However unlikely this may sound, researchers from the University of Exeter have found that drinking prosecco can actually improve your memory. (In their study, drinkers were allegedly able to remember information better when they started drinking compared to those who did not drink. Astonishingly.) In addition, scientists from the University of Reading concluded that the increased blood flow caused by drinking prosecco can decrease blood pressure and the possibility of clots forming. So now we have the story for which we have all been searching for years: wine is good for you. When combined with Aperol's own anti-malarial properties, this makes Aperol Spritz almost a health drink.

Prosecco even prospered following the global financial collapse of 2008 and the subsequent recession. Those who now found that they could not afford champagne looked for a cheaper sparkling alternative, one that was easy drinking yet at the same time distinctive. And there was prosecco: the right wine at the right time. It hasn't looked back since.

Prosecco growers in the Veneto were quick to realise they had a runaway hit on their hands, and equally quick to ensure that their golden goose was properly protected. They began with an admirably crafty viticultural sleight-of-hand. 'Prosecco' was, for centuries, merely the name of the principal grape that made the celebrated sparkling wine. Interestingly, though, while today we think of prosecco as a historically Italian drink, the town that gave the grape its name actually lies right on the border with Slovenia, not far from Trieste, in a region that is still partly Slovenian-speaking. (This area was given to Italy by the Treaty of Rapallo of 1920, one of the series of convoluted and often unstable international agreements that followed the First World War.) The word 'prosecco' is actually Slavic in origin, deriving from the Slovene *preseka*. Both the grape and the wine may well have originated in Croatia, rather than Italy; certainly the grape had been grown in the Balkans for centuries.

Following the unexpected surge in demand that followed in the wake of the 2008 recession, in 2009 the Italian government readily agreed to invent a brand-new wine region, 'Prosecco', at whose heart was a newly invented protected designation for the wine, a *denominazione di origine controllata* (denomination of origin, better known and quicker to say by its acronym, DOC). The protection afforded by the new DOC designation notionally stopped any other region or country, Italian or otherwise, from calling its wine 'prosecco'. At the same time, the prosecco grape itself was officially renamed the *glera*, an obscure term that had formerly been used as a local nickname for the fruit. Ostensibly this change was designed to avoid any confusion with the recently-created wine region; however, in truth it was mandated by European Union rules on wine appellation, which state that a grape name cannot be an appellation in itself.[73]

The creation of a newly christened, ready-to-drink wine region vastly increased the planting area available for prosecco wine. Prosecco grapes, before 2009, had (in Italy, at least) largely been confined to the hills between the small towns of Conegliano and Valdobbiadene. Now glera vines were planted across the plains of Friuli, colonising a Prosecco DOC region of over 35,000 acres that extended from the Slovak border in the east almost all the way to Verona in the west, straddling the autonomous governmental regions of Veneto and Friuli-Venezia Giulia and including the major cities of Venice, Verona and Trieste.

It may be a pure coincidence that the legislation that created this vast new habitat for prosecco was drafted by Luca Zaia, a longstanding member of the right-wing Northern League (*Lega Nord*) and minister of agriculture in Silvio Berlusconi's fourth government of 2008–10 who was born in 1968 in the town of Conegliano, at the heart of traditional prosecco country. Zaia is, at the time of writing, now on an unprecedented third term as the regional president of the Veneto. He has ambitiously vowed that he will seek 'total independence' for the region; and, while this goal seems a good way off, he did successfully achieve political autonomy for the Veneto in 2017 with a plebiscite approval rating of 98.1 per cent. Despite having made a few gaffes along the way – such as claiming that the Chinese 'eat live mice' during the early stages of the Covid pandemic of 2020 – Zaia has proved a remarkably resilient politician, given the notorious turbulence of Italian politics. He has certainly proved a good friend to the prosecco industry over the last few years.

The creation of a brand-new protected DOC for prosecco wine and the renaming of the old prosecco grape caught those countries which had also tried their hand at producing prosecco on the hop. New Zealand buckled and signed a trade agreement with the EU agreeing that they would soon no longer use a grape name nor make a wine called 'prosecco'. Australia and Argentina, though, are still holding out and persist in calling the newly christened 'glera' grape the 'prosecco'. We await the result.

2009's legal coup in creating the Prosecco DOC, which cited a centuries-old tradition of producing sparkling wine in the Veneto, has also been somewhat undermined by the prosecco producers' recent enthusiasm for promoting 'Prosecco rosé'. This newly arrived pink fizz is clearly aimed at the rapidly growing market for light rosé and 'blush' wines. Yet prosecco rosé is based not on the home-grown glera grape but on that celebrated international voyager, Pinot Noir. So it has little to do with the centuries of winemaking in the Veneto.

The story became even more complicated following Croatia's admission to the European Union in 2013. The EU, prodded energetically by the Italians, immediately banned the use of the name prošek for a traditional Croatian dessert wine. This ban was imposed despite the fact that prošek itself may well date back many centuries as well – possibly as early as Roman times. At the same time, the EU refused Croatia's application for Protected Designation of Origin (PDO) status for their wine. PDO designation was created by the EU in 1992 to protect the origin of distinctive and traditional foods and drinks, and has been applied to products as varied as champagne and Roquefort cheese in France, Gorgonzola and Sorrento lemons in Italy, and Stilton cheese and Cornish clotted cream in the UK. (Since 2021, when this agreement lapsed in the UK following its withdrawal from the EU, the UK government has continued what is effectively the same designation programme, now called the 'Geographical Indication' (GI) scheme, 'that protects the geographical names of food, drink and agricultural products.') In 2021 Croatia finally got the EU to agree to sell prošek under its original name, but four years later the battle over the wine's PDO application still raged. This heated argument wasn't just about prosecco or prošek, though. Fuelling the mutual hostility were decades of Italian resentment at the loss of the Istrian peninsula, initially to Yugoslavia and subsequently to Croatia, at the end of the Second World War. Istria was once part of the proud Venetian Republic, and its cession to the new republic of Yugoslavia in 1947 prompted the enforced emigration of the majority of the Italian-speaking inhabitants of Pula, once the Austro-Hungarian Empire's premier naval base, which in the post-war world found itself as the largest city in Croatian Istria.

In retaliation against what they perceived as a Croatian attempt to destabilise their burgeoning prosecco empire, the Italian *glerini* stressed the centuries-old heritage of their wine. They cited the first-century historian Pliny the Elder (properly Gaius Plinius Secundus, who was famously destined to perish during the Vesuvian volcanic eruption of 79 CE, whose vast encyclopedia *Naturalis Historia* of 77 CE hymned a wine he called *pucinum* as being 'rich in therapeutic properties'. Pliny also claimed that the Emperor Augustus' scheming wife Livia, widely rumoured to have murdered a number of her husband's relatives, was a big fan of a wine called *pucinum* and had attributed her longevity to its health-giving qualities, recommending it to all as 'an elixir for a long life'. (Livia died at the ripe old age of eighty-six, having, as all devotees of the television series *I, Claudius* will remember, manoeuvred all of her rivals out of the way, more often than not to an early grave.) Pliny placed the origin of his *nobile vinum pucinum* in 'the gulf of the Adriatic Sea', so roughly where prosecco is made today. Accordingly, the prosecco industry has long associated Pliny's magical wine with their sparkling prodigy. However, we have no idea whether *pucinum* was even a red or white wine. Even if it *was* a white, this wine could have been derived from a number of potential sources, including the local *ribolla gialla* grape, and not necessarily from glera vines.

Whatever its ancestry, it is hard to see modern-day prosecco being threatened by prošek or any other Balkan rival. The wine trade's specialist media periodically floats space-filling articles predicting that the prosecco bubble has burst (a punning headline that has, inevitably, appeared more than once) and suggesting that sales of the Italian fizz are about to plummet. However, to date there has been no evidence of that whatsoever. Whatever you think of 2009's audacious rebranding exercise that instantly spawned a new 'Prosecco' wine region, the vast expansion of prosecco's DOC-registered acreage that it initiated has enabled prosecco not just to keep ahead of demand but to become a massive international success. Today the region produces around 700 million bottles of bubbly every year, and sales just keep on growing annually, in double digits.

While not every bottle of prosecco is of outstanding quality, so far this hasn't bothered British consumers. As we have seen, the UK is prosecco's largest market in the world by both volume and value, importing over a third of all the prosecco shipped worldwide – approximately 131 million bottles a year.

The rising popularity of prosecco-based cocktails such as the Aperol Spritz and the Bellini (a combination of prosecco and peach purée invented by Giuseppe Cipriani at the legendary Harry's Bar in Venice some time before 1948)[74] only served to fuel prosecco's seemingly irresistible rise during the first decades of the twenty-first century. In recent years the region's producers have even invented a National Prosecco Day: held on 13 August each year, this event has now acquired a mythical provenance that appears to stretch back decades.

Britons continue to lead the world not just in their consumption of prosecco but in their eagerness to adopt the Aperol Spritz – something that could not have been foretold even twenty years ago. Almost overnight, it seems, large glasses of luridly coloured Aperol Spritz have materialised, and multiplied, in pubs, bars, restaurants and patios across the UK. The British seemingly cannot resist the chic, colourful, low-alcohol allure of this cocktail of the moment, which conjures up images of sun-drenched Italian beaches and sophisticated seaside *terrazzi* even when it is being drunk on a chilly, rainswept English summer's afternoon. For many British adults, cooped up in their homes during the Covid epidemic of 2020–1, the Aperol Spritz offered a tantalising prospect of sun, sea, sand – and freedom: a vision of sun-soaked beaches and exotic foreign 'otherness' that they were now forbidden to visit or experience. Aperol – a niche Italian vermouth that had been ignored by the British consumer for decades – now seemed to embody that fantasy of escape and excitement.

However, there is an obvious, glaring irony in the unexpected success of Aperol Spritz in the UK in recent years. For at the same time as this categorically Italian concoction was becoming Britain's most popular cocktail, one that appealed to an astonishingly wide range of demographics and audiences, many of those who so enthusiastically chugged their spritzes were the very same people who had voted to take Britain out of the European Union, whose values and qualities the Aperol Spritz incarnated in so many ways. While a majority of Britons rejected the idea of a unified Europe in 2016, it is a bizarre paradox that, increasingly, their drink of choice in the years that followed the widely unexpected Brexit 'non' was a drink that seemed to epitomise the world that they had just spurned.

-

The long, convoluted and unedifying saga of Britain's drawn-out exit from the European Union is too well known and, whichever side of the divide you are on, simply too dispiriting to be rehearsed at length here. Brexit was never expected to become a genuine reality by the Conservative prime minister who had decided to let the poll-genie out of the bottle. (The word 'Brexit', an ungainly but undeniably catchy term, was coined by television executive Peter Wilding in May 2012, four years before the actual vote took place.) David Cameron confidently predicted that a 'remain' vote would be returned in the referendum that his party manifesto had promised as it entered the 2015 general election. After all, a similar referendum held just two years after Britain had joined what was then called the European Economic Community, in 1975, had resulted in a comfortable 67.2

per cent majority in favour of staying, despite the agnostic euroscepticism of the sitting Labour prime minister, Harold Wilson. Unlike Wilson, indeed, Cameron was an unequivocal supporter of the notion of the European Union, even if – along with most Britons – he believed that may of its policies and operational systems were in need of urgent reform. Pressure from the far-right, populist UK Independence Party (UKIP), led by the irrefutably charismatic Nigel Farage, as well as from many on the right of his own Conservative Party, encouraged Cameron to offer a public referendum as a way, as he saw it, of defusing the Right's europhobia. The other main party leaders, Labour's Jeremy Corbyn and the Liberal Democrats' Tim Farron, were also in favour of remaining, as were the three previous prime ministers, the Conservatives' John Major and Labour's Tony Blair and Gordon Brown. (The Remainer camp even included two future premiers, Theresa May and Liz Truss.) In addition, once campaigning began in earnest, the 'Leave' campaign was seemingly split between rival groups, UKIP's Leave.EU and the Conservatives' Vote Leave, who both claimed to speak for those who might wish to depart the Union. What could go wrong?

In the event, of course, everything did go wrong, at least for Cameron and the Remain movement. The Leave lobby, galvanised by the controversial but inspired director of Vote Leave, Dominic Cummings, always seemed to be on the front foot and ready with a set of upbeat, optimistic messages; in contrast, the Remainers appeared to be negative, gloomy and defensive. Cummings, notoriously combative and unpredictable but a highly adept political strategist, came up with a simplistic but in the event vote-winning slogan: 'Take Back Control'. As Essex

University's Professor Paul Whiteley has noted, the Leave campaign managed to successfully target a surprisingly wide range of the discontented electorate:

> *We had the official campaign led by Boris Johnson that galvanised the part of the electorate that saw themselves as respectable and conservative. Then we had the more unofficial grassroots campaign led by Nigel Farage that appeared to galvanise those that felt left behind, giving way to the populist movement. Usually a split camp weakens a campaign – this time it served it well.*

When the vote was held on 23 June 2016, 51.9 per cent of those who voted elected to leave Europe. David Cameron immediately resigned as prime minister and, three and a half years and two premiers later, the United Kingdom left the European Union, on 31 January 2020.

Yet how many of those who toasted the result of the referendum vote, and indeed the final slamming of the European door in 2020, did so with an Aperol Spritz or three? It is highly incongruous that this most Italian of drinks should soar in popularity across Britain just when many of those same Britons were voting to abandon Italy and her other EU partners.

In the absence of reliable market research, it's difficult to define just how many Brexiteers may also have simultaneously been Aperolites (Aperolers? Aperospritzers?). But the two groups do appear to overlap significantly. The appeal of Aperol Spritz stretches across a wide range of British demographics; this includes men, who are (surprisingly) more likely to try the cocktail than women, as well as the less well off, understandably attracted by the drink's competitive pricing. It was no surprise, then, that in 2023 the apparently classless phenomenon of Aperol Spritz was hailed in Britain's national media as 'one of the most successful marketing phenomena of modern times' and an inclusive tipple that could be 'found on almost every drinks list, from the swankiest of hotel bars to the grubbiest of backstreet boozers'. Today Aperol Spritz comes pre-mixed in a distinctive, bell-shaped bottle, while some British city bars even dispense the cocktail on the bar, via a tap.

The unmistakeable colour of Aperol Spritz also ensures that it remains firmly in the public eye. Famous celebrities from Benedict Cumberbatch to Zendaya are happy to be featured as fans on social media. (Zendaya even used an Instagram post to suggest how you could dress to match your drink.) Campari Group have now developed bespoke, Aperol-branded wine glasses in which to show off its bright vermilion hue to its best advantage, to both the drinker and to the camera. This replaces the functional, unshowy glass tumblers into which Aperol was traditionally poured.

In 2023 *Guardian* journalist Dale Berning Sawa quoted one central London bar owner who described the Aperol Spritz as 'a kind of bridge' between the wine and cocktail worlds that 'has the same serve as a wine, has the same aesthetic as a wine, but also has some more nuance and intrigue.' Another London bartender admitted to Sawa that, with its distinctive physical presence yet low alcohol content, the Aperol Spritz was 'a really easy sell'.

That same year, 2023, the Aperol Spritz was voted Italy's favourite pre-dinner drink. Less positively, Eugenia Roccella, Georgia Meloni's right-wing minister for family, natality and equal opportunities, seized the opportunity of this accolade to accuse the Aperol Spritz of being responsible for Italy's population crisis, declaring that young couples now choose between 'drinking Spritz and having kids'. Aside from Buckfast Wine's allegedly detrimental effect on its less prosperous Scottish consumers, this may be the first time that an alcoholic drink has been charged with undermining a whole nation. No doubt it won't be the last.

In Britain, at least, Aperol Spritz isn't being blamed for Brexit or for national decline. Indeed, as far as the nation's booze retailers are concerned, the future's bright and orangey-red.

Bibliography

GENERAL

Briggs, Asa, *Wine for Sale* (Chicago: University of Chicago Press, 1985)

Burnett, John, *Liquid Pleasures: A Social History in Modern Britain* (London: Routledge, 1999)

Cooper, Derek, *The Beverage Report* (London: Routledge and Kegan Paul, 1970)

Harding, Julia and Robinson, Jancis, ed, *The Oxford Companion to Wine* (Oxford: Oxford University Press, 5th ed, 2023)

Matthew, Colin and Harrison, Brian, *The New Oxford Dictionary of Biography* (Oxford: Oxford University Press, 2004 and *passim* online)

CHAPTER 1: GIN AND TONIC

Buxton, Ian, *Gin* (Edinburgh: Birlinn, 2021)

Coates, Geraldine, *Classic Gin* (London: Prion, 2000)

Dillon, Patrick, *Gin* (London: Lume, 2020)

Fleming, Ian, *Dr No* (London: Jonthan Cape, 1958)

Gallagher, Paul, 'Gin on the rise to beat vodka as the spirit of the age' in *The Independent*, 14 June 2014

Khan, Yasmin, *The Great Partition* (New Haven: Yale University Press, 2007)

Larkin, Philip, *Collected Poems* (London: Faber & Faber, 2003)

Neillands, Robin, *A Fighting Retreat: British Empire 1947–97* (London: Coronet, 1997)

Porter, Roy, *English Society in the 18th Century* (Harmondsworth: Penguin 1990)

Scott, Paul, *Staying On* (Chicago: University of Chicago Press, 1977)

Simonetti, Omar et al., 'The history of the Gin and Tonic' in *InfezMed*, vol 30, no 4, 1 December 2022

CHAPTER 2: BABYCHAM

Baker, Anne Pimlott, 'Francis Edwin Showering' in *ODNB* (Oxford: OUP, 2004)

Burnett, John, *Liquid Pleasures: A Social History in Modern Britain* (London: Routledge, 1999)

Dade, Penny, *Drink Talking: 100 Years of Alcohol Advertising* (Hendon: Middlesex University Press, 2008)

Jefferys, Henry, 'Babycham is an enigma to all but the British' in *The Guardian*, 13 March 2015

Kynaston, David, *Family Britain 1951–57* (London: Bloomsbury, 2009)

Norman, Philip, *Babycham Night* (London: Pan, 2011)

Thorpe, Vanessa, 'Make mine a Babycham! Return of the drink that added sparkle to the 70s' in *The Guardian*, 26 February 2023

CHAPTER 3: HARVEYS BRISTOL CREAM

Anon, *Harveys Alphabet of Bristol Cream* (Bristol: John Harvey & Sons, 1970)

Harrison, Godfrey, *Bristol Cream* (London: Batsford, 1955)

Howkins, Ben, *Sherry* (Paris: Academemie du Vin Library, 2021)

Jeffs, Julian, *Sherry* (Cassington: Infinite Ideas, 8th edition, 2019)

Robinson, Jancis, 'Whatever happened to Harveys?', posted 1 October 2016, accessed 14 September 2024

Ruben, 'Rumasa: the dark years of sherry' in *Sherry Notes*, posted 18 November 2018, accessed 14 September 2024

CHAPTER 4: WATNEY'S RED

Baillie, Frank, *The Beer Drinker's Companion* (Newton Abbot: David & Charles, 1973)

Boak and Bailey, *Watney's Red Barrel – how bad could it have been?*, https://boakandbailey.com/2019/01/watneys-red-barrel-how-bad-could-it-have-been, accessed 31 August 2024

Boston, Richard, *Beer and Skittles* (London: Fontana, 1976)

Hutt, Christopher, *The Death of the English Pub* (London: Arrow Books, 1973)

Janes, Hurford, *The Red Barrel – A History of Watney Mann* (London: John Murray, 1963)

Farrell, T. Let's Look Again, *Over a Barrel: A History of Watney's Red*, posted 14 November 2014, accessed 31 August 2024

Parissien, Steven, ed, *Trouble Brewing: pub refurbishments – over the limit?* (Lavenham: Lavenham Press/The Georgian Group, 1991)

Protz, Roger, *Pulling a Fast One* (London: Pluto, 1978)

CHAPTER 5: BLUE NUN

Bower, Julie, 'The Evolution of the UK Wine Market: From Niche to Mass-Market Appeal' in *Beverages* 2018, 4 (4)

Burnett, John, *Liquid Pleasures: A Social History in Modern Britain* (London: Routledge, 1999)

Burr, Christopher, 'A Half-Century of Life in the UK Wine Industry' in *La Notizia* (London), 12 November 2020

Cloake, Felicity, 'The curse of the Blue Nun', *The Guardian*, 20 October 2010

Eames, Andrew, 'Whatever happened to Blue Nun…?', *The Sunday Times*, 3 November 2019

Gutzke, David, *Women Drinking Out in Britain Since the early Twentieth Century* (Manchester: Manchester University Press, 2013)

Major, Patrick, 'Britain and Germany: A Love-Hate Relationship?' in *German History*, vol 26, issue 4, October 2008

Moss, Stella, '*Continental Connotations': European Wine Consumption in 1970s Britain* (Cambridge; Cambridge University Press online, 2 November 2020)

Wittlinger, Ruth, 'Perceptions of Germany and the Germans in Post-war Britain' in *Journal of Multilingual and Multicultural Development*, vol 25, 2004

CHAPTER 6: GUINNESS

Blackhurst, Chris, 'The Renaissance man' in *The Independent*, 14 June 1997

editorial in *The Economist*, 1 September 1990

Corcoran, Tony, *The Goodness of Guinness* (New York: Skyhorse, 2009)

Mansfield, Stephen, *The Search for God and Guinness* (Cheltenham: Nelson, 2009)
Molloy, Thomas, 'Forget the Guinness publicity shots, drinks giant Diageo doesn't need us' in *The Irish Independent*, 17 June 2013
Murphy, Brenda, *Brewing Identities: Globalisation, Guinness and the Production of Irishness* (Oxford: Peter Lang, 2014)
—'Pure Genius: Guinness Consumption and Irish Identity' in *New Hibernia Review*, vol 7, no 4, Winter 2007
—'Consuming Guinness, Producing Irishness Circuits of Cultural Production' unpublished PhD thesis, Goldsmith's College, September 2002
Saunders, James, *Nightmare* (London: Hutchinson, 1989)
Warner, Jeremy, 'Ernest Saunders; Out of Jail and Back in Business' in *The Independent*, 17 May 1996

CHAPTER 7: MALT WHISKY

Botham, Noel, *Princess Margaret: The Untold Story* (London: John Blake Publishing, 1994)
Bower, Julie, 'Scotch Whisky: History, Heritage and the Stock Cycle' in *Beverages* (Basel: MDPI, 2016), published 12 April 2016
—and Higgins, David M., 'Litigation and Lobbying in Support of the Marque: The Scotch Whisky Association, c.1945–c. 1990' in *Enterprise & Society*, vol 24, no 1, March 2023
Buxton, Ian, 'Was Glenfiddich really the first ever single malt whisky?' in *Master of Malt*, posted 8 July 2019, accessed 2 November 2024

Daiches, David, *Scotch Whisky* (London: Fontana, 1976)

Finlay, Fletcher, 'Who will buy all this Scotch Whisky' in *Dramface*, 3 January 2024, accessed 2 November 2024

MacKenzie, Niall G., 'Unlocking dynamic capabilities in the Scotch whisky industry, 1945–present' in *Business History*, vol 66, no 5, 2024

Perchard, Neil and MacKenzie, Niall G., 'Behind the "tartan curtain": Cartelisation in the Scotch Whisky Industry, 1830–1960' in Martin Shanahan and Susanna Fellman (eds), *A History of Business Cartels* (Milton Park: Routledge, 2022)

Russell, Iain, 'Margaret Thatcher' in *Famous Whisky Drinkers* at scotchwhisky.com, posted 28 February 2017, accessed 4 November 2024

Wilson, Ross, *Scotch Whisky: Its History and Romance* (Newton Abbot: David and Charles, 1973)

CHAPTER 8: BEAUJOLAIS NOUVEAU

Chrisafis, Angelique, 'Beaujolais Nouveau's inventor fined for fraud' in *The Guardian* online, 5 July 2006, accessed 25 September 2024

Edwards, Amy, *Are we rich yet? The rise of mass investment culture in contemporary Britain* (Oakland: University of California Press, 2022)

Foster, Ed, 'Bringing Back the Beaujolais' in *MotorSport*, February 2008

Joseph, Robert, 'Georges Duboeuf' obituary in *The Guardian* online, 10 February 2020, accessed 21 September 2024

Mansfield, Ian, 'It's the 50th anniversary of the Beaujolais Nouveau Race' in *IanVisits*, posted 9 November 2023, accessed 25 September 2024

Robinson, Jancis, 'A toast to wine legend Joseph Berkmann' in *Financial Times* online, 21 September 2012, accessed 19 September 2024

Teague, Lettie, 'Beaujolais Isn't Nouveau for the In-the-Know' in *The Wall Street Journal* online, 14 December 2016, accessed 19 September 2024

Tempest, Rone, 'Beaujolais Nouveau Arrival a Global Affair' in *Los Angeles Times*, 18 November 1988

CHAPTER 9: BUCKFAST WINE

'Acceptable_West_3871', https://lovindublin.com/entertainment/not-a-drink-to-share-with-the-family-american-wine-enthusiast-reviews-buckfast, accessed 27 August 2024

Beacham, Peter, ed, *Buckfast Abbey: history, art and architecture* (London: Merrell, 2017)

Castle, Stephen, 'Monks' Tonic Comes With More Than a Hint of Criticism' in *New York Times*, 2 June 2015

Charles, Gemma, 'Buckfast Tonic Wine' in *Marketing*, 17 February 2010

Guthrie, Jonathan, 'Demonised Drink' in *The Financial Times*, 22 January 2010

Hands, Thora, *Drinking in Victorian and Edwardian Britain* (London: Palgrave Macmillan, 2018)

Leishman, David, '*Blame It on the Bucky!* The Positioning of Buckfast Tonic Wine between Acceptability and Transgression' in *Les Cahiers de l'ILCEA*, vol 6, no 19 (Grenoble: 2014)

Muresan, Andruta, et al., 'New Uses of Hawthorn Fruits in Tonic Wines Technology' in *Bulletin of University of Agricultural Sciences and Veterinary Medicine*, vol 73, no. 2 (Bucharest: 2016)
Murray, Gillian et al., *Living and Working in Lanarkshire* (Glasgow: Glasgow Caledonian University, 2023)
Wong, Wailim, 'Passing Bucky on Issue of Trust is Out' in *Western Morning News*, 15 November 1994

CHAPTER 10: WKD

Duffy, Jonathan, 'What happened to alcopops?' in *BBC News Magazine*, posted 9 November 2005, accessed 7 October 2024
Ferguson, Maria, *Essex Girl* (London: Oberon, 2019)
Gosling, Emily, 'JKR's WKD redesign aims for "gender inclusive" look and feel' in *Design Week*, 26 August 2016
Greer, Germaine, 'Essex Girls? We're the best' in *The Guardian*, 5 February 2006
—'Long Live the Essex Girl' in *The Guardian*, 5 March 2001
Nicholls, Jimmy, 'Can WKD create a buzz in alcoholic energy?' in *The Grocer*, 11 June 2022
Palmer, Tim, 'Out of the Woods' in *The Grocer*, 23 September 2000
Perry, Sarah, *Essex Girls* (London: Serpent's Tail, 2023)
Rohrer, Finlo and de Castella, Tom, 'The quiet death of the alcopop' in *BBC News Magazine*, posted 31 July 2013, accessed 7 October 2024
Woolfson, Daniel, 'As energy drinks soar, can boozy versions take off too?' in *The Grocer*, 26 March 2022

CHAPTER 11: THE MARGARITA

Beeson, James, 'A new dawn for tequila' in *The Grocer*, 12 October 2024

Craddock, Harry, *The Savoy Cocktail Book* (London: Constable, 1930)

'History of the Cocktail' in *The Washington Post*, 20 December 1908

Ling, David, 'The story behind the song: Marguerita Time by Status Quo' in *Classic Rock*, 15 February 2022

Sheehan, Margaret, 'The *LA Times* gets soused on its own margarita hoax' in *San Diego Reader*, 21 May 1992

Sotack, Al, 'The Myth of the Margarita and Its Many Inventors' in *Epicurious*, posted 26 April 2023

Wondrich, David, ed, *The Oxford Companion to Spirits and Cocktails* (Oxford: Oxford University Press, 2021)

—'Ancient Mystery Revealed! The Real History (Maybe) of How the Cocktail Got its Name' in *Saveur*, 14 January 2016

—*Imbibe!* (Los Angeles: TarcherPerigee, 2007)

CHAPTER 12: APEROL SPRITZ

Britner, Lucy, 'Should Campari Group change its name to Aperol Group?' in *Just Drinks Global News*, 7 November 2018

Holland, Mina, 'Greatest spritz: how a Venetian aperitif became the drink of the summer' in *The Guardian*, 30 August 2024

Jones, Gregory et al., *The power of the terroir: the case study of Prosecco wine* (Basel: Springer, 2013)

Karlsson, Per and Britt, 'How Prosecco Became the World's Most Popular Sparkling Wine: With A Name Change' in *Forbes*, 18 October 2022

Ponte, Stefano, 'Bursting the bubble? The hidden costs and visible conflicts behind the Prosecco wine 'miracle' ' in *Journal of Rural Studies*, vol 86, August 2021

Sawa, Dale Berning, '"It's the meaning of happiness": How the Aperol spritz took over the summer' in *The Guardian*, 30 August 2024

Whiteley, Paul et al., Why Britain really voted to leave the European Union', Essex University Research Case Study 60, accessed 16 October 2024

Images Credits

The publisher would like to thank the following for their kind permission to reproduce their photographs:

6 **Alamy Stock Photo:** World History Archive. 8 **Alamy Stock Photo:** Chronicle. 13 **The Advertising Archives.** 17 **Alamy Stock Photo:** Neil Baylis. 36 **Alamy Stock Photo:** Retro AdArchives. 50 **Alamy Stock Photo:** Retro AdArchives. 57 **Alamy Stock Photo:** Jeff Morgan 14. 67 **Alamy Stock Photo:** Retro AdArchives. 73 **Alamy Stock Photo:** Nicola Kota. 119 **Alamy Stock Photo:** Retro AdArchives. 143 **Alamy Stock Photo:** Chronicle. 160 **Alamy Stock Photo:** Eric D ricochet69. 165 **Mary Evans Picture Library:** Retrograph Collection. 177 **Alamy Stock Photo:** Smith Archive. 179 **Alamy Stock Photo:** 20th Century Advertising. 199 **Adobe Stock:** Jackie Davies. 203 **The Advertising Archives.** 227 **Alamy Stock Photo:** Art Directors & TRIP / Helene Rogers. 231 **Alamy Stock Photo:** Patti McConville. 243 **Alamy Stock Photo:** Greg Balfour Evans.

Notes

1. The possessions of the British Empire were customarily coloured pink on British atlases. While the imperial colour was actually red, pink allowed black-printed place names to be read more easily.

2. Although originally used in the sixteenth century to describe the global empire of the Holy Roman Emperor and king of Spain, Charles V.

3. Like so many words in the English language, this affectionately disparaging term for Britain derives from India – in this instance, from the Urdu word for 'foreign'.

4. Aside from Hong Kong, which endured as a British possession until its lease expired in 1997.

5. The founder was the first to sell artificially carbonated water, in 1783, while his firm also began to commercialise Malvern Water from 1843. The latter was a firm favourite of the British royal family until its new owners, Coca-Cola, shut its Worcestershire manufacturing plant in 2010.

6. Tanqueray Gordon was in turn bought by the Scotch whisky empire the Distillers Company in 1922, which thereafter initiated a shopping spree for British gin manufacturers, starting with Booth's in 1927.

7. Carew's Gin was actually a product of British India, made from sugar molasses, not grain. Carew & Co's distillery was founded by a Briton, John Maxwell, in 1803 in Cawnpore (Kanpur). In 1858 the firm, now in the hands of Robert Carew, became the official gin producer for the British Army as it took over the job of policing the Raj from the now-defunct East India Company. A Carew distillery still survives today in

Darshana, in former East Bengal, as the only alcohol producer in the Islamic country of Bangladesh.

8. Since 2014 it has been made at a bespoke factory at Laverstoke in Hampshire that features Thomas Heatherwick-designed greenhouses for the brand's botanicals. The brand is now owned by Bacardi.

9. Although the world's biggest gin producer is, oddly enough, the Philippines, which currently accounts for 43 per cent of the gin made globally.

10. Cadenhead of Campbeltown's 'Old Raj' gin is still flavoured and coloured with saffron – although, to Britain's embarrassment, the saffron gin market leader is now made by Boudier of Dijon.

11. VP was the brand name of cheap 'British' sherry, made from wine concentrate. It is still (just about) with us today.

12. Equivalent to what we would today call a 75-centilitre bottle.

13. Masius Wynne-Williams was formed in 1951 from Masius & Fergusson (itself created in 1943). It merged with D'Arcy MacManus to become D'Arcy MacManus and Masius in 1973 and then combined with Benton and Bowles to becomes D'Arcy Masius Benton & Bowles (DMB&B) in 1985.

14. His brand-new Rolls-Royce bore the personalised number plate JWW1. Murray Walker later wrote that this gift constituted the single most generous act that he had ever witnessed during his long marketing career.

15. Babycham's classic logo has often been attributed to one John Emperor of the famed ad agency Collett Dickenson Pearce (CDP). However, the logo was trademarked on 20 December 1955, while CDP was not founded until 1960.

16. Chinese water deer arrived at London Zoo (properly the Zoological Society of London or ZSL) around 1870 and were later bred by the Duke of Bedford (Chairman of ZSL) at Woburn Abbey. Although none survive at Shepton Mallet, there are currently about 600 water deer at ZSK's Whipsnade Zoo and 250 at Woburn, in addition to a sizeable population of escapees across Bedfordshire and East Anglia.

17. The ads featured slogans such as 'I made my début in London' and 'My picture was in all the papers' together with the tagline 'Only 59,088,038 Babycham Ads to Christmas!'

18. By 1979 apples constituted 25 per cent of the fruit that went into Babycham.

19. Showerings sued Postgate for libel but unexpectedly lost, frustrated by an unsympathetic judge who directed that the claim should be regarded as 'fair comment'.

20. This drink was still going strong, I remember, as late as 1982.

21. Mower would have been immeasurably better than the man who eventually got the gig: the Australian former car salesman George Lazenby.

22. Taken from Vikram Seth's 'I recall drinking sherry in California and dreaming of England' from his *From Heaven Lake: Travels Through Sinkiang and Tibet* of 1987.

23. Today sherry fortification is usually achieved by adding a mixture of *destillado*, distilled wine that is 95 per cent pure alcohol, and mature sherry in roughly equal proportions to the young wine.

24. The possessive apostrophe in 'Harvey's' was dropped years ago as yet another indication of modern marketing's over-simplification and infantilisation of the English language.

25. Of his nineteen children, only two survived to adulthood, while in 1991 four of his grandchildren were killed in a car accident.

26. VW initially thought it had bought Rolls-Royce, too, but soon discovered that, while it now owned the rights to the trademark portico radiator and Charles Sykes' classic 'Spirit of Ecstasy' bonnet mascot, it did not actually have the legal right to build Rolls-Royce cars.

27. Macmillan's 1985 speech, criticising Thatcher's privatisation policy, actually said: 'The sale of assets is common with individuals and states when they run into financial difficulties. First, all the Georgian silver goes, and then all that nice furniture that used to be in the saloon.

Then the Canalettos go.' While most Britons could agree with the underlying sentiment, few could relate to the analogies.

28. The apostrophe in 'Watney's' was discarded by the firm's marketing department early in the 1960s.

29. Khrushchev had actually been toppled from power in Soviet Russia seven years earlier. Presumably neither Burnett nor Watney's believed that his successor, the lugubrious and brooding Leonid Brezhnev, was as easily recognisable to the average Briton, though. It is unlikely that Brezhnev lost much sleep over his omission.

30. The SPBW is still going strong today, and publishes a quarterly magazine.

31. As journalist Simon Hoggart later revealed, Heath didn't actually mean to say this. The short-sighted Prime Minister, too vain to wear glasses, couldn't quite make out the words of his prepared speech: 'This is an unpleasant and unacceptable facet of capitalism.'

32. When neighbour Sue brings a bottle of Beaujolais to her home, Beverley consigns it to the fridge. Ironically, what was then seen as a rookie social mistake is these days considered just the right treatment for Beaujolais. So Beverley was ahead of her time.

33. Episode 1 of the sixth series of *Dad's Army*, 'The Deadly Attachment', first broadcast on 31 October 1973. The episode, unusually, featured a real German character: a U-boat captain who had survived a sinking. The unnamed German officer, played uproariously by Philip Madoc in full *übermensch* mode, is incensed by Private Pike's vulgar and ill-timed ditty denigrating Hitler ('Whistle while you work/Hitler is a twerp/he's half barmy/So's his army...') and demands the young man's name for his list of suspects.

34. First shown on 24 October 1975. For those four people who haven't seen it, the exchange continues...

    German: Will you stop talking about the war!
    Basil: Me? You started it!
    German: We did not start it.
    Basil: Yes you did, you invaded Poland...

35. In a controversial misstep, in 2020 the BBC temporarily removed this episode of *Fawlty Towers* from their UKTV streaming service on

account of its 'offensive content and language'. Most journalists got the wrong end of the stick, though, and assumed this was because of Basil's appalling anti-German comments. However, once the old major's undeniably racist comments had been removed (with John Cleese's full assent), the episode was reinstated on the channel, albeit with a content warning.

36. Actually directed by celebrated film director Alan Parker.

37. By 1990 it stood at a rather scary 32.1 pints per person.

38. Stella Moss cites a public health survey on alcohol of 1980 that concluded reluctantly that women had become the 'dominant purchasers and consumers' of wine.

39. These seemingly arbitrary vocabularies were first identified by British linguist Alan Ross in 1954 but then widely popularised in an article by the novelist Nancy Mitford.

40. The Park Royal site was closed in 2005 and subsequently demolished, despite protests from the Twentieth Century Society. All Guinness production was moved to the vast new St James's Gate plant in Dublin, which opened in 2000.

41. A pamphlet by the Whig political journalist and poet Nicholas Amhurst of 22 May 1721 mentions dining at a London cookshop 'upon beef, cabbage and porter'.'

42. CAMRA maintains that 'keg stouts like Guinness are pasteurised and then nitrogen is added to the flat beer in the keg to give it its creamy head in the pub, [which] is not a traditional way of brewing a stout.'

43. The toucan was even disinterred by the fabled British ad agency Allen Brady & Marsh in the 1980s.

44. The Provisional IRA had spun off from the traditional Irish Republican Army (IRA) in December 1969, four months after British soldiers had first been sent to Northern Ireland.

45. Quoted in his son's published apologia *Nightmare: The Ernest Saunders Story*, rushed out in 1989 before the trial's unfavourable verdict.

46. Launched by CBS in 1978 but still airing in 1990. The last of its 357 episodes was broadcast on 3 May 1991.

47. Walker's words were delivered in support of the bill that became the Scotch Whisky Act of 1988, which finally defined what Scotch whisky – as opposed to rival international spirits – actually was.

48. Not 'whiskey', a spelling reserved for Irish and American products.

49. Renowned for its jovial Scots tagline of 1925, 'Afore ye go!'

50. The ambiguous definition 'pure malt' was prohibited by the Scotch whisky industry in 2009. For example, Diageo caused confusion when their Cardhu malt was in 2003 supplemented by a 'pure malt' Cardhu that was actually a bend of malts. The malt blend was withdrawn three years later, but not before it had damaged the perception and sales of the parent brand.

51. At least with the choice of whisky, if not with the new Speaker. 'Gorbals Mick' Martin had been elected to the office in controversial circumstances the previous year, trouncing Thatcher's former cabinet minister and the bookies' favourite George Young.

52. Which in 1981 ran the world's most profitable casino, which effectively bankrolled Hugh Hefner's Playboy empire. That same year it was alleged that Freud had been gambling at the club while serving as a Playboy director, in violation of British betting regulations.

53. Master of Wine.

54. Today owned by the venerable Scottish distillers Ian Macleod, responsible for famous Scotch malts such as Glengoyne, Rosebank and Tamdhu, but still made in Norfolk, at Cawston.

55. Even today the wine claims that it contains 'a unique infusion of selected therapeutic herbs and spices… traditionally recognised for their ability to combat common ailments and alleviate their symptoms… and can have beneficial effects on the circulation system and blood pressure.'

56. In 1968 the Blessed Sacrament Chapel at the east end was completed, designed by Paul Pearn and dominated by a vast, mosaic-glass east window by one of Buckfast's monks, stained glass artist Charles Norris.

57. He also added that 'after… the iron-like metallic sweet aftertaste I just couldn't get out of my mouth even after a few glasses of water.'

58. The title of this book is borrowed with admiration and respect from that of Cooper's groundbreaking volume of 1970.

59. Rated top RTD (ready-to-drink) alcopop in the UK by market research specialists Nielsen for that year.

60. Irn-Bru's unmistakeably lurid hue partly derives from the controversial food colouring Sunset Yellow, which has been linked by some to ADHD in children. In 2011 a proposed reduction in the drink's levels of Sunset Yellow was successfully resisted by the then Scottish first minister, the late Alex Salmond.

61. First coined by *The Sunday Times* in 1995.

62. Although Irish Buckfast contains a walloping 60mg – about the same level as an espresso coffee.

63. A line from Act IV of Shakespeare's *Macbeth*, famously borrowed by author Ray Bradbury as the title for his 1962 fantasy novel.

64. Interviewed by the BBC in August 2011.

65. Yes, they spelled 'Margarita' wrongly. The song's better-known American predecessor, Jimmy Buffet's timeless 1977 single 'Margaritaville', had not made the same mistake.

66. Not to be confused with the 'marguerite' cocktail, which Craddock described as two-thirds gin and one-third 'French vermouth' (though whether this was dry or sweet, red or white, we have no idea) with a 'dash of orange bitters'.

67. The Eighteenth Amendment, prohibiting the sale or consumption of alcohol in America, came into force on 17 January 1919 and was repealed on 5 December 1933. During the period of Prohibition, Americans' consumption of spirits actually increased.

68. The highest temperature documented that summer was 35.9 degrees, in Cheltenham on 3 July. Thanks to global warming, however, that has since been surpassed on many occasions; currently the UK

temperature record, logged at Coningsby in Lincolnshire on 18 July 2022, stands at 40.3.

69. The official Aperol Spritz cocktail recipe is 75ml prosecco, 50ml Aperol and 25ml soda water on ice with a slice of orange.

70. German Aperol was sold at 15 per cent until 2021, when it reverted to 11 per cent.

71. The annual Padua Trade fair, as it's now known, is still going strong today.

72. Britain does still remain cava's fifth-largest global market by volume, however, behind Spain, the US, Germany and, surprisingly, Belgium.

73. The glera is not prosecco's only constituent grape, though: up to 15 per cent of the wine can legally derive from Chardonnay, Pinot Bianco and Pinot Grigio varieties.

74. Cipriani said that the drink's pink colour reminded him of a paint colour used by Venice's Renaissance master Giovanni Bellini. Sadly, today the cocktail is far more widely known than the artist.